DECIDING FOR OTHERS

DECIDING FOR OTHERS:
THE ETHICS OF SURROGATE DECISION MAKING

ALLEN E. BUCHANAN

and

DAN W. BROCK

CAMBRIDGE
UNIVERSITY PRESS

Published by the Press Syndicate of the University of Cambridge
The Pitt Building, Trumpington Street, Cambridge CB2 1RP
40 West 20th Street, New York, NY 10011-4211, USA
10 Stamford Road, Oakleigh, Victoria 3166, Australia

First published 1990
Reprinted 1990, 1992

Printed in the United States of America

Library of Congress Cataloging-in-Publication Data
Buchanan, Allen E., 1948–
Deciding for others : the ethics of surrogate decisionmaking /
Allen E. Buchanan and Dan W. Brock.
p.   cm.
ISBN 0-521-32422-X. – ISBN 0-521-31196-9 (pbk.)
1. Medicine – United States – Decision making – Moral and ethical
aspects.   2. Bioethics – United States – Decision making.   3. Medical
jurisprudence – United States – Decision making – Moral and ethical
aspects.   4. Decision-making – United States – Moral and ethical
aspects.   4. Decision-making – United States – Moral and ethical
aspects.   I. Brock, Dan W.   II. Title
R724.B83   1989
174'.2 – dc20   89-33209
                                                        CIP

British Library Cataloguing in Publication Data
Buchanan, Allen E., 1948–
Deciding for others: the ethics of surrogate decision
making.
1. Welfare work. Decision making. Ethical aspects
2. Medicine Decision making. Ethical aspects
I. Title   II. Brock, Dan W.
174'.9362

ISBN 0-521-32422-X hardback
ISBN 0-521-31196-9 paperback

CONTENTS

Preface

This book deals with one of the most urgent and pervasive – yet in some respects one of the most neglected – problems in bioethics: *decision making for incompetents*. Until quite recently, bioethicists have tended to focus on articulating, justifying, and implementing the rights of self-determination of competent patients. When the special problems of the incompetent have been squarely addressed it has usually been in a less than systematic fashion and often only for certain classes of incompetents, such as disabled newborns.

The present work offers a broader and more systematic account. Part One develops and defends a theoretical framework; Part Two applies the theory to the distinctive problems of three important classes of individuals, many of whose members are incompetent: the elderly, minors, and psychiatric patients. This book is directed toward an extremely broad audience. We believe it will be of considerable interest to lawyers and judges, physicians, nurses, social workers and other health care professionals, health policy analysts and health policy makers, moral philosophers, and, of course, bioethicists. Although as a whole it is written for a rather general audience, there are some sections which may be of greater interest to some rather than others. For example, much of Chapter 3 might be omitted or skimmed by those who do not have a special interest in the philosophical perplexities of personal identity and their bearing on the use of advance directives.

A very different sort of book could have been written on this same topic, a book designed primarily to expose flaws and evils in our treatment of the incompetent and in the processes by which certain individuals come to be labelled "incompetent" in the first place, a book to stir the conscience, and to inspire and mobilize forces for social reform. We have no doubt that such a book would be a worthy undertaking, although we think it quite unlikely that philosophers are the people to author it.

In each of the applications chapters we advance criticisms of current institutional practices and offer suggestions for improvement, but our self-imposed task has different primary aims. Nevertheless, it is our hope that the analytic clarity and systematic ethical reasoning we have tried to provide will, if only indirectly and in combination with the distinctive contributions of others from different fields and with different objectives, bear practical fruit in actual improvements in the lives of incompetent individuals.

This book is the result of an ongoing collaboration that has developed over several years. The authors first began thinking seriously about the problems of decision making for incompetents during their tenure as Staff Philosophers for the President's Commission for the Study of Ethical Problems in Medicine and Biomedical and Behavioral Research in Washington, DC from 1981 to 1983. In our work for the Commission, we both profitted enormously from a rare combination of two stimulating factors: the work was more collaborative and more interdisciplinary than the work philosophers usually do, and it required a constant cross-fertilization between ethical theory and concrete social problems. Much of the thinking presented in the current volume had its origin in our contributions to the Commission Report on *Deciding to Forego Life-Sustaining Treatment* (Washington, D.C.: Government Printing Office: 1983). We continued our cooperative research on this topic in a Background Study for the U.S.

Congress Office of Technology Assessment entitled "Deciding For Others: The Ethics of Decisionmaking for Elderly Individuals Who Are Incompetent or of Questionable Competence." This study, which includes contributions by Michael Gilfix, an attorney who specializes in serving the needs of the incompetent elderly and their families, appears in *Philosophical, Legal, and Social Aspects of Surrogate Decisionmaking for Elderly Individuals* (copies available from the National Technical Information Service, 5285 Port Royal Road, Springfield, VA 22161). An excerpt from it appeareed as "Deciding for Others: The Ethics of Surrogate Decisionmaking" in *The Milbank Quarterly,* vo. 64, Suppl. 2, (1986), 17–94.

Parts of Chapter 2 draw and expand upon material from the following previously published articles by Allen Buchanan: "The Limits of Proxy Decisionmaking," *U.C.L.A. Law Review* 29 (1981), 391; "The Treatment of Incompetents," in *Health Care Ethics,* edited by Tom Regan and Donald VanDeVeer (Philadelphia: Temple University Press, 1987, 215–38); and "Medical Paternalism or Legal Imperialism: Not the Only Alternative for Handling Saikewicz-Type Cases," *American Journal of Law and Medicine,* vol. 5 (Summer 1979), 97–117. Chapter 3 is a significantly modified version of "Advance Directives and the Personal Identities Problem," also by Allen Buchanan, *Philosophy & Public Affairs,* vol. 17, no. 4 (Fall 1988), 277–302, with the permission of Princeton University Press.[4] Chapters 3 and 5 build on material that appeared in Allen Buchanan's "Limitations on the Family's Right to Decide for the Incompetent Patient," in *Institutional Ethics Committees and Health Care Decision Making,* edited by Ronald E. Cranford and A. Edward Doudera (Ann Arbor, Michigan: Health Administration Press, 1984), 209–17.

Articles by Dan Brock that were drawn on for Chapter I include: "Paternalism and Promoting the Good" in *Paternalism,* edited by Rolf Sartorius (Minneapolis: University of Minnesota Press, 1983); "Case Discussion:

Competence Determinations in Emergency Settings," in *Ethics in Emergency Medicine,* edited by K. V. Iserson, A. F. Sanders, Deborah Mathieu, and A. Buchanan (Baltimore: Williams & Wilkins, 1986); "Informed Consent," in *Health Care Ethics,* edited by Tom Regan and Donald Van De-Veer (Philadelphia: Temple University Press, 1987); and "Paternalism and Autonomy," in *Ethics* 98 (1988), 550–565.

In Chapter 4, Brock's article "When is Patient Care Not Costworthy? The Case of Gertrude Handel," in *Casebook on the Termination of Life-Sustaining Treatment and Care of the Dying,* edited by Cynthia B. Cohen (Bloomington, IN: Indiana University Press, 1988) is a major source. "Children's Competence for Health Care Decisionmaking," in *Children and Health Care: Moral and Social Issues,* edited by J. Moskop and L. Koppelman (D. Reidel Publishing, 1989) is a Brock article used in Chapter 5; and "Justice and the Severely Demented Elderly," in *Journal of Medicine and Philosophy* 13 (1988) 73–99 contributes to Chapter 6. In Chapter 7, two of Brock's articles are used as references: "Involuntary Commitment of the Mentally Ill: Some Moral Issues," in *Bio-Medical Ethics,* edited by J. Davis, B. Hoffmaster, and S. Shorter (New York: Humana Press, 1979) and "Involuntary Civil Commitment: The Moral Issues," in *Mental Illness: Law and Public Policy,* edited by B. Brody and H. T. Engelhardt, Jr. (Dordrecht, Holland/Boston, U.S.: D. Reidel Publishing, 1980).

Although some portions originated in the independent previous work of each of the authors, and although each of us had primary responsibility for some chapters and for parts of other chapters, the book as a whole is an inextricably joint product. Every part of each chapter has been worked over by both authors, and we have each benefitted greatly from the critical comments of the other.

We are both indebted to Daniel Wikler for encouraging us to undertake this project, and for his detailed and probing comments on a draft of the book. We are also grateful to Nancy Rhoden and Deborah Mathieu for their valuable comments. Edwin Forman, Rosalind Ladd, and Peter Smith supplied insightful remarks on Chapter 5, while Robert Arnold and Barry Fogel contributed useful suggestions concerning Chapters 1 and 7, respectively. Thanks are also due to Michael Gillette and Sue Olivieri who served as research assistants. Terence Moore of Cambridge University Press encouraged us from the start and smoothed the way through all the stages of production. Finally, we wish to express our thanks to Lois Day, Judy Garcia, and Gale Alex for their cheerful and efficient help in preparing the manuscript, and to Rachel Hockett for her judicious copyediting.

To Dan S. and Ruth W. Brock

Introduction

I. THE QUESTION

How ought decisions to be made for those who are not competent to decide for themselves? That is the question this book seeks to answer. Our focus will be on medical treatment decision making for incompetent patients. We will mention decisions about other matters such as financial affairs, living arrangements, or participation in research either to clarify our theory for medical decisions or to show important contrasts between medical decision making and these other areas.

The scope of the problem of decision making for incompetent individuals is vast. If one focuses only on the elderly who are incompetent and, among the elderly incompetent, only on those who are incompetent due to Alzheimer's dementia, the number may be as high as two million in this country alone, and increasing. But this is only one group. When all forms of dementia are included, the total is between three and six million.[1] At the other end of life is the largest group of incompetents—those who are not competent to decide for themselves by virtue of their immaturity. In addition, there are those who are incompetent due to mental retardation, brain damage from trauma, stroke, and alcoholism, and those whose mental illness renders them incompetent to make at least some decisions, and in some cases all decisions.

Over 80 percent of Americans die in hospitals.[2] Among

those who die in hospitals, many, indeed perhaps most, are incompetent or are treated as such, for some period of time before their deaths. Ironically, the much-lauded advances of modern health care and medical intervention have swelled the ranks of the incompetent in three ways: first, by reducing the frequency of early death due to the major communicable diseases (largely through better sanitation and diet, inoculation, and, to a much lesser extent, the use of antibiotics); second, through medical interventions that prolong the lives of incompetent individuals; and third, by the use of medications (such as some highly toxic cancer drugs) which impair decision-making capacities and devices (such as respirators) that can limit the patient's ability to communicate. For these reasons, incompetence is a pervasive condition, not a special problem for a certain group. All of the readers of this book were incompetent in their earliest years, and most will be incompetent prior to their deaths. The great majority of us will be confronted with the problem of decision making for an incompetent loved one.

II. THE HISTORY OF THE PROBLEM

In this work, we focus on decisions concerning medical treatment. We do so in the conviction that the problem of decision making for incompetents is one of the most, if not the most, urgent problems of contemporary bioethics. It is not much of an exaggeration to say that from its first flowering fifteen or twenty years ago, the modern bioethics literature has focused chiefly on articulating, justifying, and implementing the rights of the competent individual. In one sense this battle has been largely won: the courts, the great bulk of writers in bioethics, and the official codes of ethics of the major health care professional organizations all explicitly recognize that the competent individual has the right to accept or refuse medical care and treatment, as well as participation in experimentation. In another sense, the struggle still continues: what is accepted in principle is still sometimes not honored in practice.[3] Nevertheless, as far as competent individuals are concerned, there is a strong convergence of opinion, grounded in a good deal of systematic ethical theorizing and a fairly solid grasp of the institutional realities.[4] The time has come to redirect the focus of bioethics toward the problem of the incompetent patient. In this volume we build on existing work in bioethics to provide a systematic account. Many of the issues explored in this book are simply basic problems of social and political philosophy and of ethical theory, even if their most dramatic and visible instantiation lies in the area of medical care and treatment. In keeping with the constitutive idea of the series in which this volume appears, we have attempted to provide a deeper and more systematic conceptual and ethical grounding for evaluating and developing different practical approaches to the problem than is usually encountered in the bioethics or health policy literature.

Just as bioethics has tended to concentrate primarily on the rights of the competent patient, so philosophical work has centered on the rights of competent persons, and the grounding of these rights in utility or in autonomy, rather than on decisions for those who are incompetent. Most philosophical work on paternalism has been directed toward the question of whether paternalistic intervention in the choice or action of *competent* persons is ever justified.[5]

John Stuart Mill's neglect of the problem of decision making for incompetents is, unfortunately, quite representative of most contemporary work on paternalism. Mill simply acknowledges that we are justified in interfering with the liberty of those who are incompetent, in order to promote their own good or prevent them from harming themselves, and adds that we may sometimes justifiably interfere temporarily with an individual's risky behavior long enough to determine whether he is competent. Mill offers no account of the principles which should guide decision making on behalf of the incompetent, nor does he offer a theory of what competence and incompetence are, or of how we are to ascertain them.

III. ETHICS AND THE LAW

Courts and legislatures have not been as successful as philosophers in evading either the problem of decision making for incompetents or the threshold issue of what competence is. But neither the law nor legal scholarship has provided an adequate theory of decision making for incompetents or a satisfactory analysis of competence. The greatest single weakness in the law and the legal literature is that they fail to develop systematically the ethical basis of our treatment of incompetents, and, perhaps to a lesser extent, fail to articulate fully the law's valuable insights into the nature of competence.

This allegation may be somewhat unfair, however. Perhaps law need not itself explicitly incorporate a particular, developed ethical theory. But the law should at least be compatible with and supported by plausible ethical theory. Thus our work here might best be viewed not so much as an implicit criticism of the law as being incomplete, but more as an attempt to ground the law more firmly in ethical theory. At certain points in the analysis, however, our ethical theory, along with what we believe to be an accurate appreciation of the institutional realities, leads us to criticize some aspects of existing law.

The distinction between ethical and legal analysis warrants further elaboration. There are two good reasons for resisting the all-too-common temptation to reduce ethical issues to legal issues. First, the law is itself insufficiently developed to provide sure guidance for some of the most urgent problems in this area. In particular, the law has frequently responded belatedly and inadequately to problems concerning the termination of sophisticated life-sustaining systems for competent as well as incompetent patients. Even fundamental and long-standing legal concepts—including the legal concept of death—have been strained and in some cases rendered obsolete by rapid technological developments.[7] Where old law must be adapted to new circumstances, and where new law must be developed, ethical guidance is essential.

Second, and just as important, there may be weighty ethical reasons for *not* attempting to extend the law into some areas.[8] Whether or not the law is an appropriate instrument for dealing with a particular problem is itself in part an ethical issue. Further, existing law, even when it clearly applies to the problems under consideration here, cannot be regarded as fixed and sacrosanct. The law itself can and should be subjected to ethical criticism.

It has been our intention, therefore, to strike a middle course between two equally inappropriate attitudes toward the law: on the one hand, a failure to evaluate the law critically from an ethical standpoint, and on the other a utopian disregard of the real constraints law places on individual choice and social policy. Law is a rather highly evolved, though of course imperfect, institutionalized form of practical reasoning about how to cope with conflicting interests. The appropriate attitude for the ethical theorist who wishes to bring theory to bear on practical problems is to recognize the power of law as an institution and the resources of law as a mode of practical reasoning, while maintaining a critical, revisionist attitude toward both.

IV. ETHICS AND PUBLIC POLICY ANALYSIS

A second error this volume is designed to combat, one which is perhaps even more common than that of reducing ethical problems to legal ones, is the mistaken assumption that "policy matters" and "ethical issues" can be separated neatly, especially at the outset of an analysis. What this assumption overlooks is that most serious policy issues, whether in health care or in other areas, involve an ethical component, often at their core. Policy analysts may not see this, perhaps because they have not made their own ethical assumptions explicit, are not trained in the analysis of forms of ethical reasoning, and mistakenly believe that their own techniques (including risk/benefit, cost/benefit, and cost/effectiveness analysis) are ethically neutral.[9]

Indeed, the distinction between ethical issues and those that are *purely* matters of policy makes sense only after a great deal of ethical analysis has been successfully completed. For example, once we have fulfilled whatever ethical responsibilities we have (both as individuals and collectively) to provide health care for those who cannot afford it, society might simply as a matter of social policy decide to spend a great deal of additional money on social support for the indigent. But the problem that must be solved before we could identify these further allocational decisions as being "merely" a matter of social policy rather than of ethics is the daunting one of delineating the scope and limits of our ethical obligations to provide health care for the indigent. Assuming a facile distinction between ethical and social policy matters can have unfortunate methodological consequences. Fundamental ethical issues may simply be overlooked, or ethical analysis may appear belatedly as a reaction to policy rather than as a vital component of policy analysis and formation.

For these reasons we have attempted to articulate a comprehensive but sensitive ethical framework for evaluating current social policy on decision making for incompetents and for developing recommendations for change. However, the ethical analysis is not restricted to social policy. It examines problems of individual ethical choice as well, and takes as one of its fundamental tasks the problem of demarcating the proper boundary between matters of individual choice and responsibility, and those of collective responsibility and social policy. Our goal, however, is to provide the ethical and conceptual framework for enlightened public policy and individual choice, not to advance comprehensive, highly specific policy proposals or to offer definitive answers or exhortations to the individual faced with hard, concrete ethical choices.

We believe work in ethical theory itself can also be greatly enriched by closer attention to matters of applied ethics and public policy. Ethics matters in the real world and reflection on real world ethical problems can also deepen our understanding of largely theoretical issues. The more applied and public orientation of much philosophical work in ethics over the last two decades, a period of renewal and broadened focus for academic work in ethics, provides many examples of the deepening of theory. There are several instances in the present work in which grappling with concrete, practical problems prompted theoretical advances. We cite just two examples here. Our account of competence and incompetence in Chapter 1 has important implications for and helps illuminate the problem of paternalism at the deepest levels of ethical theory. Our evaluation in Chapter 3 of the challenge to advance directives from common philosophical accounts of personal identity bears on broader theoretical issues concerning the implications of theories of the person and personal identity for moral theories generally. Ethical theory has been and will continue to be deepened and enriched by work in more practical or applied areas such as bioethics.

V. THE METHOD

The best way to understand our conception of ethical theory is to see it exemplified in the ethical theorizing presented in the chapters that follow. However, a preliminary, rough characterization of how we understand ethical theory is in order, even if only a rather incomplete and unfortunately abstract sketch can be offered at this point. First, our approach is thoroughly anti-Cartesian. We do not start from scratch, attempting to boot-strap an ethical theory and then use that theory as an external standard for the evaluation of institutions and policies. We begin *in medias res,* utilizing, roughly, what Rawls calls the method of wide reflective equilibrium.[10] The goal of this method, as the name implies, is to achieve a stable system of ethical beliefs and attitudes, but one whose stability is grounded in reflection and self-critical reasoning, not un-examined custom, prejudice, or blind feeling. The process is that of attempting to achieve a match between a rather small but powerful set of general ethical principles and our firmest considered moral judgments not only about the subject matter at hand, namely the treatment of in-competents, but also about other important moral issues to which the same general principles apply. The qualifier "wide" is used to signal two things: first, that the ethical principles we explore can be drawn not only from contem-porary popular morality and current law, but from the history of ethical theorizing and of jurisprudence as well; second, that besides ethical principles and more particular ethical judgments, theory here draws on related con-ceptions, such as conceptions of the person.

A second important feature of the conception of ethical theory deployed in this volume is that it takes very seriously the *institutional* aspects of ethical problems and their solutions. Russell Hardin put the point rather archly but well when he remarked that the greatest advances in contemporary ethics have come when a number of think-ers came to realize that any ethical theory that was de-veloped to cope with moral dilemmas involving (at most) two persons and a runaway trolley in an unspecified time and place, is likely to be of very limited value.[11] In other words, casuistical reasoning about the isolated decisions of individuals abstracted from institutional frameworks should give way to a more nuanced and multi-dimensional analysis of moral problems as institutionally embedded. This is especially true for decision making in health care, which takes place in such complex and powerful institutional contexts as hospitals, nursing homes, organized professions such as medicine, and the law. The chapters that follow proceed on this methodological assumption and should help to confirm its value. It has been our aim, then, both to enrich ethical theory by "institutionalizing" it and to further the evaluation and refinement of the relevant institutions by bringing systematic philosophical thinking to bear on the problems that arise within them.

VI. THE PLAN

Any theory of decision making for incompetents must begin by examining the notions of competence and incompetence. For Chapter 1 we formulate five questions:

(1) What is competence?

(2) Given an analysis of the appropriate concept of competence, what *standard* (or standards) of competence must be met if an individual is to be judged to be competent?

(3) What are the most reliable *operational measures* for ascertaining whether the appropriate standard is met?

(4) *Who* ought to make a determination of competence?

(5) *What sorts of institutional arrangements* are needed to assure that determinations of competence are made in an accurate and responsible way?

Chapter 1 focuses primarily on the first three questions; the fourth and fifth are examined in later chapters. The foundation of the first chapter is a *decision-relative* analysis of the concept of *competence as decision making capacity*. We articulate its implications and defend it against several rival analyses. We argue that the key function of the competence determination is to ascertain whether the patient's decision making capacity is sufficiently defective to war-

rant transferring decisional authority to a surrogate. Setting the proper level of decision making capacity for
competence requires balancing respecting the patient's
self-determination and protecting his or her well-being.
Consequently, a variable standard of competence for different decisions is necessary.

Chapter 2 sets forth the primary ethical framework for
decision making for incompetents. The primary framework, we contend, should be patient-centered in the fundamental sense that considerations of the incompetent's
own well-being and (where possible) self-determination,
as opposed to the interests of others, should be the primary
focus. The analysis distinguishes among different types of
principles that together constitute the primary ethical
framework.

> *Ethical value principles:* principles that specify the basic
> ethical values that are to be served in dealings with
> incompetent individuals (these include individual well-
> being and self-determination, as well as justice).

> *Guidance principles:* principles that provide substantive
> direction as to how decisions are to be made. These
> include:

> - *Advance directive:* implementing a valid advance di-
>   rective, such as a "living will" or durable power of
>   attorney, that the individual executes while com-
>   petent.
> - *Substituted judgment:* acting according to what the
>   incompetent individual, if competent, would choose.
> - *Best interest:* acting so as to promote maximally the
>   good (i.e., well-being) of the incompetent in-
>   dividual.

> *Authority principles:* principles that identify appropriate
> surrogate decision-makers for incompetent individuals.

> *Intervention principles:* principles specifying the con-
> ditions under which the courts, representatives of

government protective agencies, or others in various institutional roles are to intervene, or may intervene, so as to take decisions out of the hands of those whose presumptive authority to decide was acknowledged in the authority principles.

This chapter articulates the meaning of and justification for principles of each of these four types. It also develops a principled way of resolving conflicts among guidance principles when more than one could be applied to a particular decision.

Chapter 3, "Advance Directives, Personhood, and Personal Identity," is an analysis of a set of related and extremely perplexing philosophical issues that have a direct bearing on the use of advance directives. We defend the practice of decision making by advance directive against objections, recently pressed in the literature of law and medicine, that a correct understanding of personal identity renders advance directives intellectually incoherent. In addition, this chapter distinguishes between the right of a self to determine what happens to that self, once competence is lost, and the right of a self to determine what is to happen to its biological successor when that self no longer exists. The former right we call the broad right of self-determination proper; the latter, the right of disposal. It is our contention that in general, and other things being equal, the former right is more weighty than the latter, and similarly with the respective obligations that are their correlatives.

In Chapter 4 we qualify the patient-centered ethical framework, exploring the conditions in which the interests of others may legitimately be taken into account in decision making for incompetents. We argue that while incompetence per se does not affect an individual's status regarding claims of distributive justice, certain classes of incompetent individuals, because they lack certain morally important interests or capacities, have an inferior moral status as far as considerations of distributive justice are concerned. These include not only the permanently unconscious, but also those, such as the profoundly and permanently demented, who are not persons and who have only radically truncated interests. This chapter also explores the more general issue of when and in what manner considerations of cost may rightly be taken into account by others in making decisions for incompetents.

Chapters 1, 2, 3, and 4 constitute Part One, the *theory* of decision making for incompetents. In Part II, Chapter 5, 6, and 7, we *apply* the theory to three important classes of incompetents: minors, the elderly, and the mentally ill respectively. The purpose of these application chapters is twofold: to demonstrate the power and practical fruitfulness of the theory, and to help refine and develop the theory in greater detail and with more specificity.

Chapter 5 focuses primarily on the case of older minors, for whom the problem of ascertaining competence is especially acute. The analysis of competence from Chapter 1 is extended to adolescents, and the interests of parents in decisions about their children's health care are considered. We argue that relevant developmental evidence concerning adolescents' decision-making capacities supports an increased role for them in decisions about their health care. The case of very young minors, who are clearly incompetent, and of severely disabled newborns in particular, is also examined in considerable detail.

Chapter 6 applies the theory to a large and growing class of incompetents: those elderly individuals who are incompetent due to Alzheimer's dementia, multi-infarct (stroke-induced) dementia, or other chronic diseases frequently found among the aged. This chapter uses the theory to evaluate systematically some of the more important institutional arrangements that are now being employed to cope with problems of decision making for incompetent elderly individuals, including conservatorship, living wills, durable powers of attorney, "No Code"

("Do Not Resuscitate") orders and judicial determinations
of competence.

Chapter 7 explores the complex relationship between
mental illness and incompetence, and applies the theory
both to involuntary hospitalization for mental illness and
to psychiatric treatment decisions for the mentally ill. It
also distinguishes between paternalistic (or patient-
centered) justifications and nonpaternalistic (or other-
regarding) justifications for involuntary institutionalization and involuntary administration of psychiatric
treatment. It develops a firm ethical justification for a
controversial evolving legal doctrine according to which
some persons who justifiably have been committed involuntarily to a mental institution may refuse psychiatric
treatment. Another important conclusion drawn is that it
is justifiable to commit involuntarily some persons who
are dangerous to *others* by virtue of their mental illness'
even if there is little or no prospect that treatment will
benefit the patient himself.

The volume concludes with a brief look toward the
future. There we offer suggestions for further research,
analysis, and practice. Three of the most important suggestions are these: (1) much empirical research is needed to
ascertain more accurately how determinations of competence are actually being made—or being evaded—in a
number of different contexts, both formal and informal;
(2) sweeping and innovative institutional changes are
needed to implement more ethically responsible determination of competence and sound procedures for decision making for incompetents; and (3) if the ethical values
of individual well-being and self-determination, as well as
those of distributive justice and the responsible and efficient use of social resources, are to be well served, then the
required institutional changes must include effective incentives for all key participants. Moral exhortation alone
with not suffice.

Finally, we simply note that we do not explicitly address

in this book the complex and interesting ethical problems of experimentation with incompetent individuals. While we believe that the main implications of our analysis are largely applicable, *mutatis mutandis,* to experimentation, for the most part we do not attempt to draw those implications or to qualify them properly.

Part one
THEORY

1. Competence and incompetence

The doctrine of informed consent in medicine requires respect for the informed and voluntary treatment choice of a competent patient. This book develops a theory of decision making for incompetent persons. Thus, a crucial issue at the outset is how to determine who is properly deemed incompetent and thus as falling under our theory. As will become clear in this chapter, that is a far more complex question than may at first be apparent. In particular, the determination of competence is not simply an "objective" factual determination based on some measurable property of an individual. Nor is its complexity simply psychological or more broadly empirical and so to be sorted out by psychologists or psychiatrists *before* the ethical and legal analysis comprising a theory of decision making for incompetents is done. Instead, an analysis of competence determination is one central part of the ethical and legal analysis in a theory of decision making for incompetents.

Clarity about determinations of competence and incompetence requires distinguishing carefully among the following questions:

(1) What is the appropriate *concept* of competence?
(2) Given an analysis of the appropriate concept of competence, what *standard* (or standards) of competence must be met if an individual is to be judged to be competent?

17

(3)   What are the more reliable *operational measures or tests* for ascertaining whether a given standard of competence is met?

(4)   *Who* ought to make a determination of competence?

(5)   What *sorts of institutional arrangements* are needed to assure that determinations of competence are made in an accurate and responsible way?

Each of these questions will be addressed separately. This chapter—which is concerned with the theoretical underpinnings of determinations of competence—will concentrate on the first three questions. The last two, which raise more practical and concrete concerns, can only be addressed in detail after the ethical framework of Chapter 2 has been laid out and the realities of current practices with different kinds of patients have been described in succeeding chapters.[1]

I. THE CONCEPT OF COMPETENCE

A. Competence as decision-relative

The statement that a particular individual is (or is not) competent is incomplete. Competence is always competence *for some task*—competence *to do something*. The concern here is with competence to perform the task of making a decision. Hence competence is to be understood as *decision-making capacity*. But the notion of decision-making capacity is itself incomplete until the nature of the choice as well as the conditions under which it is to be made are specified. Thus competence is decision-relative, not global.[2] A person may be competent to make a particular decision at a particular time, under certain circumstances, but incompetent to make another decision, or even the same decision, under different conditions. A competence determination, then, is a determination of a particular person's capacity to perform a particular decision-making task at a particular time and under specified conditions.

Any individual may be competent to perform some tasks (e.g., drive a car), but not others (e.g., solve differential equations). The tasks on which this study focuses are making decisions about medical treatment; but also of concern are entering into contracts, deciding whether to continue to live on one's own in an unsupervised setting, and so forth. It is true, of course, that for some individuals, decision-making capacity is entirely lacking (for instance, when the individual is permanently unconscious), but these are the unproblematic cases.

Decision-making tasks vary substantially in the capacities they require of the decision-maker for performance at an appropriate level of adequacy. For example, even when only medical treatment decisions are considered, there is substantial variation in the complexity of information that is relevant to a particular treatment decision and that consequently must be understood by the decision-maker. There is, therefore, variation in what might be called the objective demands of the task in question—in the case of decision making, the level and specific forms of abilities to understand, reason, and decide about the options in question. But there is also variation of several sorts in a subject's ability to meet the demands of a particular decision. Many factors that diminish or eliminate competence vary over time in their presence or severity in a particular person. For example, the effects of dementia on a person's cognitive capacities commonly are at some stages not constant, particularly in cases of borderline competence. Instead, mental confusion may come and go; periods of great confusion are sometimes followed by comparative lucidity.

In other cases, the environment and the behavior of others may affect the relative level of decision-making competence. For example, side effects of medications often impair competence, but a change of medication may reduce those effects. Behavior of others may create stresses for a person that diminish decision-making capacities, but that behavior can often be altered, or the situations in which it occurs can be avoided. Further, cognitive functioning can sometimes be enhanced by familiar surroundings and diminished by unfamiliar ones. A person may be competent to make a decision about whether to have an elective surgical procedure if the choice is presented in the familiar surroundings of home by someone known and trusted, but may be incompetent to make the same choice in what is found to be the intimidating, confusing, and unfamiliar environment of a hospital.

Factors such as these mean that even for a given decision, a person's competence may vary over time, and so be intermittent. Clearly, the values that support the right of the competent person to participate in health care decisions also require that caretakers utilize periods of lucidity when they occur. Sometimes the emergency nature of the situation will not permit this, but it is no doubt possible to involve intermittently competent persons in decision making substantially more often than is done at present. Sometimes, with opportune timing or other appropriate measures (such as medications), the intermittently competent person may be able to be involved in decision making at a time when he or she is clearly competent. Often, however, the person either consistently remains in, or can only be brought to, a state of borderline competence for the decision at hand. These borderline cases of questionable competence require more careful determination. They also illustrate the need for greater sophistication on the part of health care providers and others about physical and mental problems that frequently affect patients' decision-making capacities.

B. Global conceptions of competence

Before undertaking the detailed analysis needed for clarifying the appropriate standard to be applied for determining competence in borderline cases, it is necessary to address the appropriate use of more global or general attributions of competence and incompetence. As was noted above, some task-relative specification of competence attributions, whether explicit or only implicit, is inevitable, since any person is competent to perform some tasks but not others. Our concern in this book is not with all human activities or tasks, but principally with health care decision making. With regard to health care decision making, both the law and social practice accept a *presumption of global competence* for all adults. In other words, it is presumed of any adult that he or she has sufficient decision making capacities to make these decisions for him- or herself and to warrant these decisions being respected by others.[3] The decisions are to be respected by others in the sense of not being coercively interfered with, even if others view the decisions as less than optimal, foolish, or not the decisions those others would make in similar circumstances.

To focus on the legal context, the law assigns to adults the general or global status of competence to make health care decisions unless and until there has been a specific legal finding of incompetence. Below, we consider the circumstances that appropriately trigger an evaluation of a person's decision-making competence on a particular occasion, but it bears emphasis here that to say that competence determinations are decision-specific is neither to question the general presumption of competence for adults nor to suggest that a person's competence is in every instance appropriately open to question. The general presumption of competence for adults is fully justified in comparison with the alternatives either of a general presumption of incompetence (as is the case in the law governing health care decision-making by minors) or of having no general presumption and so having to settle the competence of each instance of decision-making case by case.

The most important values that support this general presumption are individual well-being and self-determination, both of which are analyzed and discussed in some detail below. Suffice it to say here, first, that a person's important interest in making significant decisions about his or her life, specifically about health care, provides strong support for this general presumption and, second, that adults' health care decisions are in the large majority of cases reasonably in accord with their well-being and so do not warrant either an assessment of their decision-making competence in every instance, or a presumption against respecting their decisions in order to protect their well-being. Thus, in the large majority of cases persons are rightly considered to be competent to make health care decisions for themselves, and their decision-making authority ought to be respected by others with no necessity for examining their competence further in the instance at hand. It is this general and well-grounded presumption that in turn grounds and is reflected in the widely acknowledged personal right of self-determination in this area.[4]

In cases of decision-making incompetence as well, it may often be that most persons who are incompetent to make one decision, or one type of decision, are incompetent to make a wide range of decisions. Such pervasive incompetence may be recognized informally in settings like hospitals, or formally in legal proceedings in which a person is adjudicated incompetent more generally, either for all decisions in a particular area such as health care or governance of one's financial affairs, or for all forms of decision making. So the status of incompetence, like that of competence, has a general or global sense concerning capacities for all decision making, or all decision making in a given area of decisions. Thus, there is a perfectly sensible and justified use of global assignments of the statuses of competence or incompetence to most persons most of the time. However, the recognition that competence and incompetence designations are in principle decision-specific is important for the borderline cases of competence in which small differences may be important for the overall assessment, or for the cases in which there is substantial variability either in the patients' decision-making capacities and/or in the objective decision-making demands of the decisions in question.

II. CAPACITIES NEEDED FOR COMPETENCE

What capacities are necessary for a person competently to decide about health care (as well as about living arrangements, financial affairs, and so forth)? As already noted, the demands of these different decisions will vary, but it is nevertheless possible to generalize some about the necessary abilities. Two may be distinguished: the capacity for understanding and communication, and the capacity for reasoning and deliberation.[5] Although these capacities are not entirely distinct, significant deficiencies in any of them can result in diminished decision-making competence. A third important element of competence is that the individual must have a set of values or conception of the good.

Under *understanding and communication* are included the various capacities that allow a person to take part in the process of becoming informed on and expressing a choice about treatment. These include the possession of various linguistic, conceptual, and cognitive abilities necessary for receiving and comprehending the particular information relevant to the decision at hand. That information will concern, in the most general terms, the nature of and reasons for the proposed treatment. More specifically, the information will include (1) the patient's diagnosis, (2) prognoses if different treatment alternatives (including the alternative of no treatment) are pursued, including the significant risks and expected benefits with their attendant probabilities of treatment alternatives, and (3) the physician's recommendation regarding treatment. The relevant cognitive abilities in particular are often impaired by disease processes to which the elderly especially are subject, including most obviously various forms of dementia, but also aphasia due to stroke and, in some cases, reduced intellectual performance associated with depression (pseudodementia). Even when cognitive function is only minimally impaired, ability to express desires and beliefs may be greatly diminished or absent (as in some patients with amyotrophic lateral schlerosis). Special efforts may be necessary to maximize the patient's capacity to understand and communicate: for example, patients incapable of oral communication may be able to communicate in writing or with special devices like letter boards.

Understanding is not a merely formal or abstract process, but also requires the ability to appreciate the nature and meaning of potential alternatives—what it would be like and "feel" like to be in possible future states and to undergo various experiences—and to integrate this appreciation into one's decision making. In young children this is often prevented by the lack of sufficient life experience. In the case of elderly persons facing diseases with progressive and extremely debilitating deterioration, it is hindered by people's generally limited ability to understand a kind of experience radically different from their own, and by the inability of severely impaired individuals to communicate the character of their own experience to others. Major psychological blocks and illnesses—such as fear, denial, delusion, and depression—can also significantly impair the appreciation of information about an unwanted or dreaded alternative.[6] In general, understanding requires the capacities to receive, process, and make available for use the information relevant to particular decisions.

Competence also requires *capacities for reasoning and deliberation*. Since decision making is never instantaneous, but always takes place over a (sometimes protracted period of time, sufficient short-term memory capacities are needed for retaining information and allowing this *process* of decision making to take place. Reasoning and deliberation require capacities to draw inferences about the consequences of making a certain choice and to compare alternative outcomes based on how they further one's good or promote one's ends. Some capacity to employ at least very rudimentary probabilistic reasoning about uncertain outcomes will commonly be necessary, as well as the capacity to give due consideration to potential future outcomes in a present decision. Reasoning and deliberation obviously make use of both capacities mentioned earlier: understanding the information and applying the decision-maker's values.

Finally, a competent decision-maker also requires a *set of values* or *conception of what is good* that is at least minimally consistent, stable, and affirmed as his or her own. This is needed in order to be able to evaluate particular outcomes as benefits or harms, goods or evils, and to assign different relative weight or importance to them. Often, what will be needed is the capacity to *decide* on the import, scope, and relative weight to be accorded different values, since that may not have been fully determined before a particular choice must be made. Competence does not require a fully consistent set of goals, much less a detailed "lifeplan" to cover all contingencies. However, sufficient internal consistency and stability over time in the values relative to a particular decision are needed to yield and enable pursuit of a decision outcome; for example, a depressed patient subject to frequent mood changes may repeatedly consent to electroconvulsive treatment, but then change his or her mind before treatment can be carried out. Although values change over time and ambivalence is inevitable in the difficult choices faced by many persons of questionable competence concerning their medical care, sufficient value stability is needed to permit, at the very least, a decision that can be stated and adhered to over the course of its discussion, initiation, and implementation.

III. COMPETENCE AS A THRESHOLD CONCEPT, NOT A COMPARATIVE ONE

Decision-making competence, including the skills and capacities necessary to it, is one of the three components in standard analyses of the requirements for informed consent in health care decision making.[7] The informed consent doctrine requires the *free* and *informed* consent of a *competent* patient to medical procedures that are to be performed. The ideal of shared decision making underlying this doctrine is that of a patient deciding, in collaboration with a physician, what health care, if any, will best serve the patient's aims and needs.[8] If the decision is not voluntary, but instead coerced or manipulated, it will likely serve another's ends or another's view of the patient's good, not the patient's own view, and will in a significant sense originate with another and not with the patient. If the appropriate information is not provided in a form the patient can understand, the patient will not be able to ascertain how available alternatives might serve his or her aims. Finally, if the patient is not competent, either the individual will be unable to decide at all or the decision-making process will likely be seriously flawed.

Sometimes, as has already been noted, incompetence will be uncontroversially complete, as with patients who are in a persistent vegetative state or who are in a very advanced state of dementia, unable to communicate coherently at all. Often, however, deficiencies and limitations in the capacities and skills noted above as necessary to competence will be partial and a matter of degree, just as whether a patient's decision is voluntary or involuntary, informed or uninformed, is also often a matter of degree.

Does this mean that competence itself should be thought of as a matter of degree? It is certainly the case that persons are said to be more or less competent to perform many tasks, not just decision making. Nevertheless, because of the *role* competence determinations play in health care generally, and in the legal process in particular, it is important to resist the notion that persons can be determined to be more or less competent, or competent to some degree, to make a particular decision. The difficulty with taking literally the notion that competence to make a decision is a matter of degree can be seen most clearly by looking at the *function* of the competence determination within the practice of informed consent for health care, or within other areas of the law in which it plays a role, such as conservatorship or guardianship for financial affairs.

That function is, first and foremost, to sort persons into two classes: (1) those whose voluntary decisions (about their health care, financial affairs, and so on) must be respected by others and accepted as binding, and (2) those whose decisions, even if uncoerced, will be set aside and for whom others will act as surrogate decision-makers.[9] (This does not mean that surrogate decision-makers do or should completely ignore the expressed wishes of persons judged to be incompetent to make the decision in question, but only that those expressed wishes will not be accepted as binding on others.) The principal function of the competence determination, then, is to make an all-or-nothing classification of persons with regard to their competence to make and have respected a particular decision, not to make "matter of degree" findings about their decision-making capacities and skills. Persons are judged, both in the law and more informally in health care settings, to be either competent or incompetent to make a particular decision—even though the underlying capacities and skills forming the basis of that judgment are possessed in different degrees. Competence, then, is in this sense a threshold concept, not a comparative one.[10] This function of the competence determination *for a particular decision* being an all-or-nothing determination is compatible, of course, with a person's competence *for different decisions* being selective or decision-specific.

This is not to say, of course, that patients' degrees of

decision-making capacities, whether they are above or
below the threshold of competence, will not affect how
their physicians appropriately treat them. For example, it
may be appropriate for a physician to give significant
weight in formulating a treatment recommendation or in
dealing with family members to the wishes about treatment of a "nearly competent" patient who is just below
the threshold of competence. In contrast, the wishes of a
grossly psychotic or demented patient with severely impaired decision-making capacities should receive less
weight. Alternatively, for *competent patients above the
threshold,* physicians may take more time and effort to
explain a recommendation with *patients who have unusually
great capacities for understanding and reasoning.* The import of
"competence" being a threshold concept is only that
whether decisional authority is in the end left with the
patient or transferred to a surrogate is a "yes or no" not
"matter of degree" determination.

The foregoing makes clear that the crucial question in
the competence determination is *how* defective an individual's capacities and skills to make a particular decision
must be for the individual to be found incompetent to
make that decision, so that a surrogate decision-maker
becomes necessary. This is to ask for a standard of competence. In keeping with our primary emphasis in this
study, our analysis of that question focuses on medical
treatment decisions. Here the familiar doctrine of informed consent provides considerable guidance.

The central purpose of assessing competence is to determine whether a patient retains the right to accept or
refuse a particular medical procedure, or whether that
right shall be transferred to a surrogate. What values are at
stake in whether people are allowed to make such decisions for themselves? The informed consent doctrine
assigns the decision-making right to patients themselves;
but what fundamental values are served by this practice of
informed consent? In the literature dealing with informed

consent, many different answers—and ways of formulating answers—to that question have been proposed, but we believe that the most important values at stake are: 1) promoting and protecting the patient's well-being, and 2) respecting the patient's self-determination. It is in examining the effect on these two values that the answer to the proper standard of decision-making competence will be found.

IV. STANDARDS OF COMPETENCE: UNDERLYING VALUES

A. Promotion of individual well-being

There is a long tradition in medicine that the physician's first and most important commitment should be to serve the well-being of the patient. The more recent doctrine of informed consent is consistent with that tradition, if it is assumed that, at least in general, competent individuals are better judges of their own good than are others. In supporting above the global presumption of competence for adults, we have already endorsed this assumption. Of course, if patients were left completely uninformed by their physicians about the diagnosis of their present condition, their prognosis if it is left untreated, and the alternative treatments available for it with their attendant risks and benefits and associated likelihoods, then this assumption would not be reasonable. The assumption that competent individuals are usually the best judges of their own good in the context of medical treatment decisions is dependent on their having received from their physicians medical information material to those decisions in a form that facilitates their understanding and use of the information. The very notion of *informed* consent signifies this. As an expression of the ideal of shared decision making, the doctrine of informed consent recognizes that while the physician commonly brings to the physician-patient encounter medical knowledge, training, and experience that the patient lacks, the patient brings knowledge that the physician lacks: knowledge of his or her particular subjective aims and values that are likely to be affected by whatever decision is made.

As medicine's arsenal of possible interventions has dramatically expanded in recent decades, alternative treatments (and the alternative of no treatment) now routinely promise different mixes of benefits and risks to the patient. Moreover, since health is only one value among many, and different aspects of it are assigned different importance by different persons, there is commonly no one single intervention for a particular condition that is best for everyone. Which, if any, intervention best serves a particular patient's well-being will depend in significant part on that patient's aims and values. This is why health care decision-making usually ought to be a joint undertaking between physician and patient—each brings knowledge and experience that the other lacks, yet which is necessary for decisions that will best serve the patient's well-being.

In the exercise of their right to give informed consent, then, patients commonly decide in ways that they believe will best promote their own well-being as they conceive it. However, as is well known, and as physicians are frequently quick to point out, the complexity of many health care treatment decisions—together with the stresses of illness with its attendant fear, anxiety, dependency, and regression, not to mention the physical effects of illness itself—means that a patient's ordinary decision-making abilities are often significantly diminished. Thus, a patient's treatment choices may fail to serve his or her good or well-being, even as the patient conceives it. The same value of patient well-being that requires patients' participation in their own health care decision making sometimes also requires persons to be protected from the harmful consequences to them of their own choices.

There are deep and complex philosophical issues about

the best or correct account of individual well-being or good raised by our appeal to the value of individual well-being as one of the two most important values at stake in competence determinations. We can make no attempt even to explore fully, much less settle, those issues here; to do so would require a separate book.[11] We can, however, at least make clear the main alternative accounts of individual well-being and their implications for competence determinations and surrogate decision making. Much of our account of competence and of the principles guiding surrogate decision making does not presuppose one particular kind of theory of the good for persons, but we shall not attempt to specify fully when that is or is not so. Oversimplifying greatly, there are three broad and prominent theories of well-being or the good for persons in the literature of moral philosophy.

Hedonist theories hold that the only thing that is good for a person is having conscious experiences of a specified, positive sort.[12] The particular kinds of conscious experience are alternatively characterized as pleasure, happiness or the satisfaction or enjoyment that typically results from the successful pursuit of our aims and desires. On this account of well-being, health care treatment promotes a patient's well-being to the extent that it produces these valuable conscious experiences for the patient.

The second kind of theory we call a preference or desire satisfaction theory of the good for persons. In this view, what is good for persons is for them to have their desires or preferences satisfied to the maximum extent possible over their lifetimes.[13] We understand preferences or desires as taking states of affairs as their objects, and so as satisfied when those states of affairs obtain. For example, Jones's desire that her spouse be faithful is satisfied just in case her spouse is faithful, whether or not Jones knows that he is faithful or undergoes any particular conscious experience as a result. On the hedonist theory, one would have an equally pleasurable conscious experience believing

that one's spouse is faithful, whether that belief happens to
be true or false. However, the preference or desire theory
is closely related to the hedonist theory, since virtually all
persons have strong desires for happiness for themselves.

Any plausible version of a preference satisfaction theory
must allow for some *corrections* in the actual preferences
persons have at various times if the satisfaction of those
preferences is to contribute to the person's good.[14] Most
obvious is the need to correct for mistakes in reasoning
due to misinformed preferences to do or have something:
for example, a desire to eat an apparently appealing meal
not knowing that it contains a lethal dose of arsenic. Some
appeal is needed as well to the preferences a person does
not in fact have, but would have under certain conditions:
for example, the desires one would have for certain experiences if one was able in imagination to become vividly
aware of what those experiences would be like. Correction
will also be required for the way in which specific forms of
mental illness, such as severe clinical depression, can distort and alter a person's aims and values and in turn the
preferences based on them. We cannot even begin to explore here all of the ways in which preferences would be
corrected in a plausible preference satisfaction theory of
the good for persons. The feature of this theory of fundamental importance, however, is that what ultimately
makes some experience or state of affairs, such as medical
treatment, a contribution to a person's well-being is that it
contributes to his or her desire or preference satisfaction.
We shall refer below to such corrected preferences as those
supported by a person's underlying and enduring aims and
values.

Besides mistaken preferences, there is another kind of
preference whose satisfaction does not contribute to a person's well-being and which is important for our purposes
here—the preference or choice freely and knowingly to
sacrifice one's own well-being for the sake of other persons. For example, a father might freely and knowingly

choose not to pursue an expensive life-sustaining treatment such as a heart transplant in order to preserve financial resources for his children's education. We might say here that he values his personal well-being in these circumstances less than the well-being of his children. Precisely how to distinguish those preferences whose satisfaction contributes to a person's well-being from those that would sacrifice it for other values raises deep difficulties that cannot be pursued here. The rough idea is that personal well-being makes essential reference to the states of consciousness, activities, and capacities for functioning *of the person in question,* and it is these that are worsened when he chooses to sacrifice his own personal well-being for that of his child. If the informed consent doctrine requires respecting such a preference and choice, as we believe it both does and should, that *cannot* be because it contributes to the patient's well-being on the preference satisfaction account of well-being. Instead, support for respecting such a preference must come from the other principal value underlying the informed consent doctrine— self-determination—which will be discussed shortly.

The third general kind of theory of the good for persons is what Derek Parfit[15] has called an objective list theory and what one of us has called elsewhere an ideal theory of the good for persons.[16] The fundamental point of difference between ideal theories and both hedonist and preference theories is that in ideal theories some things are held to be good or bad for a person independent of whether the person him- or herself will undergo positive conscious experience while having them and independent of whether the person prefers them, even after his or her preferences have been suitably corrected. Various ideal theories of the good for persons will differ about the content of the ideals, for example whether they include being self-determined, developing one's abilities, being undeceived, and so forth, as well as about how such ideals are to be defended or justified. But it is important to note that no plausible ideal theory will deny that happiness and preference satisfaction often contribute to a person's well-being. What ideal theories deny is *only* that happiness and preference satisfaction are all there is to personal well-being.

Plainly, it will be important, at least in some cases, which kind of theory of individual well-being is employed in assessing the effects of different medical interventions on a person's well-being, as well as in any balancing of individual self-determination and well-being. Two kinds of considerations—theoretical and practical—are relevant to this choice of a theory of personal well-being that is to be employed in assessments of the appropriate level of decision-making competence. Theoretical considerations concern which is the best or correct theory of well-being. Hedonist theories have been widely criticized and, we believe, shown to be inadequate, although we will not rehearse those criticisms here.[17] Assessing corrected preference theories is more difficult because no complete and systematic account has been given of how a person's preferences should be corrected to determine his or her good. Ideal theories of the good for persons are harder still to assess, both because their proponents have differed so widely about the content of justified ideals of individual good and because there is no consensus about how those ideals are to be defended. Indeed, many of their defenders seem to fail to appreciate the need to provide arguments in defense of such ideals.

It is important to emphasize, nevertheless, that on all three kinds of theory it makes perfectly good sense to speak of persons being mistaken about their well-being *and* of persons' well-being as a subjective matter. Persons can be mistaken about what will make them happy or about what will best satisfy their underlying and enduring aims and values, and can fail to accept or choose in accord with objective ideals of the person and personal well-being. Thus, on all three kinds of theory of personal well-being, patients' treatment choices can be in conflict with their well-being. Protecting their well-being can then support setting aside their choices. Well-being is also substantially subjective on all three theories in the sense that what makes a particular person happy or satisfies his or her preferences depends ultimately on that person's aims, aspirations, and values, and since happiness and/or preference satisfaction is a substantial part of individual well-being on all three theories. These important subjective elements of well-being support the informed consent doctrine's assignment of decision-making authority to patients, as well as the advance directive and substituted judgment guidance principles that will be discussed in Chapter 2. At the theoretical level, the preference theory makes an individual's well-being ultimately fully subjective, whereas ideal theories have an element of objectivity such that some of persons' fully corrected choices could reflect mistakes about there own well-being. The subjectivity present in differing degrees in all three theories supports often accepting persons' own views of their well-being. Thus, there is a tension in all three theories between the sense in which individuals are fallible about their good and the sense in which their good is subjective and cannot be gain-said.

Practical considerations reduce the differences between preference and ideal theories by limiting substantially the extent to which ideals of personal well-being that individuals do not themselves accept should be employed in a practice designed to promote and protect their well-being. We are concerned with a theory of surrogate decision making to be employed primarily in medicine, in which there is a long and powerful paternalistic tradition to the effect that physicians know best what is good for their patients. While that tradition has come under a variety of pressures and criticisms in recent years, it remains a powerful force.[18] Sanctioning employment of ideal theories of individual well-being in the context of assessments of competence and of surrogate decision making inevitably invites substantial and unjustified abuse in which others, commonly physicians but also family members, substitute their own conceptions of where the patient's well-being lies for the patient's own conception of his or her well-being. Even if some ideal components of the good are justified or true, paternalistic interference in practice is not likely to be limited only to them.

A corrected preference account of individual well-being is also subject to considerable abuse, particularly if there is no adequate account of the sorts of corrections of preferences it should sanction. Nevertheless, a corrected preference view has the substantial practical advantage of requiring that assessments of a particular person's well-being ultimately be rooted in that person's *own* preferences and values. Consequently, it focuses attention on the person's *process* of deliberation and reasoning that has led up to his or her choice, and any errors or defects it may contain, in defense of any claims that the person's actual treatment choice is contrary to his or her well-being. Preference theories place stronger theoretical and practical constraints on unwarranted paternalism by grounding individual well-being more squarely in the underlying and enduring aims and values of the pesons in question. Thus, if worries about abuse or error are adequately appreciated, even proponents of ideal theories will see that disagreements about which ideals are correct requires some limitation of the use of objective ideals in assessments of the well-being of persons who do not accept those ideals. In practice, then, preference and ideal theories may yield very similar results.

B. Respect for individual self-determination

The other principal value underlying the informed consent doctrine is respect for a patient's self-determination, understood here as a person's interest in making significant

decisions about his or her own life. Although often conceived in the law under the right of privacy, the leading
legal decisions in the informed consent tradition appeal
fundamentally to the right of individual self-determination.[19] Since the central focus of concern in this book is on
surrogate decision making for incompetent persons, and
since surrogate decision making should take place with
persons for whom the exercise of self-determination is
either impossible or inappropriate, it is not necessary here
to analyze fully the complex of ideas giving content to the
concept of individual self-determination, nor to articulate
systematically the various values that support its importance.[20] But enough must be said about self-
determination and its value to make clear its roles in setting a standard of competence, in guiding surrogates deciding for the incompetent, and to make sense of common
judicial findings that speak of a right of self-determination
of incompetents. The central question is this: why do
persons have an interest in making significant decisions
about their lives for themselves?

There are two importantly different kinds of reasons
that should be distinguished. The first is that self-
determination is instrumentally valuable in promoting a
person's well-being. On any of the three kinds of theories
of individual well-being distinguished above, what best
serves a person's well-being often depends on the particular aims and values of that person. On the preference
theory, a person's underlying and enduring aims and values fully determine his or her good. On the hedonist
theory, it seems true that choices in accord with a person's
aims and values will usually, though of course not always,
optimally promote the person's happiness. On any plausible ideal theory, although some things are for a person's
good independent of what the person's aims and values
are, choices in accord with those aims and values will
nevertheless also usually be for the person's good, es-

pecially in light of practical or fallibilist worries about the dangers inherent in enforcing ideals on persons who do not share them.

Thus, on each of these theories, the fact that competent adults are generally the best judges of what serves their own well-being supports persons' interests in making significant decisions affecting their lives for themselves. Individual self-determination is instrumentally valuable in the promotion of individual well-being, although only on most but not all occasions of its exercise. This instrumental value of self-determination for individual well-being reflects what is often referred to as the subjective nature of individual well-being. When persons are incompetent to make a decision for themselves and others must decide for them, the instrumental value of self-determination can still be indirectly respected by guidance principles for surrogates that require them to seek to make decisions that are most in accordance with the person's aims and values while competent.

There is a second important reason why self-determination is valued, which does not depend on its instrumental value in promoting a person's well-being. Most persons commonly want to make significant decisions about their lives for themselves, and this desire is in part independent of whether they believe that they are always in a position to make the best choice. Even when we believe that others may be able to decide for us better than we ourselves can, we often prefer to decide for ourselves. The capacities for deliberation, choice and action that normal humans possess make it possible for them to form, revise over time, and pursue in action a conception of their own good. Having a conception of the good is more than merely possessing desires that support goal-directed behavior—a feature which persons share with animals. Persons have a capacity for reflective self-evaluation, for considering what they want their motivations to be, what kind of persons they want to become.

This is not to deny that there are limits to the extent to which persons can choose or change their motivations and character. In broad respects our natures are fixed and given to us by our biological endowment and our environment, but within these broad limits we adopt and affirm particular aims and values and create a unique self. In doing so, we can take charge of and take responsibility for our lives and the kinds of persons we are and will become.

This noninstrumental value of self-determination, of making significant decisions about our lives for ourselves, varies substantially depending on the particular decision being made. Particular decisions range along a wide spectrum in the importance a person may give to making and effecting his or her own choice—from inconsequential at one end to a place of central and enduring importance in shaping and directing the person's life at the other. Medical treatment decisions that affect a person's pursuit of a career, that raise conflicts with deeply held religious values, or that affect when and how one's life will end are examples of decisions at the end of the spectrum at which self-determination is of great importance.

There is another respect in which the value of self-determination varies. Self-determination is one of the most plausible candidates for an objective ideal of the person within ideal theories of the good for persons. This ideal of a self-determining agent presupposes the development of the capacities necessary for reflective choice. When these capacities are substantially limited or impaired, the value of choosing for oneself is likewise diminished because the ideal of the self-determining agent and the value it represents is less able to be realized.

Thus, the interest in self-determination, while a fundamental value in our society, should neither be overstated nor assumed to be of equal importance in all cases. The importance of our interest in deciding for ourselves will vary substantially depending on the nature of the particular decision being made. Moreover, people often wish to make such decisions for themselves simply because they believe that, at least in most cases, they are in a better position to decide what is best for themselves than others are. Consequently, when in a particular case others are demonstrably in a better position to decide for us than we ourselves are, a part, but not all, of our interest in deciding for ourselves is absent.

C. Conflict between the values of
self-determination and well-being

Because people's interest in making important decisions for themselves is not based solely on their concern for their own well-being, these two values of individual well-being and self-determination can sometimes conflict. Some people appear to decide in ways that are contrary to their own best interests or well-being, even as determined by their own settled conception of their well-being, and others may be unable to convince them of the mistake. In other cases, others may know little of a person's own settled values, and the person may simply be deciding in a manner sharply in conflict with how most reasonable persons would decide. However, it may be difficult or even impossible to determine whether this conflict is simply the result of a difference in values between this individual and most reasonable persons (for example, a difference in the weights assigned to various benefits or risks), or whether it results from some failure of the patient to assess correctly what will best serve his or her own interests or good.

In assessing which value is most important when self-determination and well-being appear to be in conflict, a tradeoff between avoiding two kinds of errors should be sought.[21] The first error is that of failing adequately to protect a person from the harmful consequences of his or her decision when the decision is the result of serious defects in the capacity to decide. The second error is failing to permit someone to make a decision and turning the decision over to another when the patient is sufficiently able to make the decision him- or herself. With a stricter or higher standard for competence, more people will be found incompetent, and the first error will be minimized at the cost of increasing the second sort of error. With a looser or more minimal standard for competence, fewer persons will be found incompetent, and the second sort of error is more likely to be minimized at the cost of increasing the first.

Evidence regarding a person's competence to make a particular decision is often ineliminably uncertain, incomplete, and conflicting. Thus, no conceivable set of procedures and standards for judging competence could guarantee the elimination of all error. Instead, the challenge is to strike the appropriate balance and thereby minimize the overall incidence of the errors noted above. No set of procedures will guarantee that in practice all and only the incompetent are judged to be incompetent.

But procedures and standards for competence are not merely inevitably imperfect. They are inevitably *controversial* as well. In the determination of competence, there is disagreement not only about which procedures will minimize errors, but also about the proper standard that the procedures should be designed to approximate. The core of the controversy is the different values that different persons assign to protecting individuals' well-being as against respecting their self-determination. There is no uniquely "correct" answer to the relative weight that should be assigned to these two values, and in any event it is simply a fact that different persons do assign them significantly different weight.

V. CONTRAST WITH A SINGLE VALUE FOUNDATION—INDIVIDUAL SELF-DETERMINATION AS SOVEREIGN

Many philosophic accounts of justified paternalism rest on a fundamental intuition that decisions for, or for the benefit of, another person must respect that person's autonomy or self-determination. These theories grounded in respect for autonomy seem to appeal only to the single value of autonomy or self-determination, and not to balance it against well-being. Perhaps the most prominent recent example of this view is the work of Joel Feinberg, who argues that whether a self-regarding decision should be left with the individual him- or herself should not be determined by a balancing of the values of personal self-determination and the protection of individual well-being.[22] Instead, when self-determination and well-being conflict, Feinberg holds that self-determination should always be sovereign and take precedence. Interference with a person's acting as he or she wishes within the self-regarding sphere is justified in order to promote or protect his or her well-being or good only if the conduct is substantially nonvoluntary, or to establish whether the conduct is voluntary. Feinberg *seems* to use "voluntary" roughly in the way others use "autonomous" or "self-determined" conduct, and so provisionally we can take him to be asserting that only whether a person's conduct is substantially self-determined is at issue. Other philosophers have also sought to develop a general account of justified paternalistic intervention that looks only to self-determination and rejects balancing it against well-being, but we shall focus here on Feinberg's account both because it is one of the most influential and carefully developed versions of this general kind of view and because Feinberg's inability to avoid the balancing that he explicitly rejects is instructive for our purposes here.[23]

Feinberg elaborates the model of a fully or perfectly voluntary choice as one "deficient in *none* of the ways that are *ever* taken into account for *any* moral or legal purpose in *any* context."[24] The general categories of factors establishing voluntariness are: the chooser is competent (minimum threshold sense); he does not choose under coercion or duress; he does not choose because of more subtle manipulation; he does not choose because of ignorance or mistaken belief; he does not choose in circumstances that are temporarily distorting. The crux of voluntariness is "the faithful expression of the settled values and preferences of the actor, or an accurate representation of him in some centrally important way."[25] Any justified paternalism in Feinberg's view must show that the person whose choices are interfered with is not getting what he or she wants, not that his or her well-being will be protected by the paternalistic intervention. Moreover, Feinberg allows that persons' fully informed and voluntary choices can be contrary to their good for any of a number of reasons. Such choices may reflect an unreasonable judgment of comparative worth, they may be due to laziness, short-term self-indulgence, and so forth. Or persons may act believing at the time that their choice is not for the best for them; or, though their choice is fully informed and voluntary, they may be mistaken nevertheless about what their good is. (This last possibility arises for Feinberg because he accepts an "objective" account of natural interests as growing out of our inherited constitutions as human beings and identifies a person's good ultimately with his self-fulfillment.[26])

In these cases in which a person's self-determination conflicts with his well-being, "he has a sovereign right to choose in a manner we think, plausibly enough, to be foolish, provided only that the choices are truly voluntary."[27] Feinberg rejects perfect voluntariness as an impossibly high standard, so the question is how voluntary is "truly voluntary" or voluntary *enough* to be protected from paternalistic interferences. What is enough will vary "depending on the nature of the interest at stake, and the moral or legal purpose to be served."[28] Feinberg offers some rules of thumb for determining the appropriate level of voluntariness, two of which are that the more risky the conduct, and the more irreversible the risked harm, the greater the degree of voluntariness that should be required if the conduct is to be permitted. This appears to trade off self-determination (Feinberg's voluntariness that comes in degrees) against well-being by requiring a higher level of voluntariness the greater and more irreversible the risked harm. However, Feinberg explicitly rejects this interpretation, insisting that it represents no independent commitment to harm prevention apart from voluntariness, but only the purpose of preventing "people from suffering harm that they have not truly chosen to suffer or to risk suffering."[29]

Feinberg's argument for the variable standard of voluntariness is an epistemic or fallibilist argument. Since we may be mistaken in our assessment of the voluntariness of another's choice, the greater the risk of a bad choice (the greater and more irrevocable the risked harm, and the higher its probability), the higher the level of voluntariness that should be insisted on in order to limit the possibility of wrongly judging the person's choice to be voluntary enough to warrant noninterference. The idea is that because we may be mistaken in our assessment of voluntariness, we raise the level required for accepting high-risk choices so as to reduce the likelihood of mistakenly accepting a choice as voluntary enough. But does this avoid balancing self-determination and well-being?

Suppose Feinberg had a principled way, apart from fallibilist considerations, of setting the proper level of voluntariness that should be required for a choice to be respected. We could then use fallibilist considerations in support of building in a greater margin for error to assure that this level is satisfied the greater the risk of the person not getting what he or she wants, or the greater the harm risked that the person may not want. But *there is no natural level of voluntariness to which fallibilist considerations could then be applied*. Indeed, if self-determination, understood as persons' interest in making significant decisions about their lives for themselves, were the *only* value or *always overrides* well-being, then fallibilist considerations would give one *no reason* for insisting on a higher level of voluntariness for choices carrying high risks of serious and irrevocable harm. While a high standard would reduce the risk of a false positive determination of voluntariness (holding a choice to be "voluntary enough" that in fact is not sufficiently voluntary), it at the same time would increase the risk of a false negative (holding a choice not to be "voluntary enough" that in fact is sufficiently voluntary). *Any* policy that risks a false negative determination of voluntariness, no matter how small that risk, cannot be justified solely by appeal to the value of self-determination, since if self-determination were *all* that is important there would be *no* reason to risk *any* restriction of it in order to reduce the risk of a false positive determination of sufficient voluntariness. Feinberg's position could only be that self-determination is the sole relevant value only when the choice is *perfectly* voluntary. If a choice is, or might be, less than perfectly voluntary, then *self-determination must be balanced against well-being.*

In setting the appropriate level of voluntariness, Feinberg holds that the greater and more irrevocable the risked harm, the higher the level of voluntariness that should be required so as to be increasingly sure that the increasingly more serious risked harm is what the person wants. This *is* to balance self-determination and well-being in *our* sense—the person's interest in making the choice for him- or herself against the person's interest in getting the alternative that in fact will best promote his or her well-being. Feinberg's assessment of voluntariness *encompasses* weighing both self-determination and well-being, as we have characterized them. Feinberg resists the balancing characterization because he accepts an "objective" conception (what we earlier called an ideal theory) of individual well-being or good, and so wants to insist that a person can make a fully or perfectly voluntary choice that is contrary to his or her good. Feinberg's insistence on restricting the decision of whether the person's choice should be respected to an assessment of the voluntariness of the choice is needed to insure the rejection of any independent commitment to promoting the person's good, defined in this objective sense.

We too have implicitly rejected balancing protecting a person's good—defined in an objective sense that can be in conflict with his underlying and enduring aims and values—against his self-determination. In discussing alternative conceptions of individual well-being above, we suggested that the two principal candidates for the best theory are the preference and ideal theories. The preference theory directly rejects this balancing because it defines persons' well-being as ultimately determined by their underlying and enduring aims and values. Ideal theories do admit objective ideals of the person that can be in conflict with persons' underlying and enduring aims and values, and so in principle allow the balancing that Feinberg rejects. However, we argued that practical or fallibilist worries about unwarranted imposition of controversial or unjustified ideals, or others' conceptions of well-being on persons who do not share those ideals or conceptions, sharply limits appeal to objective ideals in balancing well-being against self-determintion for setting the appropriate level of competence.

Thus, there is no significant disagreement between Feinberg's view and our contention that in deciding whether a person's choice is to be accepted (as competent, for us, as voluntary enough, for Feinberg), the person's interest in deciding for him- or herself must be balanced against his or her interest in obtaining the alternative that best fits his or her underlying and enduring aims and values. The factors that reduce voluntariness are just the factors that can deflect persons' choices from their well-being in this sense (although for the ideal theorist reduced voluntariness need not always deflect one's choice from the ideal). Feinberg's position, then, is that a person's self-determination is always sovereign *only when* his or her choice is sufficiently voluntary, and the voluntariness assessment *does* balance self-determination and well-being as we define them. It is clear, then, that Feinberg does *not* make self-determination sovereign, defined in our sense of self-determination as one's interest in making the choice for oneself, because to do so would require always accepting the person's choice, however much it failed to be a voluntary choice. That, for very good reason, is not Feinberg's position. Only if one values something besides choosing for oneself—for us, individual well-being, and for Feinberg, getting what one wants—can one ever have reason to set aside a person's choices, as the requirement of sufficient voluntariness does.

The result is that Feinberg's position *is* a balancing view in our sense, contrary to initial appearances, and in fact is not in substance significantly different than our own in its assessment of whether decisional authority should be left with the patient or transferred to a surrogate. We conclude that an examination of Feinberg's alternative single-value foundation shows it in fact to be a view balancing self-determination and well-being, as we have characterized those values, and shows why the balancing view cannot plausibly be avoided. Thus what at first appeared to be the most serious rival to the analysis offered here turns out to support our balancing model.

VI. DECIDING ON STANDARDS OF COMPETENCE

The proper standard of competence must be chosen; it cannot be discovered. There is no reason to believe that there is one and only one optimal trade-off between the competing values of well-being and self-determination, nor, hence, any one uniquely correct level of capacity at which to set the threshold of competence—even for a particular decision under specified circumstances. In this sense, setting a standard for competence is a value choice, not solely a scientific or factual matter.

Focusing only on the two values of patient well-being and self-determination, however, is an oversimplification.

Because other significant values are sometimes at stake, room for controversy about the proper standard of competence increases. For example, also important to the appropriate standard of competence is the value of maintaining public confidence in the integrity of the medical profession, so as to protect and foster the trust necessary to physician–patient relationships that function well.

Nevertheless, the choice need not be and should not be arbitrary. Instead, it should be grounded in (1) a reflective appreciation of the values in question, (2) a clear understanding of the goals that the determination of competence is to serve, and (3) an accurate prediction of the practical consequences of setting the threshold at this level rather than elsewhere.

People may disagree on exactly where the threshold should be set not only because they assign different weights to the values of self-determination and well-being, but also because they make different estimates of the probability that others will err in trying to promote a person's interests. Unanimous agreement on an optimal standard is not necessary, however, for workable social arrangements for determining competence, any more than it is for determining who may vote or who may drive an automobile.

VII. DIFFERENT STANDARDS OF COMPETENCE

A number of different standards of competence have been identified and supported in the literature, although statutory and case law provide little help in articulating precise standards.[30] It is neither feasible nor necessary to discuss here all the alternatives that have been proposed. Instead, the range of alternatives will be delineated and the difficulties of the main standards will be examined in order to clarify and defend the decision-relative analysis offered above. More or less stringent standards of competence in effect strike different balances between the values of patient well-being and self-determination.

A. A minimal standard of competence

An example of a minimal standard of competence is that the patient merely be able to express a preference. This standard respects every expressed choice of a patient, and so is not in fact a criterion of *competent* choice at all.[31] It entirely disregards whether defects or mistakes are present in the reasoning process leading to the choice, whether the choice is in accord with the patient's own conception of his or her good, and whether the choice would be harmful to the patient. It thus fails to provide any protection for patient well-being, and it is insensitive to the way the value of self-determination itself varies both with the nature of the decision to be made and with differences in people's capacities to choose in accordance with their conceptions of their own good.

B. An outcome standard of competence

At the other extreme are standards that look solely to the *content* or *outcome* of the decision—for example, the standard that the choice be a reasonable one, or be what other reasonable or rational persons would choose. On this view, failure of the patient's choice to match some such allegedly objective outcome standard of choice entails that it is an incompetent choice. Such a standard maximally protects patient well-being—although only according to the standard's conception of well-being—but fails adequately to respect patient self-determination.

At bottom, a person's interest in self-determination is his or her interest in defining, revising over time, and pursuing his or her own particular conception of the good life. As we noted above of ideal theories of the good for persons, there are serious practical or fallibilist risks associated with any purportedly objective standard for the correct decision—the standard may ignore the patient's own distinctive conception of the good and may constitute enforcement of unjustified ideals or unjustifiably substitute another's conception of what is best for the patient. Moreover, even such a standard's theoretical claim to protect maximally a patient's well-being is only as strong as the objective account of a person's well-being on which the standard rests. Many proponents of ideal theories only assert the ideals and fail even to recognize the need for justifying them, much less proceed to do so.

Although ascertaining the correct or best theory of individual well-being or the good for persons is a complex and controversial task, we argued above that any standard of individual well-being that does not ultimately rest on an individual's own underlying and enduring aims and values is both problematic in theory and subject to intolerable abuse in practice. There may be room in some broad policy decisions or overall theories of justice for more "objective" and interpersonal measures of well-being that fail fully to reflect differences in individuals' own views of their well-being,[32] but we believe there is *much less room* for such purportedly objective measures in the kind of judgments of concern here—judgments about appropriate treatment for an individual patient. Thus, a standard that judges competence by comparing the content of a patient's decision to some objective standard for the correct decision may fail even to protect appropriately a patient's well-being.

C. A process standard of decision-making competence

An adequate standard of competence will focus primarily not on the content of the patient's decision but on the *process* of the reasoning that leads up to that decision.

There are two central questions for any process standard of competence. First, a process standard must set a level of reasoning required for the patient to be competent. In other words, how well must the patient understand and reason to be competent? How much can understanding be limited or reasoning be defective and still be compatible with competence? The second question often passes without explicit notice by those evaluating competence. How certain must those persons evaluating competence be about how well the patient has understood and reasoned in coming to a decision? This second question is important because it is common in cases of marginal or questionable competence for there to be a significant degree of uncertainty about the patient's reasoning and decision-making process that can never be eliminated.

VIII. RELATION OF THE PROCESS STANDARD OF COMPETENCE TO EXPECTED HARMS AND BENEFITS

Because the competence evaluation requires striking a balance between the two values of respecting patients' rights to decide for themselves and protecting them from the harmful consequences of their own choices, it should be clear that no single standard of competence—no single answer to the questions above—can be adequate for all decisions. This is true because (1) the degree of expected harm from choices made at a given level of understanding and reasoning can vary from none to the most serious, including major disability or death, and because (2) the importance or value to the patient of self-determination can vary depending on the choice being made.

There is an important implication of this view that the standard of competence ought to vary in part with the expected harms or benefits to the patient of acting in accordance with the patient's choice—namely, that just because a patient is competent to consent to a treatment, it does *not* follow that the patient is competent to refuse it, and vice versa. For example, consent to a low-risk life-saving procedure by an otherwise healthy individual should require only a minimal level of competence, but refusal of that same procedure by such an individual should require the highest level of competence.

Because the appropriate level of competence properly required for a particular decision must be adjusted to the consequences of acting on that decision, no single standard of decision-making competence is adequate. Instead, the level of competence appropriately required for decision making varies along a full range from low/minimal to high/maximal. Table 1.1 illustrates this variation, with the treatment choices listed used only as examples of any treatment choice with that relative risk/benefit assessment.

The net balance of expected benefits and risks of the patient's choice in comparison with other alternatives will usually be determined by the physician. This assessment should focus on the expected effects of a particular treatment option in forwarding the patient's underlying and enduring aims and values, to the extent that these are known. When the patient's aims and values are not known, the risk/benefit assessment will balance the expected effects of a particular treatment option in achieving the general goals of health care in prolonging life, preventing injury and disability, and relieving suffering as against its risks of harm. The table indicates that the relevant comparison is with other available alternatives, and the degree to which the net benefit/risk balance of the alternative chosen is better or worse than that for optimal alternative treatment options. It should be noted that a choice might properly require only low/minimal competence, even though its expected risks exceed its expected benefits or it is more generally a high-risk treatment, because all other available alternatives have substantially worse risk/benefit ratios.

Table 1.1 also indicates, for each level of competence, the relative importance of different *grounds* for believing

Table 1.1 *Decision-making competence and patient well-being*

The patient's treatment choice	Other's risk/benefit assessment of that choice in comparison with other alternatives	Level of decision-making competence required	Grounds for believing patient's choice best promotes/protects own well-being
Patient consents to lumbar puncture for presumed meningitis	Net balance substantially better than for possible alternatives	Low/minimal	Principally the benefit/risk assessment made by others
Patient chooses lumpectomy for breast cancer	Net balance roughly comparable to that of other alternatives	Moderate/median	Roughly equally from the benefit/risk assessment made by others and from the patient's decision that the chosen alternative best fits own conception of own good
Patient refuses surgery for simple appendectomy	Net balance substantially worse than for another alternative or alternatives	High/maximal	Principally from patient's decision that the chosen alternative best fits own conception of own good

that a patient's own choice best promotes his or her well-being. This brings out an important point. For *all* patient choices, other people responsible for deciding whether those choices should be respected should have grounds for believing that the choice, if it is to be honored, is reasonably in accord with the patient's well-being (although the choice need not, of course, *maximally* promote the patient's interests). When the patient's level of decision-making competence need be only at the low/minimal level, as in the agreement to a lumbar puncture for presumed meningitis, these grounds derive only minimally from the fact that the patient has chosen the option in question; they principally stem from others' positive assessment of the choice's expected effects on the patient's well-being.

At the other extreme, when the expected effects of the patient's choice for his or her well-being appear to be substantially worse than available alternatives, as in the refusal of a simple appendectomy, the requirement of a high/maximal level of competence provides grounds for relying on the patient's decision as itself establishing that the choice best fits the patient's good (his or her own underlying and enduring aims and values). The highest level of competence should assure that no significant mistakes in the patient's reasoning and decision making are present, and is required to rebut the presumption that the choice is not in fact reasonably related to the patient's interests.

When the expected effects for the patient's well-being of his or her choice are approximately comparable to those of alternatives, as in the choice of a lumpectomy for treatment of breast cancer, a moderate/median level or competence is sufficient to provide reasonable grounds that the choice promotes the patient's good and that her well-being is adequately protected. It is also reasonable to assume that as the level of competence required increases (from minimal to maximal), the instrumental value or importance of respecting the patient's self-determination increases as well, specifically the part of the value of self-determination that rests on the assumption that persons will secure their good when they choose for themselves. As competence increases, other things being equal, the likelihood of this happening increases.

Thus, according to the concept of competence endorsed here, a particular individual's decision-making capacity at a given time may be sufficient for making a decision to refuse a diagnostic procedure when foregoing the procedure does not carry a significant risk, although it would not necessarily be sufficient for refusing a surgical procedure that would correct a life-threatening condition. The greater the risk relative to other alternatives—where risk is a function of the severity of the expected harm and the probability of its occurrence—the greater the level of communication, understanding, and reasoning skills required for competence to make that decision. It is not always true, however, that if a person is competent to make one decision, then he or she is competent to make another decision so long as it involves equal risk. Even if the risk is the same, one decision may be more complex, and hence require a higher level of capacity for understanding options and reasoning about consequences.

In the previous section, we rejected a standard of competence that looks to the content or outcome of the decision in favor of a standard that focuses on the process of the patient's reasoning. This may appear inconsistent with our insistence here that the appropriate level of decision-making capacity required for competence should depend in significant part on the effects for the patient's well-being of accepting his or her choice, since what those effects are clearly depends on the content or outcome of the patient's choice. However, there is no inconsistency. The competence evaluation addresses the process of the patient's reasoning, whereas the degree of defectiveness and limitation of, and uncertainty about, that process that is compatible with competence depends in significant part on the likely harm to the patient's well-being of accepting his or her choice. To the extent that they are known, the effects on the patient's well-being should be evaluated in terms of his or her own underlying and enduring aims and values, or, where these are not known, in terms of the effects on life and health. Thus in our approach there is no use of an "objective" standard for the best or correct decision that is known to be in conflict with the patient's own underlying and enduring aims and values, which was the objectionable feature of a content or outcome standard of competence.

The evaluation of the patient's decision making will seek to assess how well the patient has understood the nature of the proposed treatment and any significant alternatives, the expected benefits and risks and the likelihood of each, the reason for the recommendation, and then whether the patient has made a choice that reasonably conforms to his or her underlying and enduring aims and values. Two broad kinds of defect are then possible; first, "factual" misunderstanding about the nature and likelihood of an outcome, for example from limitations in cognitive understanding resulting from stroke or from impairment of short-term memory resulting from dementia; second, failure of the patient's choice to be based on his or her underlying and enduring aims and values, for example because depression has temporarily distorted them so that the patient "no longer cares" about restoration of the function he or she had valued before becoming depressed.[33]

A crude but perhaps helpful way of characterizing the proper aim of the evaluator of the competence of a seemingly harmful or "bad" patient choice is to think of him or her addressing the patient in this fashion: "Help me try to understand and make sense of your choice. Help me to see whether your choice is reasonable, not in the sense that it is what I or most people would choose, but that it is reasonable for you in light of your underlying and enduring aims and values." This is the proper focus of a *process* standard of competence.

Some may object that misguided paternalists will always be ready to assert that their interference with the patient's choice is "deep down" in accord with what we have called the patient's "underlying and enduring aims and values," or at least with what these would be except for unfortunate distortions. If there is no objective way to determine a person's underlying and enduring aims and values then the worry is that our view will lead to excessive paternalism. We acknowledge that this determination will often be difficult and uncertain, for example in cases like severe chronic depression, leading to genuine and justified uncertainty about the patient's "true" aims and values. But any claims that the aims and values actually expressed by the patient are not his underlying and enduring aims and values should be based on evidence of the distortion of the actual aims and values independent of their mere difference with some other, "better" aims and values. Just as the process standard of competence focuses on the process of the patient's reasoning, so also it requires evidence of a process of distortion of the patient's aims and values to justify evaluating choices by a standard other than the patient's actually expressed aims and values.

IX. RELATION OF REFUSAL OF TREATMENT TO DETERMINATION OF INCOMPETENCE

A common criticism of the way physicians actually practice, often noted with some cynicism, is that patients' competence is rarely questioned until they refuse to consent to a physician's recommendation for treatment. (Here, our discussion of treatment refusal is limited to medical patients; we discuss refusal of psychiatric care in Chapter 7.) It is no doubt true that patients' competence when they accept physicians' treatment recommendations should be questioned more often than it now is, because consent without understanding provides little basis for believing the choice is best for the patient, and because the physician's judgment about what is best is fallible. Nevertheless, some treatment refusal does reasonably raise the question of a patient's competence in a way that acceptance of recommended treatment does not. We believe that it is a reasonable assumption that physicians' treatment recommendations are more often than not in the interests of their patients. Consequently, it is in turn a reasonable presumption—although rebuttable in any particular instance—that a treatment refusal is contrary to the patient's interest. Exploration of the reasons for the patient's response, including determination of whether the decision was a competent one, are appropriate—although reassessment by the physician of the recommendation is often appropriate as well. Since some studies suggest that most treatment refusals are withdrawn once a more adequate explanation of the reasons for the recommendation is provided, the first response of physicians to refusals should be a further attempt to provide that explanation.[34]

It is essential to distinguish here, however, between grounds for calling a patient's competence into question and grounds for a finding of incompetence. Treatment refusal usually does reasonably serve to *trigger* a competence evaluation. On the other hand, a disagreement with the physician's recommendation or refusal of a treatment recommendation is *no basis or evidence whatsoever* for a finding of incompetence. This conclusion follows from the premise supported earlier that the competence evaluation, as well as evidence in support of a finding of incompetence, should address the *process* of understanding and reasoning of the patient, *not* the *content* of his decision.

Another essential distinction is between two quite different types of treatment refusal: refusing all the treatment options offered, and refusing the one treatment that the physician believes to be best while accepting an alternative treatment that lies within the range of medically sound or acceptable options. If there is more than one medically sound treatment option—in the sense that competent medical judgment is divided as to which of two or more treatments would be optimal or if some treatments not medically optimal are still reasonable in view of their expected benefits and burdens—then the patient's refusal to accept the option that the physician believes is optimal should not even raise the question of the patient's competence, much less entail a finding of incompetence, at least so long as the option the patient chooses lies within the range of medically sound options.

X. CONTRAST WITH A FIXED MINIMUM THRESHOLD CONCEPTION OF COMPETENCE

Before elaborating the implications of our analysis for operational measurements of competence, it will be useful to contrast it in this section and the next with two alternative analyses that have been implicitly rejected here. According to one widely-held alternative conception—which may be called the "fixed minimal capacity" view—competence is *not* decision-relative. The simplest version of this view holds that a person is competent if he or she possesses the relevant decision-making capacities at some specified level, regardless of whether the decision to be made is risky or nonrisky, and regardless of whether the information to be understood or the consequences to be reasoned through are simple or complex. This concept of competence might also be called the "minimal threshold status concept," since the idea is that if a person's decision-making capacities meet or exceed the specified threshold, then the status of being a competent individual is to be ascribed to that person. According to this view, competence is an attribute of persons dependent solely on the level of decision-making capacities they possess (although these may vary, of course, from day to day or even from hour to hour, depending upon the effects of disease, medications, emotional states, and so on), and so is compatible with a person making a particular decision that is sufficiently foolish, imprudent, or otherwise flawed as to warrant paternalistic interference with the decision for the patient's own good.

In contrast, according to the conception of competence espoused here, competence is a *relational property* determined by a *variable standard*. Whether a person is competent to make a given decision depends not only upon that person's own capacities but also upon certain features of the decision itself—including risk and information requirements. Central to the case for our approach is the function of the competence evaluation in allocating decisional authority to the patient or a surrogate. There are at least five specific points in favor of our approach.

First, a concept that allows a raising or lowering of the standard for decision-making capacities depending in part upon the risks of the decision in question is clearly more consonant with the way people actually make informal competence determinations in areas of judgment in which they have the greatest confidence and on which there is the most consensus. For example, you may decide that your five-year-old child is competent to choose between a hamburger and a hotdog for lunch, but you would not think the child competent to make a decision about how to invest a large sum of money. This is because the risk in the latter case is greater, and the information required for reasoning about the relevant consequences of the options is much more complex. It is worth emphasizing that incompetence due to developmental immaturity, as in the case of a child, is in many respects quite different from the increasing incompetence due to a degenerative disease such as Alzheimer's. However, these and other cases of incompetence do have in common the relevance of the degree of risk for determining the appropriate level of competence.

Second, the decision-relative, variable-standard conception of competence also receives indirect support from the doctrine of informed consent. The more risky the decision a patient must make, and the more complex the array of possible benefits and burdens, the greater the amount of information that must be provided and the higher the standard of understanding required on the part of the patient. For extremely low-risk procedures, with a clear and substantial benefit and an extremely small probability of significant harm, the information that must be provided to the patient is correspondingly less. It might seem that there are very low-risk but also very complex decisions that we rightly let people make, despite their inability to understand them, because nothing significant for their well-being rides on the outcome of their decision. This might seem a case in which the person is incompetent to decide but is still given the authority to decide. Instead, we consider this a case in which the lowest standard for competence applies since only the person's self-determination and not well-being is at stake in his choice between options.

Third, perhaps the most important reason for preferring the decision-relative concept of competence is that it better coheres with our basic legal framework in two distinct respects. First, in its treatment of minors, the law has already tacitly adopted the decision-relative concept and rejected the minimum threshold concept (see Chapter 5). The courts as well as legislatures now recognize that a child can be competent to make some decisions but not others—that competence is not an all-or-nothing or global status—and that features of the decision itself (including risk) are relevant factors in determining whether the child is competent to make that decision. This approach is increasingly popular, and is utilized in, for example, "limited conservatorships," where some decision-making authority is expressly left with the conservatee (see Chapter 6).

In addition, the law in this country has in general steadfastly refused to recognize a right to interfere with a *competent* patient's voluntary choice on purely paternalistic grounds—that is, solely to prevent harms or to secure benefits for the competent patient him- or herself. Instead, the law makes a finding of incompetence a necessary condition for justified paternalistic interference with the patient's choice. According to the decision-relative concept of competence, the greater the potential harm to the individual of accepting his or her choice, the higher the standard of competence. From this it follows that a finding of incompetence is more likely in precisely those instances in which the case for paternalism is strongest—cases in which great harm can be easily avoided by taking the decision out of the individual's hands. The variable standard leaves patients with some right to make bad choices, but does not make that right unlimited without regard for the patient's well-being. Thus the concept of competence favored here allows paternalism in situations in which the case for paternalism seems strongest, while at the same time preserving the law's fundamental tenet that in health care people may be treated paternalistically only when they are incompetent to make their own decisions.

The alternative minimum threshold conception of competence both misplaces where, and misunderstands in what form, the question of paternalistic interference in the patient's choice arises, either in formal legal adjudications of incompetence or in the more common, informal assessments of competence within health care settings. It is compatible with the fixed minimum threshold conception that a person satisfy this minimum threshold requirement of decision-making capacities, yet at the same time on a particular occasion have made a choice about treatment that is foolish, confused, or, more generally, sharply in conflict with his or her own good, even as he or she under better circumstances understands that good. If the consequences for the patient of accepting his or her choice are serious enough, then paternalistic interference with this *competent* patient's choice for his or her own good may be justified. This alternative conception makes the questions of the patient's competence and of paternalistic interference with his or her choice distinct and independent.

Our own conception of competence, however, locates the issue of paternalistic interference where it in fact occurs in legal adjudications of competence, as a part of the determination of the appropriate standard of competence to be applied to the patient's decision for the purposes of judging whether the patient's decision will be honored or whether instead a surrogate decision-maker will be appointed to decide for the patient. Informal determinations of the patient's competence by physicians in health care settings are guided by this legal framework as well. Here too, there are not two distinct questions of whether the patient is competent and then whether, even if competent, paternalistic setting aside of the patient's choice about treatment is justified. Instead, there is the one question of whether the patient's exercise of decision-making capacities on this occasion has been sufficiently defective and has yielded a decision sufficiently contrary to the patient's good to warrant setting aside the patient's choice by deeming him or her incompetent. Normal adults will be permitted to make their own decisions, even if others with "above normal" decision-making capacities might make them better, just because the capacities for choice of normal adults make their self-determination paramount.

The fourth reason for preferring the decision-relative concept of competence is that it allows a finding of incompetence for a particular decision to be limited to that decision, and so it is not equivalent to a change in the person's overall status as a decision-maker. In principle, a fixed-threshold standard of competence could be selective and not global, but unlike our variable standard, a fixed-threshold standard is in practice likely to be generalized to other cases and/or areas of choice. Consequently, the decision-relative concept of competence contains a built-in safeguard to allay the fear that paternalism—even if justified in a particular case considered in isolation—is likely to spill over into other areas, eventually robbing the individual of all sovereignty over his or her own life. Further, any finding of incompetence is likely to evoke strong psychological reactions from some patients because to be labeled as "an incompetent" is to be returned to a childlike status. By making it clear that incompetence is decision-relative and hence may be limited to specific areas or even decisions, the concept of competence used here can at least minimize the potentially devastating assault on self-esteem that a finding of incompetence represents to some individuals.

Finally, the decision-relative concept of competence has another clear advantage over the minimum fixed threshold concept. It allows a better and more sensitive balance between the competing values of self-determination and well-being that are to be served by a determination of competence. The alternative concept, on its most plausible interpretation, also represents a balancing of these fundamental values, but in a cruder fashion.[35] Setting a minimal threshold of decision-making capacities also represents a choice about the proper balance or tradeoff between respect for self-determination and concern for well-being, but it does so on the basis of an extremely sweeping, unqualified generalization—about the probability that unacceptable levels of harm will occur if individuals are left free to choose—over an indefinitely large number of highly diverse potential decisions.

But as indicated earlier, decisions can vary enormously in their information requirements, in the reasoning ability needed to draw inferences about relevant consequences, and in the magnitude of risk involved. Hence any such sweeping generalization will be very precarious, and will inevitably be insensitive to significant differences among individual instances of decision making. If the generalization errs in one direction—by underestimating the overall harm that would befall individuals if the threshold for competence were set at one level—then the minimal threshold of decision-making capacities will be set so low that many people who are judged competent will make disastrous choices. If the generalization errs in the other direction—by overestimating the harm that would result if the threshold were set at a particular level—then many people will be interfered with for no good reason. Thus, regardless of where the minimal threshold is set, it seems likely that it will provide either too much protection or too little. The decision-relative concept of competence avoids relying upon such crude generalizations about likely harms, and permits a finer balance to be struck between the goods of protecting well-being and of respecting self-determination.

XI. A TWO-STEP MODEL OF PATIENT DECISION-MAKING AUTHORITY— THE COMPETENCE OF THE DECISION-MAKER AND THE RATIONALITY OF HIS OR HER CHOICE

Charles Culver and Bernard Gert have recently argued that a variable level standard of competence of the sort we have developed here mistakenly conflates two distinct issues—the competence of the decision-maker and the rationality of the choice he or she makes on a particular occasion.[36] In most borderline cases, they hold that it is the rationality of the person's decision, not whether the person is competent, that should determine whether the person retains decisional authority. While they reject a broadly global account of decision-making competence, they do insist that competence is a property of a *person* to make a *kind* of decision, not a property of a particular decision a person makes. In principle, competence should be determinable prior to the person making the particular decision in question. Culver and Gert define competence "exclusively as an ability to carry out certain mental tasks: to understand the information relevant to making the decision; to appreciate that this information applies to oneself in one's current situation; and to realize that one is being asked to make a decision about the treatment(s) being suggested."[37] So understood, competence makes no reference to the decision the patient makes, and can be determined wholly independently of what that decision turns out to be.

The decision itself is to be evaluated principally in terms of its rationality, where "a decision or action is irrational if its forseeable results are that the person will suffer evil(s) without an adequate reason."[38] They define evils or harms as 'a finite set of conditions: death, pain (both physical and mental); various disabilities (physical, mental or volitional); and loss of freedom, opportunity or pleasure."[39] A reason "is a conscious belief that one's decision or action will help oneself (or someone else) avoid or relieve some evil or gain some good" and it is adequate "when the evils avoided (or the goods gained) by suffering the evils of a contemplated act compensate for the evils caused by that act."[40]

Culver and Gert believe it is necessary to distinguish between the competence of the person and the rationality of the person's choice in order to deal with cases like that of a deeply depressed person who is refusing medication to treat his depression and who then refuses all food and fluids. The patient may suffer no delusions, understand his situation and his physician's recommendation of treatment quite well, but be so depressed that he does not want to be cured but wishes instead to die. This patient would satisfy their conception of competence, yet be making a decision that they would in the circumstances characterize as irrational. It is the irrationality of the patient's decision, they argue, that would justify removing decisional authority from him and treating him against his will. Furthermore, they note that if this patient happened to be feeling a little less hopeless and agreed to treatment his consent would be accepted as competent. Yet if his mood changes again and this ambivalent patient now refuses treatment his refusal again would not and should not be accepted. Since Culver and Gert define competence essentially in terms of a capacity to understand relevant information, this patient remains competent throughout his mood swings and ambivalence. Consequently, they believe that incompetence cannot be what justifies not accepting his treatment refusal.

Culver and Gert's account of competence is an example of a minimum threshold conception of competence, although the threshold is not "fixed" in the sense that whether the patient has the capacities required for competence will depend, at least in borderline cases, on the particular decision that is to be made. Consequently, we believe that the consideration we advanced in the preceding section against a fixed minimum threshold conception and in support of our own variable conception apply to their account of competence and its separation from the evaluation of the rationality of the patient's choice and whether that choice is to be respected. However, their account of competence does bring out an important consideration in support of a minimum threshold conception, and in turn further focuses the nature of the choice between it and our own conception. Culver and Gert are correct, we believe, that in the ordinary use of "competence" in many contexts it is a property of a person, not a decision, and is a minimum threshold requirement. They are correct as well that criticism of a person's choices or actions is often in other terms, such as that they are irrational. If we were starting afresh to decide in what terms patients' treatment choices are to be evaluated for whether they should be respected or set aside, and with no prior constraints on how these questions are framed in the law or in medicine, then this fit with ordinary usage would be a reason in favor of Culver and Gert's alternative account of competence. However, we are not starting afresh, but instead are analyzing an ongoing legal and medical practice of evaluating patients' treatment decision making.

As we argued in the previous section, questions of the

competence of a patient's treatment decision are substantially framed by the general position in the law that
patients' competent and voluntary choices must be respected, and their voluntary choices only set aside for their
own benefit *if* deemed to be incompetent. Since competence and incompetence are formally legal statuses, their
informal evaluation in medical settings is in turn shaped by
this feature of the law. It is our single-finding analysis of
competence, not Culver and Gert's two-step "competence
and rationality" analysis, that best fits this legal and medical framework. We believe that this consideration strongly
supports our analysis. Moreover, there are additional considerations—both theoretical and practical—that support
our account of competence.

At the theoretical level, Culver and Gert could argue
that our analysis of competence fails to give an appropriate
place to all relevant considerations which should be
weighed in the determination of whether to respect the
patient's decision regarding treatment or instead to transfer that decision to a surrogate of the patient. However,
we that believe our analysis of competence in this chapter
succeeds in this respect. For example, in Culver and Gert's
case of the deeply depressed patient refusing food and
water because he no longer wants to live, our view that
competence evaluations should be directed to the process
of the patient's decision making would focus on how the
depression has distorted the patient's underlying and
enduring aims and values, leading him to a choice that will
not get him what he otherwise wants and values when his
aims and values are not distorted by his depression. When
he is feeling less hopeless and accepts treatment, our analysis supports a finding of competence both because the
depression then is having less of a distorting effect on his
enduring and underlying aims and values, and because a
lower standard of competence is appropriate since his
choice now has a very positive expected effect on his
well-being. Conversely, when his mood swing and

ambivalence again lead him to refuse the treatment, our analysis again supports a finding of incompetence because there is again a more severe impact of the depression on his values and, in turn, choice, and because a high standard of competence is now appropriate in light of the very adverse expected effect of his refusal on his well-being. Our account does provide a clear and principled basis for plausible findings about the patient's competence in these cases.

Two practical or policy considerations also support our analysis in comparison with that of Culver and Gert. First, if we are correct that our analysis of competence fits the general legal framework that shapes its determination in medicine, then an important practical difficulty for Culver and Gert's view is that it would require a fundamental change in the law of informed consent—the rejection of the principle that the voluntary and informed treatment choices of a competent patient must be respected, in favor of the principle that a competent patient's voluntary and informed treatment choices can be set aside on paternalistic grounds if sufficiently irrational. Such a change would not easily be brought about. Second, even if this change in the law required by their account were possible, there is an important practical or policy consideration that would militate strongly against it. The principle that a competent patient's voluntary choices can be set aside if sufficiently irrational would likely be subject to an intolerable level of abuse in practice. While Culver and Gert seek to define and restrict the grounds for deeming a choice irrational, "rationality" is a term both in wide common use and without any clear and fixed, agreed-upon meaning, not a technical term whose meaning and application is easily restricted. Patients who make unusual treatment choices based on unusual values would often find, as already happens now, their choices criticized as irrational by others because those others do not share their values. If the irrationality of the choice is accepted as grounds justifying paternalistic interference with it, it is virtually certain that choices accur-

ately reflecting a patient's own aims and values would
frequently and wrongly be interfered with by others who
have different values and preferences and different view of
what is best for the patient. Since our account of competence evaluation requires focusing instead on the *process*
of the patient's decision making and, roughly, on whether
the patient is getting what he or she wants, that is, what
conforms to the patient's underlying and enduring aims
and values, it should be less subject to unwarranted sub-
stitutions by others of their different view of what is best
for the patient. Here again, a proponent of an ideal theory
of well-being will accept some appeals to ideals not shared
by the individual in question; and Culver and Gert are
probably ideal theorists in our sense. But the problematic
theoretical status of ideals together with practical worries
concerning disagreement about justified ideals should limit
appeal to such ideals.

XII. OPERATIONAL MEASURES
IN THE MEDICAL SETTING

The next question to be addressed is whether competence
can be measured, and if so how. In medical settings, initial
judgments about patients' competence are commonly
made in an informal and commonsense way by their
attending physicians, other health care personnel, family
members, and others. These judgments are often based on
rough estimates of the patient's general mental status and
of the patient's understanding and reasoning in the decision at hand. It has already been noted that a common
factor triggering a competence evaluation is the patient's
refusal of the physician's treatment recommendation.
When a patient's competence appears questionable or borderline, psychiatric consultations are commonly sought, at
least when they are readily available, as they are in many

hospital settings. Psychiatric evaluations of a patient's competence commonly include both formal and informal components.

A. Use of formal tests to determine competence

In psychiatric literature, practice, and research, a number of different tests have been developed and employed to measure formally a person's cognitive impairment and to quantify its severity. A recent study[41] found the most frequently-used tests to be the Mini-Mental State Examination,[42] the Cognitive Capacity Screening Examination,[43] Mattis Dementia Rating Scale,[44] Kahns Mental Status Questionnaire,[45] and the Short Portable Mental Status Questionnaire.[46] While they differ in details, these instruments test for such functions as orientation to time and place, attention and calculation, repetition, short-term verbal recall, and language use. Though the rating methods differ—for example, on the Mini-Mental State test a score below twenty-four suggests cognitive impairment, while the Short Portable Mental Status Questionnaire categorizes patients as intact or mildly, moderately, or severely impaired—none of these tests purports to provide more than a crude measure of mental status.

No attempt will be made here to assess the validity and reliability of these tests, which will, of course, vary among the different tests.[47] Rather, our concern is this: assuming that some such tests are reasonably reliable and valid measures of general mental status, what role should they play in competence evaluations?

Primarily because competence is decision-specific in the sense explained earlier, in borderline cases such tests can usually serve only as a somewhat crude initial screen of the patient's competence. When patients are non-testable due to unconsciousness, or when a patient's organic mental disorder or cognitive impairment is severe, this will be a reliable indication that the patient is not competent to give or refuse consent for treatment. However, when brain damage and cognitive impairment are less debilitating, these tests can at best serve as guides for determining whether further examination of the patient's understanding and reasoning in the specific decision at hand is called for. The process of questioning and discussion with the patient will inevitably be more informal than any standardized test, with the special content being tailored to the decision in question.

Even when properly used only as initial screening devices for cognitive impairment, these tests have significant limitations.[48] They tend to show significant false positive results for culturally disadvantaged and poorly educated patients, thereby leading to underestimates of these patients' decision-making capacities. Conversely, they show significant false negative results for particularly intelligent or well-educated patients, thereby leading to a failure to question adequately the competence of a patient whose decision-making capacities are seriously impaired. Here, good performance on a formal test may rest on over-learned skills irrelevant to current capacity to make an informed judgment about treatment. Another aspect of the false negative problem is that these tests are quite insensitive to circumscribed local brain damage that may nonetheless have major effects on judgment and so on decision making. Finally, since these tests all focus on cognitive impairment, they are of little help in focusing on affective disorders that, especially but not only in psychiatric patients, impair decision-making competence.[49] Thus, clinicians who are called upon to evaluate patients' competence need to bear in mind the serious limitations of the common tests for cognitive impairment even when their use is properly limited to an initial crude screen of decision-making capacities.

B. Importance of informal evaluations
of competence

Even when such screening tests fail to indicate any organic mental disorder or general cognitive deficits, there may nevertheless be reason to examine further a patient's competence to make a specific decision. For example, incompetence may sometimes result not from organic brain damage, but from psychological processes—such as severe depression, denial, or anxiety—that prevent a patient from achieving adequate understanding and reasoning in the particular decision at hand. Since the denial may function in a relatively limited area, discussion with the patient about the decision in question will likely be necessary to reveal its presence. These psychological factors provide an additional reason—besides their experience in administering mental status exams and diagnosing and assessing organic mental disorders—for psychiatrists to play a part in competence evaluations. Psychiatrists are professionally trained and experienced in the diagnosis of various psychological factors that may have a significant adverse effect in a particular decision. Moreover, they are commonly more skilled than many other health care professionals at ameliorating or removing the impact of such psychological factors on a patient's decision making.

In cases of genuinely questionable competence, general mental status exams will always need to be supplemented by an evaluation of the patient's understanding and reasoning in the specific decision at hand. The general tests may serve as useful guides for defects to look for in the decision making at hand, but the organic disorders and cognitive impairments that they measure are often sufficiently variable and uncertain in their effects in a particular instance of decision making to require more specific evaluation.

Does the necessity for this more specific and informal evaluation of a patient's particular decision mean that competence does not in the end admit of measurement? It is a common criticism of competence evaluations that they are intuitive and lack any theoretical basis because they are based on no single, uniform, and precise measure of competence. And, of course, if they are merely intuitive in this way, they are likely to be particularly susceptible to evaluator bias, prejudice, and discrimination, and to the use of widely varying standards for competence.

The fact that no one has proposed a single unified scale or numerical measure of competence applicable to every decision and decision-maker does not indicate, however, that judgments of competence rest on nothing more than intuitive criteria. Instead, the lack of such a scale merely reflects the reality that competence involves too complex a meshing of various capacities and skills of each patient with the demands of a specific decision situation to yield a single, unified, formal summary. The potential situations are too numerous and the potential arrays of patient decision-making abilities and disabilities are too varied. But in any particular case, the various capacities and skills of understanding and reasoning noted above as necessary to competence in decision making can each be measured on a relative scale and reasons can be offered for the importance of specific deficiencies that limit a person's overall competence to make that decision. Thus, although decisions about a patient's competence to make a given decision are complex and not amenable to simple codification by any single measure, they need not be intuitive in the sense of being inchoate, arbitrary, or purely subjective.

An important question for empirical research is the degree to which different competence evaluators attempting to apply our theory of competence would reach the same conclusions about the competence of real patients. A related question concerns what procedures and practical guidelines might increase interpersonal evaluator reliability. There is a general dearth of empirical research concerning competence determinations in medicine, which is particularly unfortunate given the importance of these determinations. Even without this needed research, however, we believe it is clear that health care institutions need to develop policies that assign responsibility for making competence determinations and specify procedures by which they should be made.

XIII. COMPETENCE DETERMINATIONS IN NONMEDICAL SETTINGS

So far, our analyses both of the concepts of competence and incompetence and of appropriate standards and measurements have focused on the case of medical care decision making. That is the central focus of our study, and a significant body of literature, both medical and legal, exists on competence for medical treatment decision making. However, there are at least three other broad classes of related decisions of which mention can be made here: (1) decisions about participation in research protocols, (2) decisions concerning financial affairs, and (3) decisions about living arrangements. The conceptual analysis developed thus far, as well as the account of the manner and extent to which competence can be measured and the argument for a decision-specific and variable standard of competence, hold as well for these other kinds of decisions. Here, too, the objective is to protect persons' well-being—often primarily physical well-being in the case of research participation and living arrangements, financial well-being in the case of financial affairs and other contractual matters—when their own decision-making capacities may be deficient and their decisions threaten them with significant harm or loss of benefit, while at the same time respecting their interest in self-determination, in directing their own lives for themselves and according to their own conception of their good.

One principal difference between these kinds of decisions and those about medical treatment lies in *who* should be called upon to make competence determinations, as well as the appropriate procedures for surrogate decision making in the case of incompetence. These issues will be addressed in greater detail in Chapter 2. One other important difference regarding competence determinations for these other kinds of decisions should be noted here, however. The persons who may be involved in a competence evaluation in these other types of decisions—investigators in the case of research, family members in the case of financial and living arrangements— are probably in general more likely to be subject to conflicts of interest with the person whose competence is in question than are physicians in the case of medical treatment. Although medicine has a powerful historical commitment to serving the patient's interests, the principal commitment of research investigators is to further knowledge, and family members will naturally be concerned with their own interest, which may often be in conflict with the person whose living arrangements or control over financial affairs is in question. Consequently, in such cases a person's disagreement with the recommendations of others provides *no grounds* for calling the individual's competence into question or triggering evaluation of his or her competence. Independent grounds for questioning the person's competence are necessary.

Furthermore, the increased potential for conflicts of interest in these other kinds of decisions argues strongly against reliance on the informal determinations that are common in medical care decision making. Determinations of competence for decisions about financial matters and living arrangements should commonly be judicial ones. The decision to place an unwilling patient in a nursing home is not itself simply a *medical* decision—although, of course, medical judgment commonly will be one basic component of the decision. Consequently, more formal safeguards are needed for this type of decision than for medical decisions in general. For the same reasons, com-

petence determinations for research participation should at
the very least involve disinterested third parties.[50]

XIV. VARYING STANDARDS OF
COMPETENCE

Although the proper standard for decision-making competence is always to be determined by a balance between
protecting a person's well-being and respecting his or her
self-determination, the particular harms and benefits in
prospect from the decisions will, of course, differ with
these other kinds of decisions. In the case of research
participation, or at least of nontherapeutic research, there
will rarely be major benefits secured or harms averted for
the subject by agreement to participate, and so there will
be little if any place for the minimal standard of competence. Other considerations—such as that noted earlier
of maintaining public confidence in the research enter-
prise—also argue against use of a minimal standard for
competence, such as mere awareness of what is to be done
and assent, with its potential both for exploitation of subjects and for giving the appearance of exploitation.

In the case of decisions about financial affairs and living
arrangements, the weight that should be given to self-
determination would appear to be at least as great, *if not
often greater,* than with medical treatment decisions. Financial matters and living arrangements often have as great an
impact on an individual's life, and on control over major
aspects of life, as do most medical decisions, with the
exception perhaps of decisions to forego life-sustaining
treatment. As one writer on guardianship laws and practices has noted:

> It may be difficult to underestimate the psychological
> impact of depriving an individual of the right to
> manage his own property as he sees fit. Surrogate
> management of one's finances has been described as

"the kind of intervention [which] is a basic deprivation of a right cherished in a free society: the right for an individual to self-determination." For an elderly person struggling to maintain his independence and self-esteem in the face of forced inactivity due to mandatory retirement, the loss of control over assets accumulated during a working lifetime may be a critical blow to the individual's sense of integrity. The right to "acquire, enjoy, own and dispose of property" has received judicial recognition as a fundamental attribute of citizenship: an essential precondition to the realization of other basic rights and liberties.[51]

It is therefore ironic that so much ethical analysis and public attention have focused on medical treatment decisions and so little on "mere" financial or placement decisions. (Our own treatment in this book suffers from this same imbalance, but that is a result only of the focus we have set for ourselves, not from any assumption about the lesser importance of these other decisions.)

Moreover, many decisions about the use of an individual's financial resources or about where and how to live are more clearly questions of personal preference, about which there is no objectively correct answer, than are decisions about medical care. Thus, there may be an even stronger case for respecting individual choices in these cases.

A. Difficulties raised by determinations regarding the incompetent's finances

In the case of the financial affairs of the elderly, competence is often *not* treated in the law as decision-specific in the way that our analysis of competence for medical decision making supports—at least in cases of persons of borderline, questionable, partial, or intermittent competence. Of course, even in medical matters, perhaps most persons will be either clearly competent (for example, normal adults) or clearly incompetent (for example, unconscious or severely demented patients) to make *any* treatment decisions.

But in financial matters, there is a factor external to the condition of the patient that makes the decision-specific treatment of competence difficult even in cases of borderline competence. This factor is the common involvement in a person's financial dealings of other persons, often many other persons. It is important that these others be able to know whether they can rely on agreements, undertakings, and contracts with the person in question. Understanding competence as decision-specific in financial matters would sometimes make financial dealings with the person in question unacceptably unpredictable and unreliable. Together with special worries about financial exploitation of marginally competent persons, this consideration must at the least substantially limit the extent to which competence about financial matters should be treated as a decision-specific determination. Nevertheless, "limited conservatorships" that designate a surrogate to manage limited and specific financial matters can sometimes be used to recognize a person's capacity to handle some but not all of his or her financial affairs.

There is a painful dilemma here for individual conduct and public policy in competence determinations regarding financial affairs. On the one hand, the need to avoid disruption of the legitimate expectations of others who are affected through contractual relationships argues for global, rather than decision-specific, determinations of incompetence with respect to financial decisions. On the other hand, global determinations of incompetence for individuals who are in fact competent to make some financial decisions can lead to "total takeovers" of their lives by others—not only violating their right of self-determination, but also in some cases precipitating a decline in physical and psychological well-being. The fundamental ethical issue here is one of distributive justice: to what extent may the right to make decisions that a person is competent to make be compromised by considerations of the rights and interest of others?[52] Issues of distributive justice are addressed in more detail in chapter 3.

Despite these qualifications, essentially the same conceptual framework developed here for medical treatment decisions can generally be applied to these other kinds of decisions. Of course, in the concrete application of that framework, exactly what capacities for understanding and reasoning will be called on, and exactly how particular conditions of the person may affect those capacities, will vary depending on the kind of decision in question. Similarly, the institutional procedures that are feasible and appropriate for surrogate decision making will vary as well.

XV. THE NEED FOR INSTITUTIONAL POLICIES FOR THE DETERMINATION OF COMPETENCE

Once the significance of the competence determination is appreciated, the need for appropriate institutional policies is clear. The specific content and mode of implementation may vary from institution to institution, but we believe that the core of an adequate policy will be a written set of guidelines that will include at least the following elements. The paragraph that precedes the numbered items is offered as an example of a preamble to introduce such guidelines.

Minimal Guidelines for
the Determination of Competence

Ascertaining the patient's status with respect to competence is of utmost importance because it determines the primary locus of decision-making authority. The competent patient is the primary decision-maker regarding his or her own care: legally and ethically the competent patient has the right to accept or reject any form of care or treatment (at least so long as this does not endanger the health of others, as in the case of communicable disease). If a patient is judged to be incompetent, then a suitable surrogate decision-maker—usually a member of the family or a legal guardian—must be identified, unless the patient when competent issued a valid advance directive, such as a living will, which clearly governs the decision or decisions in question.

1. The attending physician (that physician who has principal responsibility for the care of the patient) is responsible for ensuring that the status of the patient with respect to competence is accurately ascertained and for documenting this status in the chart.

2. With the exception of certain classes of patients who are clearly incompetent, such as the comatose, the severely demented or the severely retarded, as well as younger minors, patients are to be presumed to be competent unless there has been an explicit and documented determination of incompetence.

3. The determination of competence is in essence a commonsense judgement about the adequacy of the patient's decision-making abilities for the decision task at hand. As such it is neither a legal judgment nor a psychiatric judgment. However, in some cases the attending physician may find it appropriate to seek the opinon of a psychiatric consultant, especially if there are indications that the patient's decision-making abilities are being impaired by psychiatric disorders (e.g., depression or acute anxiety). Similarly, it may sometimes be necessary to seek a judicial determination of competence, for example, if there is ir-

reconcilable disagreement between the medical team and the family or within the medical team as to the patient's status, or if the patient has been judged to be incompetent but protests against the judgment even after its basis has been explained to him or her. In the great majority of cases, however, a judicial determination of competence should not be necessary.

4. Competence is adequate decision-making capacity, not perfect rationality. The chief elements of patient competence are these:

   a. the ability to understand the relevant options,

   b. the ability to understand the relevant consequences for the patient's life of each of the relevant options,

   c. the ability to evaluate the consequences of the various options by relating them to his or her own values.

5. In general, the presence or absence of the appropriate levels of the three decision-making abilities can only be ascertained by carefully discussing the decision with the patient. Simple cognitive tests, such as mental status exams, are of only limited value. Failure of such a test should trigger concern over competence and prompt further investigation, but passing such a test is no guarantee of competence. Efforts to ascertain competence should focus on questions designed to elicit information about the patient's decision-making process, not primarily upon the outcome of that process. The patient's disagreement with the physician's preference as to treatment should never be taken as evidence of the patient's incompetence, although it may trigger an investigation of the patient's competence.

6. Competence, strictly speaking, is decision-relative: the same individual may be competent to

make one decision but incompetent to make another. In general, the appropriate levels of the three abilities that constitute competence, understood as adequate decision-making capacity, will vary as a function of two factors: the complexity of the information a reasonable person would require in order to make the decision in question, and the risk the individual incurs as a result of his or her choice. Risk is the product of the magnitude of the harm that would result from the decision and the probability that the harm will result if the decision is followed. Other things being equal, the greater the complexity of the information required and the greater the risk, the higher the levels of decision-making abilities it is reasonable to require for a judgment that the patient is competent to make the decision in question.

7. Competence may also be intermittent: the same individual may be competent to make a particular decision at one time and incompetent to make that same decision at another time due to fluctuations in his or her mental state. From this two important consequences follow:

   a. The attending physician is responsible for seeing that the patient's status regarding competence is re-evaluated appropriately; and

   b. The attending physician is responsible for making every reasonable effort to maximize the patient's competence (by appropriate control of medications, by improving the patient's ability to communicate through the use of special techniques or equipment where appropriate, and by making a sincere effort to provide relevant information to the patient in a manner which he or she can understand and evaluate and in a decision-making context which is supportive).

XVI. SUMMARY OF CONCLUSIONS
CONCERNING COMPETENCE

As our study is of surrogate decision making for people who are incompetent to decide for themselves, it is necessary to clarify at the outset the nature of the judgment that an individual is incompetent. Since so much will hang upon whether a person is determined to be competent or incompetent, this task of clarification is of the greatest importance. The major conclusions established in this regard are the following:

- Competence is competence *for some task,* competence *to do something.* More specifically, the concern is with competence *to made a decision* (e.g., regarding health care, living arrangements, financial affairs, and so on).
- The necessary decision-making capacities include:

  Understanding and communication

  Relatively stable values or a conception of the good life

  Reasoning and deliberation

- Appropriate standards for competence will focus primarily on the *process* of reasoning, not on the content of the decision itself.
- The function of a competence determination is to sort people into two classes: those whose decision must be respected, and those whose decision will be set aside and for whom others will be designated as surrogate decision-makers. Competence, then, is not a matter of degree—a person either is, or is not, competent to make a particular decision. Thus competence is a *threshold* concept, not a comparative one.
- Setting the proper level of decision-making competence involves balancing two important values: protecting and promoting the individual's well-being, and respecting the individual's self-determination. In balancing these two values, it is important to avoid two types of

errors: (1) failing to protect the well-being of an in-competent person, and (2) failing to respect the self-determination of a competent person. The looser the standard for competence, the more common will be the first type of error; the stricter the standard for competence, the more common will be the second type of error. Deciding how to set the standard for competence so that it avoids both types of errors is not solely a scientific or factual matter, but rather a value choice (although not an arbitrary one).

- No single standard for competence is adequate for all decisions. The standard depends in large part on the risk involved, and varies along a range from low/minimal to high/maximal. The more serious the expected harm to the patient from acting on a choice, the higher should be the standard of decision-making capacity, and the greater should be the certainty that the standard is satisfied. In particular, the following should be noted:

  > If the net balance of the expected benefits and risks from the patient's choice is substantially more favorable than for possible alternatives, then the level of decision-making capacity required is low/minimal.

  > If the net balance of the expected benefits and risks from the patient's choice is roughly comparable to that of other alternatives, then the level of decision-making capacity required is moderate/median.

  > If the net balance of the expected benefits and risks from the patient's choice is substantially less favorable than for other alternatives, then the level of decision-making capacity required is high/maximal.

- Some treatment refusals may reasonably trigger competence investigations, but refusal of treatment itself is not ever proof or even evidence that a patient is incompetent. A patient's rejection of the physician's first choice for treatment should not even trigger an inquiry into the patient's competence if the patient chooses instead a treatment that also falls within the range of medically sound options.

- In cases of questionable competence to decide on medical treatment, general mental status exams are not sufficient, and must be supplemented by an evaluation of the patient's understanding and reasoning in the specific decision at hand.

- Because of the potential for conflicts of interest, judicial determinations of competence for decisions about financial matters and living arrangements are generally necessary. Competence determinations for research participation must involve disinterested third parties. Determinations in medical settings may remain somewhat more informal, except when ineliminable conflict about competence requires referral to the courts for a formal adjudication of competence.

2. The primary ethical framework: patient-centered principles

I. THE NEED FOR AN ETHICAL FRAMEWORK

Once it has been determined that an individual is incompetent to make all or some decisions of a given type, a number of perplexing ethical issues arise. The most obvious questions that must be answered are these: Who should decide for the incompetent? According to what principles should decisions be made? The issues are, however, considerably more complex than this. What is needed is a systematic ethical framework capable of distinguishing and answering not only these but other equally important questions as well. It is useful to think of such a framework as a *theory* of surrogate decision making—by "theory" we mean a coherent set of principles related to one another in a systematic way, and with sufficient power to resolve a wide range of important issues.

It is essential to distinguish among different types of elements that together constitute the needed theory. The most fundamental of these are the following:

- *Underlying ethical values:* The basic ethical values that are to be served in dealing with incompetent individuals. These values are primarily: respect for individual self-determination, concern for the individual's well-being, and distributive justice. Of course, other important values, such as community and charity, are also sometimes relevant.[1]

- *Guidance principles:* Principals that provide substantive direction as to how decisions are to be made. These include:

  advance directive: implementing an advance directive, such as a "living will" or durable power of attorney, that the patient executed while competent

  substituted judgment: acting according to what the individual, if competent, would choose

  best interest: acting so as to promote maximally the good of the individual

- *Authority principles:* principles that specify who is to make decisions concerning incompetent individuals.

- *Intervention principles:* principles specifying the conditions under which physicians, the courts, representatives of government protective agencies, or others in various institutional roles are to intervene so as to take decisions out of the hands of those whose presumptive authority to decide was acknowledged in the authority principles. An example might be a principle stating that the court may remove an individual from the care of his or her spouse and appoint a public guardian if it is believed that the spouse is clearly acting contrary to the individual's important interests.

Failure to distinguish these four elements of a theory of decision making for incompetents can lead not only to conceptual confusion but also to grave practical errors. For example, there are many cases in which the best interest principle is appropriate to guide a surrogate's decision, but this same principle would be wholly inappropriate if taken as specifying the conditions under which others may rightfully intervene and wrest decision-making power from the surrogate. Even if a surrogate ought to *try* to act in the incompetent's best interest, *requiring success* in this effort is too stringent. This holds true in general, not just for decisions concerning elderly incompetents. Although parents ought primarily to be guided by what is best for their children, it is generally recognized that it would be intolerably intrusive to intervene to transfer custody whenever doing so would result in a net increase of benefit to the child. The fact that another, wealthier couple could provide a *better* education is not a sufficient reason for removing a child from his or her natural parents, even if this could be done without psychological harm to the child.

To think of the task as that of constructing a *theory* of surrogate decision making is helpful because it enables us to sort out various issues that arise at different levels. However, a fully adequate theory, complete with crisply formulated principles to cover every contingency, must be understood as a regulative *ideal,* not as a realistic expectation. Any actual set of social arrangements for dealing with these complex issues will necessarily involve imperfections and compromises, and any set of principles will leave some questions unanswered.

Even a theory that is fully internally consistent and that provides answers in principle to all crucial questions would not be enough unless it satisfies what may be called *feasibility constraints.* For example, a theory that makes unrealistic moral demands on people by ignoring human psychology and the financial and institutional incentives under which individuals operate is of little practical significance. On the other hand, a theory should enable criticism of the existing institutional framework within which decisions are now made. Throughout this study, we attempt to tread a narrow line between utopian moral exhortations that ignore the inertia of existing practices, on the one hand, and a premature pessimism concerning the possibility of changing defective arrangements, on the other.

II. UNDERLYING ETHICAL VALUES

In Chapter 1 the values of individual self-determination and well-being, as well as their interrelationships, were already explored in some detail. In a later section of this chapter (in our analysis of the best interest principle) and also in Chapter 3, the finer contours of an analysis of the concept of the individual's well-being will be provided. Chapter 5 is devoted entirely to issues of distributive justice. In the present chapter we focus primarily on how the values of self-determination and the individual's well-being are to be reflected in a proper understanding of (a) the individual's right to decide about treatment and care, and (b) the content of the guidance principles and the relations among them.

The dominant tendency, both in recent legal doctrine and in the bioethics literature, has been to view the rights of incompetent individuals as an extension of the rights of competent individuals, through arrangements by which these rights are exercised for the incompetent by others. Although many bioethicists, including the authors of this book, are sharply critical of attempts to apply this approach to those incompetent individuals who were never competent, it is generally agreed that the appropriate starting point for a theory of decision making for incompetents is the rights of competent individuals. And here, as in the analysis of competence in Chapter 1, decisions concerning medical care will be the point of departure and primary focus.

A. The scope of the competent patient's right to refuse treatment

There is now a rather broad consensus agreement in public opinion, in the writings of bioethicists, and in the law that a competent patient has the right to refuse medical care, even life-sustaining medical care.[2] Although the majority of cases in which courts have affirmed this right involved situations in which most would agree that prolonging life was of dubious net benefit to the patient, several influential rulings have held that a competent patient has the right to refuse treatment that most reasonable people would accept.[3] However, practice still often lags behind theory. Several recent studies indicate that many physicians continue to behave paternalistically, even while professing to respect the patient's right of self-determination.[4]

The ethical foundations of the competent person's right to refuse treatment, as has already been suggested in Chapter 1, are the values of individual self-determination and well-being. First, self-determination is, generally speaking, of considerable instrumental value for a competent individual – the assumption being that a competent person's own choices, at least under conditions of informed consent, are more likely to promote whatever particular interests that person has than are choices made by others. Second, self-determination is said to be of considerable value, independently of whether it does in fact enable an individual to promote other interests. Recognizing the right of the competent person to accept or refuse medical care or treatment is simply a concrete way of showing respect for self-determination as such and as a contributor to well-being in one important area of decision making.

This understanding of the ethical basis of the right to refuse care and treatment for competent individuals makes the right a very broad one. It applies to medical treatment and care generally, and to all life-sustaining care and treatment in particular. More specifically, the right to refuse care or treatment itself acknowledges no distinction between the refusal of life-sustaining treatment and the refusal of life-sustaining care, including nutritional support (whether it be ordinary feeding or "artificial" nutrition by nasogastric tube, intravenous tube, or gastrostomy). From the standpoint of respecting individual self-determination and promoting individual well-being, extending a competent patient's life by forced feeding is no more acceptable than forcibly maintaining that individual on a respirator.[5] Our purpose here, however, is not to provide a comprehensive account of the ethics of feeding, but rather to avoid an arbitrarily restricted understanding of the scope of the right to refuse care or treatment. Our chief conclusion is that both morally and in the developing case law, the right of self-determination includes the right to refuse any form of care or treatment, including that which is needed to sustain life.

B. Limitations on the competent person's right to refuse care or treatment

The most obvious and uncontroversial limitation on the right of the competent person to refuse care or treatment, recognized both in the law and in bioethics, is that it does not include any unlimited right to subject others to significant health risks. A person, for instance, must either accept effective treatment for a highly communicable serious disease, or be subject to quarantine.

Another important limitation is that the right to refuse treatment or care is not a right to receive whatever services the patient demands. Whether or not there is a general moral right to health care is a much disputed question.[6] It is clear, however, that at present in the United States there is no recognized constitutional or general statutory legal right to health care.[7] Even if there is a moral basis for the legal recognition of such a right, the right in question would be distinct from the right to refuse treatment and care. The former would be a positive right, a right to have desired medical services rendered; the latter is a negative right, a right not to have medical treatment or care provided to an individual without his or her consent.[8]

For the same reasons, the right of self-determination in medical treatment and care decisions does not include the right to active euthanasia. Whether or not taking positive actions, such as administering a lethal injection at the voluntary and informed request of a competent person, is ever ethically or legally permissible is a different question altogether on which we take no position here. At present the law in this country, as well as prevailing professional standards of practice and formal professional codes of ethics, prohibits voluntary active euthanasia, thus limiting the patient's right of self-determination.[9]

To summarize: the competent individual's right of self-determination with respect to medical decisions is a right to refuse all forms of medical treatment and care, including nutritional support by ordinary or artificial means, except when refusal imposes significant health risks on others. It is not a right to demand whatever services one desires, nor a right to active euthanasia.

As will become apparent, a proper understanding of the competent individual's right to decide provides an important – albeit far from complete – basis for an ethically and legally sound theory of decision making for those who are incompetent. The strategy here will be first to examine the issue of what principles ought to direct decision making for incompetent persons (guidance principles), and then address the question of where decision-making authority ought to be located (authority principles). Only when the scope and limitations of the various guidance principles are appreciated will it be possible to demarcate accurately the proper division of decision-making responsibility as well as the sharing of decision-making authority.

We now turn to an analysis of the guidance principles for decision making regarding incompetents that will clarify not only the principles themselves but also their relationships to one another and their connections with the underlying values of self-determination and well-being.

III. GUIDANCE PRINCIPLES

As in other areas of ethical theory, the task is to see whether it is possible to formulate a small set of plausible general principles that will yield more or less determinate results when appropriately applied, results that accord with our firmest considered moral judgments while shedding new light on hitherto problematic cases. Fortunately, there is no need to start from scratch. Three distinct guidance principles are widely endorsed and discussed in the bioethical-legal literature: (1) the advance directive principle, (2) the substituted judgment principle, and (3) the best interest principle. Each of these principles has deep roots in commonsense morality and each has received more determinate expressions in the rapidly evolving law concerning surrogate decision making. The chief questions to be addressed here are these: (a) How are these rather abstract principles to be understood, and (b) what should be done when two or more of them apply to the same situation but yield conflicting guidance?

The best interest principle states that a surrogate is to choose what will best serve the patient's interests, in other words, that which will maximally promote the patient's good. The qualifier "best" indicates two important factors: Some interests are more important than others in that they make a larger contribution to the patient's good, and a particular decision may advance some of the patient's interests while frustrating others. Thus, according to the best interest principle, the surrogate must try to determine the net benefits to the patient of each option, after assigning weights reflecting the relative importance of various interests affected when subtracting the "costs" from the "benefits" for each option.

In contrast, the substituted judgment principle states that a surrogate is to choose as the patient would choose if the patient were competent and aware both of the medical options and of the facts about his or her condition, including the fact that he or she is incompetent. Thus a surrogate who must decide whether antibiotics should be given to an unconscious man with terminal cancer might consider the following as a test of the substituted judgment principle: "If the patient miraculously were to awaken from this coma for a few moments, knowing that he would soon lapse back into it, would he choose to have antibiotics administered?"

A third guidance principle may be called the advance directive principle: It states that where a clear and bona fide advance directive is available, it is to be followed. There are two broad types of advance directives: instructional and proxy. An instructional advance directive is an instrument whereby a person, when competent, specifies, perhaps only in rather general terms, which types of treatment he or she wishes to have or, more commonly, not have, under certain circumstances, should he or she become incompetent. So-called living wills are the most familiar instances of instructional advance directives. In a proxy advance directive, often called a durable power of attorney for health care, a competent individual designates some other individual or individuals to serve as the surrogate should the person become incompetent. These two types of advance directive may be combined: An individual might designate his or her spouse as proxy but include instructions that place limits upon that person's discretion to decide the individual's fate.

A distinctive feature of the advance directive principle is that it – unlike the best interest and substituted judgment principles – provides an answer not only to the question of how decisions are to be made, but also who is to make them. It locates decision making authority in the formerly competent individual or, in the case of a proxy directive, enables the formerly competent individual to determine who shall decide. Thus the advance directive principle offers the simplest extension of the competent patient's right of self-determination to the problem of decision making for incompetents. It is at best a partial solution, however, for three reasons. First, and most important, at present and in the foreseeable future the vast majority of those who are or will become incompetent have issued no advance directives.[10] Second, some incompetent in-

dividuals (such as very young children and those severely
retarded from birth) never were competent, and hence
never were qualified to issue advance directives. Third,
even where advance directives exist, it is still necessary to
locate authority and responsibility for interpreting and
implementing them. Each of these problems will be explored in detail in what follows.

IV. CONFLICTS AMONG GUIDANCE PRINCIPLES

Which guidance principle is followed can make a difference – in some cases, the difference between life and death.
Acting in the patient's best interest can be incompatible
both with choosing what the patient would choose if competent and with following an advance directive, whether it
be of the instructional or proxy variety. This is not surprising, since the best interest principle focuses exclusively
on the patient's good, while both the substituted judgment
and advance directive principles require that respect for the
patient's former choices and values be decisive. As the
debate over paternalism shows, concern for the individual's good and respect for his or her self-
determination can be incompatible.[11] Since competent
persons sometimes make choices contrary to their own
best interest, both following an advance directive and
choosing what the patient would choose if competent can
be incompatible with acting in the patient's best interests.

In addition, substituted judgment can yield a decision
that is incompatible with following the patient's advance
directive. What a person now (at the time of incompetence
and illness) would choose were he or she competent may
be different from what, at an earlier time before the person
was either incompetent or ill, that person said he or she
wished to be done if incompetence and illness occurred.

It might be thought that if an advance directive conflicts
with the decision yielded by substituted judgment, then
the discrepancy between the two must be the result of

either one or both of two circumstances: failure on the part of the patient, when competent, to envision concretely and accurately the circumstances in which the treatment decision must be made, or a change in the individual's values after the advance directive was issued (and before the person became incompetent). Thus it might be assumed that where the two conflict, the surrogate should use substituted judgment and not follow the advance directive – on the grounds that if the patient had not suffered from a lack of imagination or information, or if the patient had anticipated the change in values, he would have issued a different advance directive.

This amounts to a decision to view advance directives merely as *evidence* of what the patient would choose if competent, and robs the advance directive principle of its status as an independent guidance principle. On this view, if it is thought that the patient's values did not change during the interval between the issuing of the advance directive and the onset of incompetence, and that at the time of issuing the advance directive the patient did accurately envision the later treatment situation, then the advance directive is taken as conclusive evidence of what the patient would (now) choose if competent. Later we shall challenge and reject the view that advance directives are merely evidence of preferences, arguing instead that, when valid, they are *performances* that constitute acts of will.

The discrepancy between an advance directive and substituted judgment, however, may have an altogether different source. An individual might issue an advance directive stating that he or she is not to be sustained by treatments such as dialysis if severely brain-damaged, because of a desire to spare other family members the psychological and emotional burdens of continued, long-term care, or because of a moral conviction that the resources that would be used to keep the person alive ought to be used for others who are normal or who have less serious mental impairments. Yet if the individual were miraculously to regain competence for a few moments, the person's self-interested motivation might override the familial concern or moral conviction, and the patient might choose to be given antibiotics and other forms of life support. In such a case, there is a genuine and inescapable conflict between the advance directive and substituted judgment, one that cannot be resolved by saying that the advance directive should be overridden because it was issued without an adequate appreciation of what the future would be like or because the patient's values changed.

Since different results may emerge, depending upon which guidance principle is followed, some way of ordering these principles in situations in which more than one could be applied is needed. One seemingly plausible rule has been proposed by the recent Presidential Commission on Medical Ethics, and enjoys widespread support: Where a valid (i.e., bona fide) and clear advance directive applies, it is to take precedence over any other guidance principle, including best interest and substituted judgment.[12]

V. THE ADVANCE DIRECTIVE PRINCIPLE

The popularity of giving priority to a clear and bona fide advance directive is not hard to understand. The same strong reasons for affirming the right of the competent patient to accept or reject treatment offered when the person is competent seem to weigh heavily in favor of following an advance directive. Society affirms the right of the competent patient to refuse or accept treatment, because self-determination is valued both for its own sake and as something of great instrumental value. A person can exercise self-determination not only by accepting or rejecting treatment that is now offered, but also by making decisions that will influence what is to happen in the future, when the person becomes incompetent.

Consequently, following an advance directive can be viewed as a case of respecting self-determination, even if the individual has no self-determination to respect at the time the advance directive is carried out. Further, although exercising substituted judgment can also be seen as a way of respecting self-determination, the often highly conjectural nature of attempts to ascertain what the patient would want if competent is so subject to abuse and error that the most reliable way to show respect for self-determination is, at least in general, to follow an advance directive where one exists. Those who know the patient best may have a serious conflict of interest that may distort their speculations about what the patient would want if competent.

To appreciate fully the attractions of reliance on advance directives, we must answer a seemingly simple question: what values are they supposed to promote? Either of two answers is usually given. First, as we have already noted, advance directives are valued because they respect self-determination, which is said to be valuable for its own sake. Second, advance directives are said to serve individual well-being by protecting us from unwanted, virtually futile medical interventions that at best may prolong a miserable or meaningless existence. These answers specify the most important and widely appreciated values of advance directives, but they miss an additional, widely overlooked value and so are seriously incomplete. Indeed, they give a foreshortened picture not only of the value of advance directives, but also of the moral life.

In addition to protecting its author from unproductive bodily invasions and allowing him or her to exercise self-determination, advance directives can allow a person to relieve emotional and financial burdens that would otherwise fall on others. By issuing an appropriate advance directive one can *do good to others*. For a person who takes a direct interest in the good of others who will be affected by what is done to him or her after becoming incompetent, an advance directive can make a significant contribution to its author's own good in two ways. First, the issuance of an advance directive can contribute to its author's good *while he or she remains competent* by reducing anxiety about the distress his or her loved ones would experience in making difficult decisions without the person's guidance, and by assuring him or her that they will not be subject to crushing and wasted financial costs. Second, there is a sense in which our interests can survive us. One may have an interest in how one's family will fare after one's death, and that interest survives one in the sense that whether or not it is satisfied will depend upon events that occur after one is gone. An advance directive can help one ensure that one's "surviving interests" are satisfied. To the extent that one's good or at least the goodness or success of one's life, depends on how one's interests in general fare – including one's surviving interests – an advance directive can make an important contribution to it.

To view the value of advance directives in these ways can be liberating. Instead of being seen exclusively as devices for protecting the patient or for exercising self-determination for its own sake, they might in addition become vehicles for *new forms of altruism,* new ways of exercising the virtue of charity. For example, instead of specifying that if one comes to be in a persistent vegetative state, all means of life-support are to be withdrawn, a person with a strong sense of social obligation might instead request to be sustained in such a condition until his or her organs and other transplantable tissues were needed to save or enhance the lives of others. (This is not to say, of course, that this use of advance directives will be the most important for most people.) For several reasons, then, advance directives are of great potential value. Nevertheless, serious objections can be raised against allowing them unlimited authority.

A. The case against always giving priority to advance directives

Objections to a blanket policy of following advance directives – including objections to giving priority to them where doing so conflicts with other guidance principles – can be grouped rather roughly under two broad headings: practical problems, and moral objections.

1. Practical problems. The most obvious reservation about adhering to an advance directive, especially when doing so will result in the patient's death, is that the directive may not be valid for any of several reasons. Doubts may exist as to whether the person who issued it was *competent* at that time to make the decision expressed in the advance directive, *adequately informed* about the situations covered by such directives, or *voluntarily* issuing the directive. In the case of proxy directives, there is the additional problem that the designated surrogate must also be competent and adequately informed. None of these concerns about validity is unique to advance directives, however. Each has an analog in the conditions for informed consent on the part of a competent patient who must accept or refuse treatment offered while competent.

Without denying the potential seriousness of any of these problems, it is important to emphasize that the institutional, procedural safeguards that are needed to ensure informed consent for competent patients' choices can be adapted for advance directives. There is, however, at least one difficulty that is peculiar to advance directives. Although the competent patient need only have adequate information about the actual treatment decision that must be made, the individual formulating an instructional advance directive must draft it so as to cover an indeterminate range of contingencies and will not be able to be informed fully about each in advance. In addition, the instructions about treatment included in an advance directive may be ambiguous and therefore difficult to apply.

One salient advantage of proxy over instructional directives is that by designating in advance a surrogate decision-maker, the individual can avoid the impossible task of attempting to envision all treatment decision situations that might arise should he or she become incompetent, and can leave some matters of interpretation up to the proxy. This advantage, however, comes at a price. First, it would be unfortunate, as well as ironic, if an instrument designed to help people determine their fates in accordance with their own distinctive values concerning death and dying became a means to evade the question of what those values are or ought to be by simply throwing the responsibility onto a proxy, without adequate discussion and without limiting the authority of the proxy by carefully considered instructions. In other words, proxy advance directives might for some people serve as a means for relinquishing their self-determination and for the denial of death. Respect for self-determination requires that this price be paid, for a voluntary and informed decision by a competent individual to displace the task of planning for his or her own death may nevertheless be an exercise of self-determination. What is important is that those who wish to use proxy advance directives to exercise direct control over their fate are allowed to do so.

Second, and more important, although an individual who uses a proxy directive needs to know less about particular choice situations that may arise than someone who employs an instructional advance directive, he or she must know a good deal about the decision making capacities and moral character of the surrogate. There are two sources of error in this regard. The individual may unwittingly designate a proxy who, even at that time, is not primarily concerned either with the patient's best interests or with choosing in accordance with the patient's values. For example, a resident of a nursing home might designate as her proxy a staff member who is under the control of the owner of the facility and who may act in the interest of the owner, to the patient's detriment. Or the very process that renders the individual in need of a treatment decision but unable to decide on it may change the surrogate's motivation, by creating or exacerbating a conflict of interest. Financial and emotional slavery to a demented and chronically ill spouse or parent, for example, may erode even the deepest loyalties. Like the problems concerning the validity of advance directives, the worry that the interests of those other than the patient may inappropriately influence treatment decisions are not unique to decisions for incompetent patients. The greater vulnerability of the incompetent patient, however, argues for special legal and institutional safeguards. Any recommendations concerning appropriate safeguards must rest on a clear appreciation of current practices, which are examined in Chapter 3.

2. *Moral objections.*   Moral considerations favor limiting or overriding the authority of advance directives, even in some cases where there are no doubts about the validity of the document. It can be argued that an advance directive that clearly runs contrary to the individual's basic interests may sometimes be overridden on paternalistic grounds – because the reasons that support the right to refuse medical care and treatment in the case of a competent patient who is now making a decision have less force in the case of a choice about a decision to be implemented in the distant future under radically altered circumstances. The paternalistic arguments challenge the simplistic assumption that if the competent individual has the right to refuse life-sustaining treatment, then the same choice always ought to be considered binding by others if the individual makes it concerning a future decision situation in an advance directive.

This assumption is flawed because it overlooks several morally significant asymmetries between the contemporaneous choice of a competent individual and the issuance of an advance directive to govern future decisions. First, even if, at the time an advance directive was issued, an

individual was well-informed about the options available
should he or she develop a particular disease, therapeutic
options and hence prognosis can change between the time
the advance directive is issued and the time it is to be
implemented. For example, granted the current lack of a
cure for Alzheimer's disease, some persons might issue an
advance directive stating that if they are diagnosed as having this condition, certain life-sustaining measures (from
respirators to antibiotics) are not to be used. However, in
the interval between the issuance of such a directive and
the point at which the need for such measures arises,
unforeseen successes in treatment might develop. Similarly, had advance directives been widely used ten or
fifteen years also, some individuals might have requested
withholding of some life-sustaining measures should they
become afflicted with Hodgkin's disease or testicular cancer – two diseases that previously were regarded as a
virtual death sentence but that now are treated with considerable success in some cases.

Requiring that advance directives by reevaluated and
reaffirmed or modified periodically (say every five years)
may reduce the problem, but the sometimes rapid and
unpredictable changes in therapeutic options ensure that it
will not be eliminated. Another way of mitigating this
problem would be for legislation concerning advance directives to exclude those that mention specific diseases.
Although there is never any guarantee that a competent
individual making a decision to refuse treatment that is
now being offered will choose on the basis of an adequate
understanding of the full range of currently existing
therapeutic options and prognostic predictions, the problem is clearly greater in the case of advance directives, and
weakens the case for a virtually unlimited right to refuse
future treatment.

A second related but distinct problem may also arise for
advance directives that specify that a specific treatment or

intervention is not to be used. Advance directives are often framed with certain implicit assumptions in mind about the expected condition of the patient when a treatment decision must be made. When the patient's actual condition is substantially different, this calls into question the authority of the advance directive. For example, a person, when competent, might stipulate that he is not to be given cardiopulmonary respiration (CPR). It is likely that such an individual chose to reject this intervention because he assumed that it would be administered in circumstances which would make it of very doubtful benefit – where it would probably at best prolong life only very briefly and with very low quality in the final stages of his last illness.

But cardiac arrest might occur and the question of whether to administer CPR might arise in entirely different circumstances, in which the prospects for genuine benefit are much greater. For example, the individual might suffer cardiac arrest due to trauma (an automobile accident or a near drowning) or because of a reaction to a drug which produced a transient arrhythmia. Such circumstances may be covered by the letter of the advance directive, yet applying the advance directive to them may conflict with the individual's intent. Moreover, attempting to formulate a directive with so many qualifications and exceptions as to eliminate the possibility of such a conflict seems hardly feasible.

The third morally relevant difference is that the assumption that a competent person is the best judge of his or her own interests is weaker in the case of a choice about future contingencies under conditions in which those interests may have changed in radical and unforeseen ways than it is in the case of competent individual's contemporaneous choice. What is in an individual's interest – what contributes to his or her good – depends in part upon what that individual's capacities are for activity, pleasure, and enjoyment. Competent persons, at least usually and in the long run, are thought to be the best judges of what is conducive to their good in part because they are best acquainted with their own capacities.

However, severe illness or trauma of the sort that extinguishes or diminishes an individual's competence to make various decisions often also radically changes the individual's other capacities. For example, the active forty-year-old university professor who relishes enjoyments requiring complex cognitive and social skills may be unable to appreciate adequately the less sophisticated pleasures and enjoyment that would constitute his or her well-being were he or she to suffer serious loss of some higher brain function due to stroke or other illness. The professor may, in fact, confuse the judgment that he or she, given current interests in the kinds of sophisticated enjoyments now pursued, would find life intolerable if paralyzed and unable to speak, with the quite different judgment that if he or she lost both the capacity for those sophisticated enjoyments and the desire to pursue them, he or she would find life not worth living. The first judgment might be accurate and the second quite mistaken. Just as it might be difficult for an executive to appreciate the value of life of the confused, incontinent, socially isolated elderly person who lies about a filthy home, surrounded by thirty wailing cats, so a competent individual may fail to appreciate the value of his or her own future life under greatly altered conditions.

A fourth and equally significant asymmetry is that in the case of an advance directive, important informal safeguards that tend to restrain imprudent or unreasonable contemporaneous choices by a competent individual are not likely to be present, or if present, to be as effective. If a competent patient refuses life-sustaining care, those around the person who are responsible for care can and often do urge the patient to reconsider his or her choice. The well-known bias of health care professionals toward prolonging life, as well as their tendency to be optimistic about prospects for relief or cure through further treatment, can sometimes prevent a patient from giving up too soon. In some cases, an expression of concern by the family and the health care team – a clear message that they believe the patient's life is valuable and that they are committed to the person – can correct for distortions in the patient's decision making due to the depression and loss of self-esteem that often accompany serious illness.

Thus, although the decision to refuse or accept treatment must ultimately rest with the competent patient, everyone may benefit from a health care system in which the patient who refuses life-sustaining care or treatment must face a degree of opposition in doing so. So long as those who express initial disagreement with the decision do so by rational discussion rather than manipulation or coercion, the patient's self-determination is respected. This sort of initial opposition, as a safeguard against imprudent decisions to forego treatment, is unlikely to come into play as forcefully, if it occurs at all, during the process of drawing up an advance directive. The decision to forego life-sustaining treatment is a remote and abstract possibility, the mere contemplation of which is unlikely to elicit the same protective responses that are provoked in family members and health care professionals when they are actually confronted with a patient whom they believe should live but who chooses to die.

These four differences between the contemporaneous choice of a competent individual and an advance directive support the conclusion that *more* confidence should be accorded to the assumption that an individual is the best judge of his or her own interests in the former case than in the latter. To the extent that the case for self-determination rests upon this assumption, this right is of narrower scope in the case of advance directives than for the contemporaneous choice of a competent patient. Even if a competent patient has the right to refuse life-sustaining treatment or care when others believe it is fundamentally contrary to the patient's own interests to do so, it does not follow that the same choice ought always to be respected if embodied in a valid advance directive. Thus, in principle there is a special limitation on the moral authority of advance directives. The more serious one or more of these four special concerns about a particular advance directive, the less moral weight, in principle and other things equal, that advance directive has. The question for policy, however, is what is the practical significance of this special limitation.

One of the most unsettling cases for according advance directives absolute authority would be of the following sort. An apparently valid advance directive specifies that no life-sustaining treatments, including antibiotics, are to be used on the individual if he or she suffers a serious loss of cognitive function. The patient does suffer a serious loss of cognitive function due to a discrete neurological injury, such as a stroke: The person is now moderately mentally handicapped. However, the patient is otherwise healthy, and apparently quite happy. Then the patient develops a life-threatening pneumonia. Following the advance directive will result in the easily avoidable death of a happy and healthy, though mentally handicapped, individual. Cases like this challenge the assumption that the moral authority of advance directives may never be limited on paternalistic grounds.

Yet the combination of factors that makes cases such as this one so troubling will probably be quite rare. An individual who is in the advanced stages of terminal cancer or of Alzheimer's disease is not an otherwise healthy person whose only disability is a loss of cognitive function. Moreover, many, if not most, of these individuals do not appear to be happy – as many mentally handicapped people apparently are – but instead suffer anger, frustration, and terror resulting from disorientation and confusion, as well as physical ailments.

It seems unlikely, then, that many cases will arise in

which the special limitation on the moral authority of advance directives should actually come into play. In most cases, the expressed intention of the individual who issues an advance directive is to avoid a prolongation of life that would involve burdens that are disproportionate to benefits, not to reject treatment or care that would clearly serve the individual's best interests. If this intention is clearly expressed in the advance directive, then there will be no need to override it on paternalistic grounds. Therefore, acknowledging in principle the special limitation on the moral authority of advance directives need not undercut the authority and usefulness of these directives in general. At least in the great majority of cases, those in which following the advance directive would not be clearly contrary to the patient's most basic interests, an advance directive, like the contemporaneous choice of a competent patient, can provide a justification for withholding any form of life-support, including feeding (whether by artificial means or otherwise).

Some physicians may in fact make the mistake of thinking that an advance directive for termination of life support is contrary to the patient's basic interest because they uncritically assume that life itself – the mere continuation of biological existence, regardless of its quality for the individual – is a basic, indeed overriding interest for all people. But this assumption seems impossible to defend, whether it is understood as an objective or a subjective theory of the good. As a subjective theory of the good it is quite implausible, since many people, and in particular most who issue advance directives for termination of life-support, do not in fact place a preeminent value on the continuation of life as such. As an objective theory it is equally unconvincing: Among the candidates for preeminent objective goods, self-determination and a life of conscious purposeful activity or at the very least one in which pleasures outweigh pains and disabilities are much more plausible than biological life as such.

The central dilemma for public policy, then, is that of developing institutional safeguards that adequately reflect these moral reservations about advance directives without so weakening their authority as to rob them of value. If the conditions for issuing an advance directive are made too demanding, or if physicians and families are granted wide discretion to override them, then the advantages that made them attractive in the first place will be lost.

B. Conclusions: The scope and limits of the moral authority of advance directives

Advance directives are subject to all the same limitations as the right of a competent patient to refuse medical care and treatment. In neither case, for instance, is there a right to active euthanasia. Nor is there an unlimited right to demand services. Hence if an individual stated in an advance directive that he or she wanted all possible means of support continued for as long as there is any prospect of survival, no matter how small, the advance directive itself would not create any obligations on the part of others to supply the services in question – unless the individual had made arrangements to pay for them – nor to act against their deeply held professional or moral standards. And, like the right of the competent patient, the right to determine future treatment and care decisions by an advance directive is not a right to refuse treatment when doing so would impose significant health risks to others.

Further, even in cases in which there is an ongoing physician-patient relationship that creates special duties to provide care on the part of the physician, the competent patient has no right to demand unorthodox treatment or treatment that falls below the accepted standard of care, regardless of whether the patient chooses such treatment through a contemporaneous decision or in an advance directive.

The moral authority of advance directives is, as we have seen, in principle subject to one further limitation that does not apply to the competent patient's right to refuse care or treatment. Because the arguments from the value of well-being and self-determination that support the competent patient's right have less force in the case of advance directives, it may sometimes be appropriate to refuse to implement an advance directive when doing so would result in the death of an individual who, though impaired, would with proper care and treatment lead a life that clearly contains more pleasure and enjoyment than suffering and pain, In Chapter 3 this difficult issue will be plumbed in greater depth.

It is important to note, however, that a social and legal policy that acknowledged that advance directives in some rare cases may be overridden on paternalistic grounds might be subject to serious abuse. The long struggle to guarantee the rights of competent patients provides ample evidence that many physicians tend to be unduly paternalistic. Even if a paternalistic limitation on the authority of a small class of advance directives is justifiable in principle, efforts to restrict the limitation to *just those cases in which it is appropriate* may fail. If this occurs, then most of the value of advance directives as a means of exercising individual self-determination would be lost.

The most urgent ethical problems concerning advance directives are the need to ensure that the conditions of validity are met and to embed the practice of implementing them in a set of effective but not unduly cumbersome institutional safeguards that will minimize the effects of conflicts of interest. In the case of proxy advance directives (durable powers of attorney), the problem of conflicts of interest is especially acute because the person who is close enough to the principal to be chosen as a proxy is most likely to have interests that are in conflict.

The most highly developed existing instance of a proxy advance directive – the Durable Power of Attorney for

Health Care created by statute in California – is likely to be duplicated, at least in general outlines, in many other jurisdictions in the next decade. The Durable Power of Attorney for Health Care allows the individual great flexibility in planning his or her future and can avoid costly, time-consuming, and intrusive guardianship proceedings that might otherwise be required for certain treatment decisions. At the same time, it bestows on private individuals unprecedented freedom to make life-or-death decisions for others, and also provides a great measure of protection to physicians who carry out the choices those individuals make. Thus the very features that make the Durable Power of Attorney for Health Care so attractive also create a special need for carefully crafted institutional safeguards. These more concrete, practical issues will be addressed in detail in Chapter 5.

VI. THE SUBSTITUTED JUDGMENT STANDARD

Even if the considerable attractions of the advance directive approach are fully acknowledged, substantive standards for decision making will still be needed, not only for cases in which there is no directive to rely upon, but also for cases in which the advance directive does not provide adequate instructions to cover all decisions that must be made. In the case of proxy advance directives, the same respect for self-determination that justifies the recognition of the authority of an advance directive in the first place suggests that the proxy ought (unless otherwise instructed) to attempt to make decisions according to the substituted judgment standard – choosing as the incompetent individual would choose in the circumstances were he or she competent. Where sufficient evidence is lacking to exercise substituted judgment, the proxy ought to rely on the best interest standard, discussed in detail in the next section. Later we shall complicate this simple picture, arguing for a more nuanced approach in which the substituted judgment and best interest principles cannot be so sharply separated in their application.

Where there is no advance directive, there is no one guidance principle appropriate for all cases. Several recent influential court rulings have failed to recognize this fundamental point, applying the substituted judgment standard to cases in which it was wholly inappropriate.

The source of this error lies in two landmark judicial decisions: the New Jersey Supreme Court's ruling in the Quinlan case[13] and the Massachusetts Supreme Judicial Court's ruling in the Saikewicz case.[14] Both cases appeared to hold that substituted judgment is the appropriate guidance principle for decision making for all incompetent patients (at least where no valid advance directive is available). Their assumption was that all incompetent individuals have the same rights as competent persons, including the right to refuse medical treatment. Reasoning that only through substituted judgment could a surrogate exercise of this right be achieved for those who cannot exercise it for themselves, the *Quinlan* and *Saikewicz* courts concluded that to fail to apply substituted judgment to an incompetent would be to deny him or her a fundamental right.

What the courts failed to appreciate is that a surrogate exercise of the right of self-determination is not possible for incompetent individuals in two types of cases. In the first, although substituted judgment is in principle applicable because the incompetent patient was at some earlier time competent and capable of making a decision about the treatment or care in question, sufficient evidence of what the patient would choose now, if competent, is lacking. This may often be the case simply because many individuals have not clearly expressed the relevant preferences prior to the onset of incompetence, or because they have expressed relevant but contradictory preferences. For such an individual, no responsible application of substituted judgment – and hence no surrogate exercise of the right of self-determination – is possible. By tenaciously clinging to the assumption that a failure to exercise the right of self-determination on the patient's behalf is to discriminate against the incompetent individual, the courts have sometimes stretched beyond reason what counts as sufficient evidence for a decision according to substituted judgment.

The *Spring* case shows how far this lowering of standards of evidence or prior wishes has progressed.[15] Earl Spring, an allegedly senile seventy-eight-year-old man suffering permanent total kidney failure, was expected to live about five years if his dialysis treatments, which had begun before he allegedly became senile, were continued. His wife and son petitioned a Massachusetts probate court for authorization to terminate the dialysis. The Appeals Court found that Spring, if competent, would not wish to be kept alive in his present condition.

The authors of an *amicus curiae* brief correctly observed at the time that "the evidence provided by family members, in an attempt to indicate what Mr. Spring would choose, is virtually non-existent." The only consideration adduced was that Mr. Spring was now unable to live the active, vigorous life he had enjoyed when he was competent. But there are convincing reasons for rejecting this vague and anecdotal evidence. The brief's authors point out that

> It is almost always true as people get older that their level of activity declines, and is often severely curtailed. It does not follow from this that such a person would prefer to cease living because of the curtailment of such activities.[16]

The second type of error in the application of substituted judgment embodies a more profound confusion. In the case of Joseph Saikewicz, the court attempted to determine whether a sixty-seven-year-old with leukemia – who had been severely retarded from birth, with an estimated mental age of about one and an IQ of 13 – would, if competent, choose to refuse or accept chemotherapy. The court somehow overlooked the fact that Saikewicz's lifelong mental disability was so severe that he was never capable of forming the preferences in question because he lacked the concepts those preferences presuppose.[17] Although the Massachusetts Supreme Court subsequently in effect acknowledged this mistake, a close examination of the reasoning employed in *Saikewicz* is highly illuminating.

Critics of the Court's decision have noted that Joseph Saikewicz's right of self-determination could not be exercised by proxy because he never had the conceptual capacities required for anyone to infer his preferences about whether or not to be given chemotherapy (or, more generally, to have his life prolonged at the cost of considerable pain). Yet the error is more fundamental. The very notions of self-determination, and hence of a right of self-determination, only apply to beings who have, or at least have the potential for developing, certain rather complex cognitive functions: the ability to conceive of the future, to discern alternative courses of action, and to make judgments about their own good. Above all, it makes sense to ascribe a right of self-determination only to beings who are capable of conceiving of themselves as agents – beings distinct from, and capable of changing, their environment. Instead of clearly acknowledging the inapplicability of substituted judgment in cases like that of Joseph Saikewicz, the court made a heroic but confused attempt to ascertain the conceptually sophisticated preferences of an individual who never possessed the requisite concepts, in order to protect a right of self-determination that could never be ascribed coherently to him.

There is another way in which substituted judgment, or more precisely, its relationship to advance directives, has been misunderstood. Sometimes advance directives are mistakenly viewed as one especially important kind of *evidence* concerning what the individual would choose. The error here is that of failing to see that advance directives are *performative,* not merely evidentiary.

The crucial point is that evidence concerning *preferences,* especially if it is indirect and inferential, does not have the same moral weight as evidence of a *deliberate choice.* A deliberate choice is an act of will or commitment. A preference is merely a pro-attitude, a desire to have one thing rather than something else. Sometimes a person deliberately chooses not to do that which he or she prefers, either out of prudence or because the person thinks it would be morally wrong to do so. The contemporaneous choice of a competent individual under conditions of informed consent is an act of will, not the mere expression of a preference. An expression of preference that falls short of deliberate choice is *mere evidence* of what the person would choose if competent.

Like the contemporaneous choice of a competent patient under conditions of informed consent, a properly executed advance directive is not merely evidence of an individual's preference. The issuing of the advance directive is a *performance,* an act of will, in just the way in which drawing up an ordinary will for the disposition of one's property is a performance, not a mere expression of preference. Similarly, when a competent patient deliberately and unambiguously refuses life-sustaining treatment under conditions of informed and voluntary consent, his refusal is not merely evidence that he prefers not to have the treatment; it is, under these conditions, an act of will.

The practical import of the distinction between an expression of preference and an act of will may be seen by contrasting the moral (and legal) significance of two utterances that might be given in reply to the question, "Will you take this women to be your wife?" Under certain circumstances, the question might be taken as a straightforward factual inquiry about what a person will in fact do at some time in the future. And, absent any assumption of deceit or duress, the prediction made in answering, "I will" might reasonably be taken as evidence of a man's preferences for the woman in question. However, in other circumstances (when standing at the altar before witnesses) the same utterance ("I will") would not only express a preference but also constitute an act of will – in this case the making of a promise and commitment – which has different moral and legal implications.

Similarly, while a competent person's statement that he or she would not wish to be sustained if severely brain-damaged may be an accurate expression of preferences at that time, it may not have the same moral force as the deliberate choice, or act of will, of a competent patient who, in the presence of witnesses and after serious deliberation, explicitly chooses not to have a particular treatment. In so choosing, the individual is waiving his or her right to the care or treatment in question and thereby releasing others from their duty to provide it, and in addition creating at least a prima facie obligation that they *not* impose it. A mere expression of preference may not be sufficient to waive a right or release anyone from an obligation, much less to create an obligation.

VII. SCOPE AND LIMITS OF THE MORAL AUTHORITY OF SUBSTITUTED JUDGMENT

As a legal standard, substituted judgment first emerged in probate court rulings concerning financial decisions on behalf of incompetent individuals.[18] These rulings recognize an important limitation on substituted judgment. A gift may be made to another from an incompetent's estate if the ward would have made this gift if competent, but *only if* the gift is not so large that it would deprive the ward of the basic necessities of life, even if the ward, if competent, would have been more generous. Presumably the rationale for this limitation is that the inherently speculative nature of substituted judgment, along with the vulnerable position of the incompetent, require that substituted judgment may not be used to justify a course of action that serves the interests of others at the expense of the ward's basic interests. It is important to note that this "basic interest" limitation does not *reduce* substituted judgment to best interest: a decision may satisfy the rather minimal condition of not being clearly contrary to the individual's basic interests and yet not be in his or her *best* interest. The "basic interest" limitation does, however, blur the sharp distinction between the ranges of application of the two principles.

The "basic interest" limitation, as found in the law concerning the estates of incompetents, appears to be a very strong and general principle: the need to secure the basic interests of the incompetent is to be given absolute precedence whenever it conflicts with what the incompetent would choose if competent. It should not be assumed, however, that this absolute precedence version of the basic interest limitation should be applied in medical contexts, even if it is plausible in matters of estate management.

A sensitive approach to the issues requires distinguishing several types of cases in which the substituted judgment principle might be invoked. At one extreme there are cases in which the individual when competent issued only an oral advance directive before witnesses. No written form was used, but the individual clearly and voluntarily performed an act of will – made a choice and let it be known to others. One can imagine circumstances in which this might occur. For example, a person might express his or her choice orally rather than in writing if he or she was illiterate or physically unable to write, or perhaps lived in a jurisdiction in which there was no legally recognized written form for advance directives. Of course, one of the chief reasons for developing authorized, written forms for advance directives was to minimize opportunities for fraud or duress and to reduce ambiguity, and written advance directives are for these and other reasons preferable.

Nevertheless, it would be a mistake to make the sweeping generalization that advance directives must be written. If there is a bona fide advance directive, oral or written, it should, as we have argued earlier, be treated as having performative, not merely evidentiary status, as an act of will, not as a mere expression of preference to be used as one bit of evidence among others for applying the substituted judgment principle.

At the other end of the spectrum are cases in which there is no advance directive, oral or written, and in which substituted judgment is highly reconstructive, even speculative. Perhaps the individual never spoke directly to the issue, but did on several occasions express judgments that provide indirect evidence that he or she would not choose to be sustained with a respirator or feeding tube if he or she were seriously demented. Referring to an aged relative in a similar condition, the individual may have said "they shouldn't have kept Aunt Mary alive that way – they should have let her die." Or he or she might have expressed a strong but somewhat indeterminate preference about him- or herself, saying that he or she definitely did not want to be sustained by "extraordinary means" at an advanced age. Thus, the evidential base for substituted judgment can run from such indirect and indeterminate testimony at one extreme, to a person's direct and determinate expression of preference at the other, with the latter approaching the status of an oral advance directive.

Our proposal for coping with these complexities is that the range of cases which fall short of being oral advance directives should be treated differently, depending upon the overall strength of the evidential base. In those instances in which the overall strength of the evidential base is weaker, the "basic interest" limitation found in estate law should be given proportionately greater weight; where the overall strength of the evidential base is greater, the "basic interest" limitation should be accorded less weight. This may be called the variable weight version of the basic interests limitation, as opposed to the absolute precedence version employed in estate law and advocated by the President's Commission. Its virtue is that it recognizes the dangers inherent in speculative and reconstructive applications of substituted judgment, without imposing an absolute blanket restriction which would in effect unduly discount the respect for self-determination which makes substituted judgment attractive in the first place. If the variable weight approach is correct, then the substituted judgment and best interest principles cannot be so neatly separated as first appeared. In cases in which the evidential basis for substituted judgment is relatively weak, not simply what the individual would want, but his interests – at least the more basic interests – are relevant to the decision.

It is not our aim here to provide an analysis of the notion of the overall strength of an evidential base. The general features of such an account are the subject matter of epistemology, the philosophy of law, and the philosophy of science. Here we need only indicate, very briefly, some of the dimensions for assessing the strength of evidence in the sorts of cases that concern us. These are perhaps best expressed as the following rules of thumb.

(1) Other things being equal, the more determinate the preference expressed, the greater its evidential weight (e.g., a statement by Jones that he would not want to be sustained on a respirator if he were permanently unconscious has more weight than Jones's statement that he wouldn't want to be "kept alive by machines").

(2) Other things being equal, the more direct the preference, the greater its evidential weight (e.g., a statement by Jones that he would not want *himself* to be kept alive, by such and such means, under certain conditions, has greater evidential weight than his

statement that *Smith* shouldn't have been kept alive by those means under those conditions).

(3)   Other things being equal, the greater the number of sources of the evidence, the greater the evidential weight. (If Thomas and Harris both independently report that Jones expressed a certain preference, this is stronger evidence than if only one or the other did.)

(4)   Other things being equal, the more reliable the source of evidence, the greater the evidential weight. (If Thompson is a more reliable witness than Brown, Thompson's testimony is to be given more weight.)

(5)   Other things being equal, repeated expressions of the same preference over longer intervals of time and after careful consideration are to be given more evidential weight (e.g., if Jones expresses a desire not to be sustained on a respirator on several occasions over a period of months, this is stronger evidence than if he stated the preference only casually once or stated it twice in a short interval).[19]

Perhaps the single most important consideration which has led some to insist on an absolute basic interest restriction on substituted judgment rather than the variable weight restriction we advocate, is fear that the family, whether intentionally or not, may misrepresent what the individual would want if competent. This worry is exacerbated by the fact that the physician may have no independent evidence, apart from the family's statements, of what the individual would want.

The physician and other members of the health care team in such settings often are not well acquainted with the patient's preferences and "value history" when he or she was competent. If this is the case, then the health care professionals treating the patient will not be in a position to serve as an independent check on the accuracy of the family's claims about what the patient would want if competent. This is very troubling because the family, more than anyone else, may have a serious conflict of interest that distorts their testimony about what the patient would want.

Granted the potential for deliberate abuse or unintended bias, safeguards are clearly needed. One approach is to extend to medical decisions the absolute version of the "basic interests" limitation that probate court law places on financial decisions. An alternative is to rely on the variable weight version of the "basic interests" limitation while at the same time constructing *institutional safeguards* to avoid undue reliance on the family's claims about what the patient would want if competent (or upon the claims of the institutional caretakers of patients who have no family).

It would be a mistake to assume that the only adequate institutional safeguard is to require that substituted judgment must be exercised by a judge or by a court-appointed guardian *ad litem* in all or even most cases. As will be shown later in Chapter 5, some of the safeguards provided by direct judicial involvement can be achieved by less formal – and less intrusive and cumbersome – institutional arrangements, including hospital ethics committees (see section X.B. below).

VIII. THE BEST INTEREST PRINCIPLE

In cases in which there is no valid advance directive and in which substituted judgment is inapplicable, the best interest principle ought to guide decision making for the incompetent individual. The qualifier "best," as was noted earlier, signals the complex and comparative nature of the judgment: Some interests (such as the interest in avoiding death or chronic pain) are generally more important than others in that advancing them makes a greater contribution to the individual's good, and a particular decision can advance some of the individual's interests while thwarting others. Thus the best interest principle instructs us to determine the *net* benefit for the patient of each option, assigning different weights to the options to reflect the relative importance of the various interests they further or thwart, then subtracting costs or "disbenefits" from the benefits for each option. The course of action to be followed, then, is the one with the greatest net benefit to the patient. The mere fact that a treatment would benefit the patient is not sufficient to show that it would be in the individual's best interests, since other options may have greater net benefits, or the costs of the option to the patient – in suffering and disability – may exceed the benefit.

Since the effects of medical decisions and decisions about the incompetent person's financial assets are sometimes interdependent, a package of decisions must be considered, rather than individual decisions in isolation. This greatly complicates matters and limits attempts to divide the labor among surrogates according to their areas of expertise.

The best interest principle is clearly patient-centered because it focuses primarily upon the current and future interests of the incompetent individual. As such it must take into account *quality-of-life* judgments. Whether a particular treatment is in a patient's interest depends upon how it affects that patient's life. Whether a particular life-sustaining treatment is in a patient's interest depends upon whether life under the conditions that would exist if the care in question were provided would be worth living for the patient. Quality-of-life judgments are unavoidable because whether life would be worth living for the patient depends not only upon the length of time that life would be extended but also upon the character of the life for the patient during that period. The factors that must be considered will vary, depending upon the physical and cognitive capacities of the individual. For those with severely reduced cognitive capacities, life may be worth living if there is a balance of simple pleasures or contentment over pain and discomfort.

Several influential court rulings, including *Saikewicz*, as well as the "Baby Doe Regs" have purported to exclude quality-of-life considerations altogether from decision making for incompetents. Quite understandably, many physicians and families have taken this exclusion to be inhumane because it seems to overlook the important fact that in some cases prolonging life can subject the patient to burdens that are disproportionate to any benefits that person receives.

The courts that have attempted to exclude quality-of-life judgments, and those who have criticized them for doing so have commonly failed to distinguish carefully two very different sorts of quality-of-life judgments. The first may be called the *social worth* or *interpersonal* sense. To make such a quality-of-life judgment is to assign some comparative value to the life of an individual – to rank the worth of that individual relative to the worth of others, usually for the purpose of calculating the costs and benefits of expending resources upon the person. The second sense of quality of life may be called the *intrapersonal* or *noncomparative* sense, in which a judgment is made about the value or quality of an individual's life *to that individual,* regardless of how society or would-be calculators of social utility evaluate it.[20] Moreover, in the case of life-sustaining treatment, the intrapersonal quality of life judgment is very carefully circumscribed. The question is not whether the patient's quality of life is below average, or worse than it used to be, or anything of this sort. Instead, the proper quality of life judgment is only whether the quality of the patient's life with the life-sustaining treatment will be so poor as to be not worth living or worse than no further life at all.

Nothing in the reasoning the *Saikewicz* court actually went through in making its decision appears to exclude intrapersonal quality-of-life considerations. Indeed, the only coherent reconstruction of that ruling is that it *requires* that intrapersonal quality-of-life judgments be made in the effort to determine what the patient would choose, were he or she competent, or, where this cannot be ascertained, what would be in his or her best interest. Since Joseph Saikewicz had never been competent, no judgment could be ventured as to what *he* as an individual would choose were he competent. Instead, the appropriate task for the Massachusetts Supreme Judicial Court would have been to recognize explicitly the inapplicability of substituted judgment and to affirm the lower court's judgment that treatment was not in Saikewicz's best interest.

Although it claimed to be exercising substituted judgment, the Massachusetts Supreme Judicial Court in fact seems to have based its decision to allow treatment to be withheld on the fact that the quality of Saikewicz's life to him would be extremely poor during the period of its prolongation, thus tacitly appealing to his best interest. The usual suffering produced by chemotherapy would be increased by the patient's inability to comprehend what was being done to him.

> He . . . would experience fear without the understanding from which other patients draw strength. The inability to anticipate and prepare for the severe side-effects of the drugs leaves room only for confusion and disorientation.[21]

This passage from the *Saikewicz* ruling expresses a quality-of-life judgment of the intrapersonal type and assigns it a crucial role in the decision. Indeed, it would be very difficult to understand the court's decision against treatment in this case except as being based on such a judgment. More generally, no reasonable interpretation of acting in the interest of an incompetent, or of doing what he or she would choose, were he or she competent, could exclude this sort of quality-of-life judgment.

How, then, can this interpretation of the case be reconciled with the court's statement that quality-of-life judgments are *not* to be allowed to influence the decision? The answer is quite simple: The quality-of-life judgments that the court correctly sought to prohibit were *interpersonal* (social worth) judgments, not *intrapersonal* judgments.

A. Beyond the scope of the best interest principle: Permanently unconscious patients

In some patients neurological damage is so extensive and irreversible that the application of the best interest principle – and with it the concept of quality of life – becomes extremely tenuous. Attempts to apply this principle to those in a persistent vegetative state – who are permanently and completely unconscious but not legally dead because some lower brain function remains – have sometimes resulted in confusion and in the erroneous conclusion that such individuals must be maintained indefinitely on life-sustaining measures such as respirators and nasogastric tube-feeding.

A patient in a persistent vegetative state (permanently lacking all consciousness) will experience no pain or discomfort from life-sustaining efforts. So it cannot be said that it is in the patient's best interest to withhold such systems because the pain and discomfort would outweigh any benefit to the individual. Instead, the best interest principle, if taken literally, might seem to require *perpetual* life-sustaining efforts for *everyone* in a persistent vegetative state. This conclusion was in fact drawn by a guardian *ad litem* recently appointed by a Massachusetts court to represent the interests of a Mr. Brophy, a forty-seven-year-old former firefighter who lapsed into a persistent vegetative state after surgeons attempted to repair damage caused by an aneurysm that had burst in his brain two years earlier. The guardian *ad litem,* who challenged a request by the patient's wife to remove a feeding tube, is quoted as saying, "I can't believe it is in Mr. Brophy's interest to be starved to death."[22]

His conclusion was incorrect, for three reasons. First, if the testimony of his family and friends was accurate, Brophy had expressed a very strong and clear desire not to be maintained under such conditions. If, employing the whole-brain concept of death, it was correct to say that Brophy was not dead, then it could have been said *even then* that it was in his interest not to be maintained, if avoiding a prolongation of irreversibly unconscious life was extremely important to him when he was conscious. Second, since he derived no benefits from the bare preservation of his vegetative functions – being permanently unconscious – there was no current interest in gaining such benefits that could outweigh his previously expressed interest in avoiding a prolongation of permanently unconscious life. Third, the unstated implication that being "starved to death" would entail suffering was incorrect for a permanently unconscious patient. So the guardian *ad litem's* conclusion that it cannot be in the patient's interest to die of malnutrition is simply false.

In Brophy's case, again assuming that the testimony of his family and friends was correct, the appropriate guidance principle was substituted judgment. But in the Quinlan case – and others in which a decision must be made concerning a permanently unconscious patient who had not previously clearly expressed a preference not to be maintained – the appropriate guidance principle is best interest.

Now, it might appear implausible to say that ending a patient's life – a life without suffering or discomfort – would be in the patient's best interest. Thus, the best interest principle might *seem* to forbid the withholding of support in cases in which the individual when competent did not express a desire to be sustained in a persistent vegetative state. This unsettling result arises from the un-examined assumption that the notion of *interest* relevant to the best interest principle applies to the individual in a persistent vegetative state. It is probably less misleading to say that the permanently unconscious, as such, have no interests, certainly no experiential interests. If these individuals could be said to have interests at all, this is only because the word "interest" was being used in a very attenuated and misleading sense. We do sometimes speak of what is good or bad for rudimentary forms of animal life or plants (saying, for instance, that sunshine is good for a tree). Even when one indulges in the somewhat misleading language of saying that a tree has interests (rather than simply saying that some things are good for it and others not), it does *not* follow that there is any moral obligation to promote its "interests" (or to do what is conducive to its good).

Whether the tree's "interests" are promoted or not, indeed whether it lives or dies, *does not matter to the tree* — because it lacks, has never had, and never will have consciousness of any sort. And the fact that it does not matter to the tree whether it lives or dies does and should *matter to us*. We do not have positive obligations to use scarce human and natural resources to promote the "interests" of (to do what is good for) beings whose good can never matter to them. The best interest principle, however is a principle that expresses a *positive obligation,* a duty to do what best promotes someone's interests or is most conducive to his or her good. As such, the best interest principle does not apply to beings who permanently lack the capacity for consciousness and whose good can never matter to them, and this includes human beings who are in a permanent vegetative state.

The last claim requires an important qualification. Although it is true that the individual who is in a persistent vegetative state *as such* has no interests, or at least none covered by the best interest principle, some persistently vegetative individuals may have certain interests, if this condition is satisfied: the individual, prior to becoming permanently unconscious, had certain future-oriented interests which will be satisfied or thwarted depending on what happens to him or her after becoming permanently unconscious. For example, because of stable religious values he or she cherishes, a person may have an interest in being sustained in a persistent vegetative state for some period of time. If this condition is satisfied, then we can say that the permanently unconscious individual has an interest in being sustained on life support.

It is nevertheless true that the permanently unconscious individual *as such,* that is, simply by virtue of his present condition of permanent unconsciousness, has no interests. Whether or not a permanently unconscious individual has interests in virtue or having previously been conscious is a different matter and will depend upon what the individual's values were when he or she was conscious. Chapters 3 and 4 consider the complications that arise on the assumption that some permanently unconscious individuals may have interests – namely the future-oriented interests they had prior to becoming unconscious. Here we bracket these complications and concentrate upon the implications of the fact that the permanently unconscious as such have no interests. If the permanently unconscious patient as such has no interests, or no morally considerable interests, then such interests cannot serve as a basis for making claims of distributive justice on his or her behalf, including claims to the use of scarce resources for sustaining his or her unconscious life.[23]

The reasons for concluding that the permanently unconscious patient as such has no interests to ground claims of distributive justice are worth explicating in further detail. The chief goals of medical care are these: the promotion or restoration of opportunity through the prevention or treatment of disability; the prevention or palliation of discomfort, pain, and suffering; the extension of life or the prevention of unwanted death; and the provision of valuable information about one's health status. For the permanently unconscious patient the first goal cannot be achieved since disability is total and opportunity is irretrievably lost. Prevention or palliation of discomfort, pain, or suffering, is irrelevant because the patient is permanently bereft of all sentience and awareness. No matter how fascinating physicians and others may find the information about the patient yielded by sophisticated monitoring techniques, the permanently unconscious patient, unable to receive any information, can derive no benefit. The extension of life – the life of a human being (a homo sapiens), though not a person or even a sentient being – does remain possible so long as we grant the controversial claim that the relevant criterion of death is the permanent cessation of all brain activity (i.e., whole brain death).

It might be suggested that so long as the probability is greater than zero that the prognosis is erroneous, there is a perfectly robust, unattenuated sense of "interests" that is applicable – namely, the interest that an individual has in returning to a cognitive state. If there is a chance of recovery, be it ever so slim, the best interest principle might be thought to yield the result that every comatose patient must be sustained for as long as possible. Given the apparently tremendous value of the favorable outcome for the individual, acting in the patient's best interest seems to require sustaining him or her indefinitely, so long as there is any hope at all. Such an application of the best interest principle would exacerbate the already grievous dilemmas of allocating scarce medical resources, especially since advances in medical technology are making it possible to sustain larger numbers of individuals in a persistent vegetative state for longer periods of time.

However, this argument overlooks two important factors. First, to determine what maximizes the patient's expected net benefit, we must not only consider the (very small) probability that he or she will return to a cognitive, fully functional state; we must also take into account the very high probability that the individual will be severely disabled if he or she ever regains consciousness. The only well-documented cases of adults regaining consciousness after having been judged by experts as being permanently unconscious for over one year illustrate this point graphically: One person is paralyzed in three limbs, emotionally unstable, and totally dependent on others for the remainder of his life; the other is severely depressed and remains in the so-called locked-in condition, completely paralyzed except for the ability to blink his eyes.[24] These can hardly be called miraculous recoveries.

Second, even ignoring the high probability that disability will be severe, indeed almost total, if the patient regains consciousness after an extended period in a vegetative state or deep coma, it would still not follow that a reasonable employment of the best interest principle requires that every effort be made to maintain such patients for as long as possible so long as there is any possibility, no matter how miniscule, that they will recover. Just as an individual or a society is not obligated to continue the search for a lost hiker or a shipwrecked sailor indefinitely, regardless of cost, so neither society nor the individual's family can be reasonably viewed as being obligated to engage in ceaseless efforts to "save" an individual whom we believe – beyond a reasonable doubt – to be permanently unconscious. Thus even if it were true that being sustained indefinitely is in the best interest of the vegetative patient, a general endorsement of the best interest principle should not be understood as requiring perpetual support. We can express this point either by acknowledging that the best interest principle can be overridden by considerations of distributive justice or by noting that the principle does not apply, or does not bind, in cases in which the probability of benefit is extremely low and the costs of attempting to secure the benefit are extremely high.

It should be clear, then, that the best principle, properly

understood, does *not* require that permanently unconscious patients be sustained indefinitely. It does require,
however, that such individuals be maintained on life-
support long enough to make reliable prognoses that consciousness will not return.[25] But once this has been done,
the fact that the prolongation of vegetative functions
brings no benefit to the patient justifies withdrawal of life
support. The proper questions for such patients then is not
"Would withdrawal of life support best serve the patient's
interest?" but rather "Would continued support provide
any benefit?" The best interest principle applies, strictly
speaking, only to cases in which treatment or nontreatment can either serve or thwart the patient's interests.
Permanently unconscious patients as such have no interests, or at least no interests of the sort that the best
interest principle is designed to protect.

B. The individual's interest in the good of others

Several important court decisions have addressed the issue
of whether, in determining what would be in the best
interest of an incompetent individual, an individual's interest in the good of others ought to be considered.[26] The
cases in question have involved minors or mentally handicapped nonelderly adults who were potential organ or
bone marrow transplant donors for relatives. Those seeking permission for the transplantation argued that it was in
the interest of the incompetent to preserve the life of the
relative, either because failure to do so would cause psychologically damaging guilt or, somewhat more plausibly,
because the loss of the relative would deprive the incompetent of a satisfying and supportive relationship.

Although most of these cases involved younger individuals, it is not hard to see how the issues they raise
extend to other incompetents as well. The President's
Commission on Medical Ethics drew this implication,
suggesting that since most people have an interest in the

welfare of their families or closest associates, the patient's interest in avoiding severe financial and emotional burdens for his or her loved ones ought to count in determining whether termination of treatment is in the incompetent's best interest. Aware of the potential for abuse, the Commission went on to suggest that – at least in cases in which acting according to what is taken to be in the individual's interest in the good of others is contrary to that person's important self-regarding interests – a high standard of evidence should be required for showing that the individual does in fact have an interest in the good of others.[27]

Although it is correct to note that the potential for abuse is great, the approach the Commission recommended is flawed. If there were sufficiently weighty evidence that the individual did take a strong enough interest in the good of others to justify a decision that runs contrary to the patient's self-regarding interests, then this evidence would presumably be strong enough to justify the use of substituted judgment instead of the best interest principle. It appears, then, that when decision-makers must rely on the best interest principle (rather than an advance directive or substituted judgment), the determination should focus on the individual's self-regarding interests, not upon his or her alleged interests in the good of others.

C. The dependence of the patient's well-being on institutional options and others' interest in the patient

Whether a particular decision would be in the best interest of an individual often crucially depends on what institutional options are available, and on the interests and preferences of others with whom the individual is closely associated, even if he or she does not take an interest in their well-being. It might be said that psychosurgery or a massive dose of tranquilizer that reduces a patient to docility at the expense of his or her personality are nonetheless in the patient's best interest because they eliminate behavior that would lead to serious abuse or neglect by caretakers or retaliation by fellow patients. Similarly, some would justify withholding life-sustaining treatment from a severely demented elderly individual with no family on the grounds that it would not be in that individual's best interests to live in an inadequately funded state institution that is little more than a "human warehouse."

These two examples vividly illustrate the enormous potential for abuse inherent in construing the best interest principle so as to include in the patient's interests the effects of the preferences and interests of others, or the effects of defective institutional arrangements. It would be a tragic irony if adherence to a principle designed to protect the individual incompetent served only to perpetuate attitudes and social practices that systematically disadvantage incompetents as a class. What these cases show is the importance of altering institutional environments so that their current deficiencies do not serve as a rationale for nontreatment.

On the other hand, neither the attitudes of others nor the defects of existing institutions can be ignored in determining what is in the incompetent's best interest. In applying the best interest principle, a thin line must carefully be tread between passively accepting existing attitudes and institutions, which in some cases severely constrain the good that can be done for the incompetent individual, and making a decision as if those constraints did not exist.

IX. AUTHORITY PRINCIPLES: WHO SHOULD DECIDE?

The need to fix primary decision-making authority and responsibility is most obvious in cases in which the appropriate guidance principle is either best interest or substituted judgment. Instructional directives are by definition an attempt to make the individual, when competent, the principal decision-maker, while the purpose of a proxy advance directive is to identify a surrogate decision-maker in advance. However, since instructional advance directives can neither cover every contingency nor be fully self-explanatory, someone must be identified as having principal responsibility for interpreting and applying the instructional advance directive as choices arise. Only proxy advance directives provide an answer to the question of who the surrogate decision-maker is to be and, as noted earlier, only a very small minority of persons currently issue such directives.

Unless there is a clear locus of authority, decision making is liable to be lacking in coherence, continuity, and accountability. Nevertheless, it is important to recognize that regardless of which guidance principle is followed, decision making is likely to be more or less shared. The principal decision-maker will not, and generally should not, operate in isolation. Physicians traditionally have played an important role in shaping decisions because families have often relied heavily on their advice, deferring to the physician's technical expertise, but probably also because families often wish to diffuse the responsibility for making painful decisions under conditions of uncertainty. Attorneys, bank trust officers, and other financial advisors may exert considerable influence on their client's decisions for similar reasons. One of the main conclusions to be drawn about authority principles is that shared decision making is highly desirable – if properly structured by appropriate institutional arrangements and procedural safeguards to ensure accountability and combat conflict of interest. The task at hand, therefore, is to ascertain who the *principal* decision-maker should be and to delineate the structure within which that person should operate.

A. The family as decision-maker

In general, the appropriate presumption is that the family of the incompetent individual is to be the principal decision-maker, except in those emergency situations in which the family cannot be consulted without a delay that puts the patient at serious risk. The "family" is usually considered to be the individual's closest biological relation(s) or spouse. However, it is essential to recognize that the fundamental notion here is broader. For purposes of surrogate decision making, the family is whomever the individual is most closely associated with. This point is especially important at a time when alternatives to marriage and the nuclear family are becoming more common. Neither the law nor less formal practices on the part of physicians or attorneys should be allowed to discriminate against those who have chosen to participate in nontraditional or non-legally sanctioned intimate associations.

The chief reasons in support of the presumption that the family is to serve as surrogate decision-maker are both obvious and compelling. The family is generally both most knowledgeable about the incompetent individual's good and his or her previous values and preferences, and most concerned about the patient's good. Furthermore, especially in a society in which impersonal relationships have replaced most other forms of community, participation in the family as an intimate association is one important way in which individuals find or construct meaning in their lives. Since intimate relationships can only thrive under conditions of privacy, society should be reluctant to intrude in the family's decisions concerning its own members, unless others are adversely affected. (A more detailed account of the role of the family follows in Chapter 5.)

The presumption in favor of the family as surrogate is stronger in the case of decisions about medical treatment or care than in those about the disposition of the incompetent individual's financial assets. There are two reasons for this: (1) In general there is more likely to be a serious conflict of interest in the latter case (as noted earlier), and (2) the context in which the more serious medical treatment or care decisions are usually made typically provides significant safeguards to inhibit decisions that promote the family's interest at the expense of the incompetent person's welfare – safeguards that are not usually present in decisions regarding the incompetent's financial affairs.

The professional norms of health care providers, which tend to focus their concern primarily on the welfare of the patient, as well as widespread fear of legal liability should they fail to safeguard patients' interests, provide significant safeguards against self-interested decision making by the family in the medical context. Moreover, the relatively public institutional environment in which many of the more serious medical decisions are made, especially in large tertiary care facilities, makes it less likely that at least the most flagrant abuses will go undetected. In contrast. decisions about the management of an incompetent's estate and about where he or she will live and with whom he or she will associate – although as momentous for the individual as some of the most serious medical decisions – are often made in more private settings with little or no institutional safeguards or accountability. As will become apparent in Chapter 6, current procedures for guardianship and conservatorship do not always provide adequate protection for the incompetent elderly against the conflicting interests of family members who seek to control their financial affairs. Nevertheless, the contrast with decisions in the health care context ought not to be overstated. Many important medical decisions for incompetents are made in nursing homes that are sorely lacking in the safeguards often present in hospital settings.

B. Disagreements within the family

In some cases, disagreements among family members are so intractable that the family cannot function as a coherent decision-making unit. If the conflicting members stand in roughly the same degree of closeness to the incompetent, recourse to probate court for a formal determination of guardianship will generally be appropriate.

In other cases, there will be no family, or no family-member who is willing to serve as surrogate. This was the case with Joseph Saikewicz – his two sisters were alive but had not had contact with him in many years and were unwilling to assume responsibility for the decision to administer or withhold chemotherapy for this profoundly retarded elderly man who was terminally ill with leukemia. As noted earlier, the Massachusetts Supreme Judicial Court issued a ruling that seemed to require that all decisions concerning withholding of treatment that is expected only to prolong the life of a terminally ill incompetent patient must be made by a probate court judge after a full adversarial hearing in which a guardian *ad litem* represented the rights and interests of the incompetent. Just as troubling as the *Saikewicz* ruling's attempt to extend the substituted judgment principle to an individual who was never competent to make the decision in question was this apparent denial of the presumption that the family of the incompetent is to be the principal decision-maker. In apparently holding that life-sustaining treatment decisions for all terminally ill incompetents were to be made by judges, the Massachusetts court failed to restrict its ruling to cases, like that of Joseph Saikewicz, in which there is no functioning family.

The requirement of formal judicial proceedings makes especially good sense for individuals like Saikewicz, who not only have no functioning family but who also have been long-term inmates of "total institutions" such as mental hospitals or prisons. The long and dismal record of neglect, abuse, and outright exploitation of the permanently institutionalized supports the conclusion that – at least for the more serious decisions – the role of surrogate decision-maker should not be assumed by health care professionals or administrators of the institution in question (except where medical emergencies make this unavoidable).

In *Dinnerstein,* a decision which in other respects seemed to reverse the *Saikewicz* ruling's apparent insistence on judicial decision making, the Massachusetts Supreme Court again infringed the right of the family to decide by construing a moral decision as to whether to resuscitate as a purely medical decision, within the sphere of the physician's technical expertise.[28]

C. Physicians and judges as decision-makers

The presumption that the family is to be the principal decision-maker for the incompetent concerning medical care and treatment has been challenged from two quite different perspectives. On the one hand, some legal scholars have contended that, at least for critical medical treatment decisions, neither families nor physicians, but only judges, should decide. Both the medicalization and judicialization approaches have been criticized in detail.[29] This section summarizes the main considerations that favor rejecting these competing models of decision-making authority and endorsin;g the presumptive family authority view.

The chief difficulties with the view that the physician should be the principal decision maker for the incompetent patient are: (1) that it overestimates the knowledge that physicians usually have of their patient's interests and values, while underestimating the families' ability, when properly informed, to make reasonable decisions, and (2) that it confuses medical judgments, which physicians' special training uniquely qualifies them to make, with moral decisions, for which physicians as such possess no special credentials. The judgment that an individual in the advanced stages of Alzheimer's disease is in a persistent vegetative state is a medical judgment expressing a prognosis. The judgment that a patient who is in a vegetative state may be allowed to die is not a medical, but rather a moral, judgment.

The confusion between medical and moral judgments stems in part from a failure to sort out different kinds of costs and benefits that must be taken into account in making a judgment about what is best for a patient who cannot express his or her own preferences. Whether a certain treatment would be in the best interest of the patient depends not only upon the medical effects of treatment but also upon the relationship between those effects and the interests and previously expressed values of the patient. Physicians' professional expertise makes them more knowledgeable about the former, but not about the latter.

The proposal that decision making for incompetent patients be routinely judicialized is scarcely more plausible. Aside from the high financial costs of requiring court proceedings for all such decisions or even only for all termination of life-support decisions for incompetents, the process would be cumbersome and slow. In addition, and perhaps most importantly of all, routine judicialization would fail to take seriously the special moral relationship that usually exists between the incompetent patient and his or her family. As noted earlier, the family is generally more likely to be most knowledgeable of and most concerned about the patient's interests. Moreover, members of a family typically have a special responsibility for each other's welfare, a responsibility that emerges from the intimate nature of their union and long-standing patterns of cooperation. By entirely removing the decision-making process from the family and shifting it to a public form of debate among legal professionals who typically have no such special connection with the patient, the judicialization approach inappropriately denies any special role and standing to the family. As will be seen in Chapter 5, the right of the family to decide is, of course, a defeasible right, not an absolute one; but the point to be noted here is that routine judicialization ignores the legal and moral *presumptive* authority of the family.

The strength of the judicialization approach is that judicial proceedings in general exhibit four important characteristics that tend to improve decision making, none of which is likely to be present in purely private, informal decision making, unconstrained by institutional rules. (1) They are *public;* (2) the judge's decision must be supported explicitly by *principles;* (3) efforts are made to ensure that the decision-maker is *impartial* (only certain types of facts are allowed as being relevant and decision-makers who are in conflict of interest are excluded); and (4) judicial proceedings are *adversarial* in nature.[30]

While it is quite true that these features are largely or wholly lacking if decision making for incompetents is medicalized, it does not follow that the benefits they tend to produce can only be achieved by embracing the opposite extreme of judicialization. A more plausible intermediate approach is to attempt to protect the privacy and legitimate standing of the family (or other designated surrogate) while at the same time embedding their decision making within institutional arrangements that assure the quality of decision making and protect the vulnerable incompetent patient. How best to achieve this delicate balancing act is explored in some detail in the application chapters to follow (especially Chapters 5 and 6). In the sections that immediately follow we discuss the principles that specify conditions under which the presumptive authority of the family is defeated, as well as one important type of safeguard, the institutional ethics committee.

X. INTERVENTION PRINCIPLES:
ATTEMPTS TO SPECIFY CONDITIONS
THAT REBUT THE PRESUMPTIVE
AUTHORITY OF THE FAMILY

Plausible intervention principles fall into three types.[31] First, there are those that specify conditions that disqualify the family from the role of surrogate decision-maker altogether. The family should be disqualified if there is abuse or neglect of the patient, if there is a serious conflict of interest likely to bias their decisions against the patient's rights and interests, or if the family itself is incompetent to decide. If a member of the health care team or anyone else involved in the care of the patient believes that any of these disqualifying conditions is satisfied, he or she should notify the appropriate authorities within the institution, such as the medical chief of staff or the chief of nursing, or an institutional ethics committee where one exists. If these persons or bodies concur with the judgment that the family is disqualified, then they should seek the court intervention to see that a suitable guardian is appointed.

The second type of intervention principle specifies certain classes of cases as deserving special scrutiny, by virtue of the especially vulnerable position of the incompetent patient, the momentousness of the consequences of the decision, and/or the especially high likelihood of conflicts of interest between patient and surrogates. The first subcategory would include (1) incompetents who are candidates for removal of tissue or organs for transplantation, and (2) incompetent patients who are long-term residents or inmates of institutions such as mental hospitals, state institutions for the retarded, or prisons, or incompetents who reside in nursing homes and have no family or none willing or able to serve as a surrogate and advocate for them. The second subcategory would include two types of "momentous decisions": first, decisions that are likely to result in a preventable and considerable shortening of the patient's life[32] (for example, when parents refuse to sign a surgical permit for correction of the blocked intestine of an otherwise healthy Down syndrome baby); and second, decisions that are likely to result in permanent and avoidable loss or impairment of important physical or psychological functions (for example, sterilization or psychosurgery). The third subcategory would include cases where strong familial attachments between patient and surrogate do not exist and some treatment alternatives would impose great burdens on the surrogate, such as some life-sustaining treatment decisions for seriously impaired newborns. If a case falls into any of these special scrutiny categories, some sort of institutional review – for example, referral to a hospital ethics committee – should be mandatory.

So far we have discussed two types of intervention principles: those that state the conditions that disqualify the family from being the decision-maker and those that single out certain types of cases as deserving unusual safeguards. In addition to these, a third type of intervention principle may be distinguished. This type of principle focuses on *the decision the surrogate makes* and specifies the very general conditions that this decision must satisfy.

There is at least one condition which the family's decision should always satisfy. Regardless of whether the decision is made by following the patient's advance directive or according to the substituted judgment or best interest principles, the medical treatment (as opposed to nontreatment) the family or guardian chooses must be within the range of medically sound alternatives, as determined by appropriate medical community standards. To deny this is to make the mistake of viewing the physician as a passive vendor of services and to overlook the physician's right to refuse requests for bad or inadequate medical care. But so long as the family's choice of a particular treatment falls within the range of medically sound options, physicians should not insist that the particular option they favor be employed, nor should they seek intervention by a hospital ethics committee or other institutional or government agencies to challenge the family's decision. If competent medical opinion is divided as to which of two or more options for achieving a therapeutic goal is best, due recognition of the family's role as decision-maker requires noninterference. If physicians' personal standards forbid them to employ what they take to be second-best means, or if they have serious moral objections to the procedure, they should see that the patient is safely transferred to the care of another physician.

The additional conditions which the family's decision must satisfy may differ depending on which guidance principle is being employed. If the appropriate guidance principle is the best interest principle, it is tempting to assume that any departure from the single most beneficial course is sufficient for intervention. This, however, would be a mistake, for the reasons discussed earlier. Neither the law nor commonsense morality dictates that society should intervene whenever the family's treatment of its dependent member merely fails to *maximize* his or her interests. (Intervention by the state to transfer a child to the custody of a richer family simply because this would maximize his or her interests in higher education would be wholly inappropriate.) The fact that a decision concerns medical treatment does not itself prove an exception to this general policy of allowing some latitude in the family's determination of what is best for its incompetent member.

It is one thing to acknowledge that in employing the best interest principle the family should sometimes be allowed to depart from what would, strictly speaking, maximize the incompetent's interest. It is another to say that what counts as the best interest of the incompetent should be left wholly to the judgment of the family. In general, the degree of latitude that should be accorded to the family's determination of the incompetent's best interest should be governed by two distinct types of factors: first, the severity of the harm (or the magnitude of the foregone benefit) that might result from the family's decision and the likelihood that the harm will actually occur (or that the benefit will actually be lost); and second, the strength of the evidence that most reasonable and informed persons would choose differently from the family in applying the best interest principle.

The greater the preventable harm (or loss of benefit to the patient) and the more likely its occurrence, the stronger the case for intervention. (This is analogous to our account of how a standard for competence should be set: other things being equal, the greater the risk of allowing the individual to decide for him- or herself, the higher the level of decision-making abilities necessary for a judgment that he or she is competent.) But even if the likelihood that the family's choice will result in harm to the patient is small, intervention may be appropriate if the severity of the harm is very great and if there is strong evidence that most informed and reasonable persons, in applying the best interest principle, would choose differently.

If there is a consensus among reasonable persons who are informed about the relevant facts of the case that the family's choice is *not* in the best interest of the incompetent, then intervention may be appropriate. Even where such a consensus exists, however, intervention would not be appropriate if the harm (or loss of benefit) to the patient that would result if the family's choice were respected is rather slight and very unlikely to occur.

If the surrogate decision-maker simply implements a properly prepared, documented, unambiguous advance directive set out by the patient when he or she was competent, there will in general be no grounds for intervention. For if there is no doubt about the nature of the instructions, their application to the decision at hand, or the patient's competence when he or she issued them, then, for reasons noted earlier, the advance directive should generally be followed. Consequently, the qualified surrogate's accurate execution of the explicit, unambiguous, well-documented instructions of a formerly competent patient should not be overridden simply on the grounds that following them will result in an avoidable shortening of the patient's life.

In the case of substituted judgment, however, additional safeguards are needed and a different intervention principle will be appropriate. This is because substituted judgment, a judgment about what the patient would want if competent, is always to some degree *reconstructive* and *speculative;* it is a hypothetical statement developed from evidence about the patient's past preferences and values. As such, it does not carry the same moral weight as the actual choice of a patient when he or she is competent, nor even the same moral force as a clear and well-documented advance directive. There are at least two conditions under which it is appropriate to intervene in the family's exercise of substituted judgment. First, if there is a consensus among reasonable and informed persons that the family's construction of what the patient, if competent, would choose is an unreasonable inference from the evidence about his or her former general preferences and values, and if there would be significant harm or loss bereft to the patient if the family's choice is respected, then the family's decision should be challenged and the case should be referred to the appropriate appeal body or person within the institution. In applying this intervention principle, it is important to emphasize that there may be a *range* of reasonable interpretations of the patient's prior instructions, rather than *one* uniquely reasonable interpretation. If there is no consensus among reasonable and informed persons as to what the range of reasonable constructions is, then substituted judgment should not be attempted and the best interest principle should be employed.

Second, even if the family's attempt to decide according to substituted judgment falls within the range of reasonable inferences from the evidence about the patient's former values and preferences, it may still be challenged if the decision is likely to result in severe harm to the patient and if the evidence for what the patient would choose is indirect and/or less than fully decisive and consistent. This restriction, like the first, reflects the fact that substituted judgment does not carry the same moral force as the informed decision of a competent patient, nor of an advance directive.

Nevertheless, it does not follow that a family's attempt to use substituted judgment should be challenged whenever it yields a decision that is not strictly in the patient's best interest. Instead, the same latitude should be tolerated here as in the application of the best interest principle, so long as the decision made according to substituted judgment falls within the range of reasonable inferences from the evidence of the patient's former general preferences and values. The reasons for allowing this latitude in the family's application of the two guidance principles are the same reasons that ground the presumption that the family is the appropriate decision-maker: the fact that the family is generally more knowledgeable about the patient's preference and values and more interested in his or her good, and the need to protect the family from unnecessary intrusions.

A. Challenges to the family as decision-maker

The person in a position to challenge the family's role as surrogate if any of these conditions obtains will vary depending upon the setting in which decision making occurs. In the medical context, the members of the health care team – including physicians, nurses, and social workers – all bear an obligation to see that surrogate decision making is ethically sound. Outside the medical context, it will often be a social service or protective agency caseworker or the family attorney who will be in the best position to monitor the family's performance of the role of surrogate. Some states also have institutional offices, such as ombudsman for the elderly or mental health advocate, specifically charged with protecting the rights and interests of special classes of persons. In some jurisdictions, health care professionals and social service personnel have legal duties to report neglect or abuse of children or the elderly, but not all of the conditions that should trigger scrutiny of the family's fitness to serve as surrogate fall neatly under the heading of neglect or abuse. The moral obligation to protect the defenseless holds regardless of whether it is explicitly recognized in statute law.

No single answer can be given to the question of what form intervention should take if any of the conditions listed above is met. In some cases – for example, where there is evidence of abuse – direct notification of the court or of the appropriate government protective agency is in order. In others, however, it may be more appropriate to rely, at least initially, upon less formal, less coercive, and less adversarial institutional safeguards for the decision-making process. Perhaps the most widely discussed of these is the institutional ethics committee.

B. The institutional ethics committee

Institutional ethics committees can perform several valuable functions: They can serve as a focus for bioethics education in the institution and the community; they can provide ethics consultation services for staff, patients, and family; and they can serve as a forum for complaints about the decisions of any of the parties involved in treatment decision making, sometimes achieving a satisfactory resolution of conflicts without recourse to the courts or other government agencies. Further, they can serve to refer otherwise intractable cases to the appropriate state agencies. For example, the committee might initiate court appointment of a legal guardian for an incompetent patient.

Perhaps the most important function of the institutional ethics committee is that it facilitates, indeed should insist upon, *principled* decision making. Once the rationale for current methods of decision making in the institution is made explicit in the course of the committee's discussions, those practices can be subjected to criticism and revised and improved over time. If properly composed of persons with diverse professional and disciplinary perspectives, including some who are independent of the health care institution in which it operates, the committee can improve the impartiality of the decision-making process by exposing biases and by calling into question unarticulated assumptions. Since those who appear before the committee will be expected to give reasons for the courses of action they endorse, the opportunity for principled, consistent decision making may be enhanced. Where decision making is either entirely private, with no standards or policy guidelines shared by those working in a particular health care institution, or where it is taken completely out of the hands of the institution and assigned to courts or government agencies, there is little opportunity for developing better decision-making practices within the institution.

With respect to the problem of providing safeguards against abuses of the family's authority to serve as surrogate, the institutional ethics committee can play an important role. It can serve as an initial focus for challenges to the family's decision-making authority short of full-scale legal proceedings or official complaints to government agencies. In addition, it can act as a filter to determine which cases ought to be referred to the courts or to government agencies. If, for example, after discussing the matter with the family and the health care team, a committee is unable to resolve a dispute over treatment between two members of a family, each of whom has a reasonable claim to serve as surrogate, then the matter should be referred to probate court for a determination of guardianship. The same action by the committee would be appropriate if its investigations substantiated a report by a

nurse that the spouse of an incompetent was not competent to decide for him or her. It is worth emphasizing
that there is now substantial agreement that the proper role
of an institutional ethics committee is not to make treatment or care decisions, but rather to facilitate sound decision making by families and legal guardians, and, where
this fails, to refer cases to court or to protective agencies.

It is also important to understand that the advantages of
reliance on institutional ethics committees are comparative. Even their most enthusiastic supporters must
acknowledge that they are no panacea, but at best only one
element of a complex set of social arrangements needed to
assure responsible decision making for incompetent people. The chief virtue of institutional ethics committees is
that they can provide some of the impartiality and critical
scrutiny of judicial proceedings in a way that is less
cumbersome, less expensive, less adversarial, and less in-
vasive of the patient's and the family's privacy.

Whether or not useful analogs of institutional ethics
committees can be developed to enhance *nonmedical* decision making for incompetents remains to be seen, but the
need is so great that the experiment seems well worth
undertaking. At present, institutional ethics committees
are not even available as a resource in most hospitals,
much less in nursing homes and residential care facilities.

Given the lack of institutional ethics committees or
alternative intrainstitutional mechanisms for facilitating
sound decision making for incompetent patients, the contrast drawn earlier between decision making in medical
and nonmedical contexts should not be exaggerated.
Allowing the family to exercise broad authority for medical decisions is *only* acceptable if there are reliable safeguards within the health care institution itself. Where
strong disagreement arises among family members and the
health care team concerning critical decisions it is more
likely that the courts, protective agencies, or other disinterested parties will become involved in an effort to pro-

tect the incompetent individual. On the other hand, the mere absence of disagreement among the key parties to the decision is no guarantee of sound decision making. Indeed, perhaps the most troubling case is that in which the family and the physician agree in a biased decision to withhold life-sustaining care or treatment.

3. Advance directives, personhood, and personal identity

I. THE VALUE OF ADVANCE DIRECTIVES

In the preceding chapter it was noted that advance directives can serve several important values. They can preserve well-being by protecting the individual from intrusive and futile medical interventions; they can promote self-determination; and they can serve as vehicles for altruism by authorizing termination of treatment that would impose financial or emotional costs on others. Nevertheless, weighty objections have been raised against advance directives, and a more probing analysis of their moral authority is warranted.

II. THE MORAL AUTHORITY OF ADVANCE DIRECTIVES

Those who have shown unreserved enthusiasm for the use of advance directives have perhaps made the following assumption: If, as the courts and most bioethicists now agree, the competent individual has a virtually unlimited right to refuse treatment, even life-sustaining treatment, then the same choice ought to be respected when a competent individual makes it concerning a future decision situation through the use of an advance directive.

It was argued in Chapter 2 that this assumption is dubious because it overlooks several morally significant asymmetries between the contemporaneous choice of a competent individual and the issuance of an advance directive to cover future decisions. First, even if at the time an advance directive was issued an individual was well informed about the options available should he or she develop a particular disease or be in a certain condition, therapeutic options and hence prognosis may change between the time the directive was issued and the time at which it is to be implemented. A second morally relevant difference is that the assumption that a competent person is the best judge of his or her own interests is weaker in the case of a choice about future contingencies under conditions in which those interests have changed in radical and unforeseen ways than it is in the case of a competent individual's contemporaneous choice.

A third and equally significant asymmetry is that important informal safeguards that tend to restrain imprudent or unreasonable contemporaneous choices are not likely to be present, or, if present, to be as effective in the case of an advance directive. If a competent patient refuses life-sustaining treatment, those who are responsible for his or her care can and often do urge the patient to reconsider this choice, and in some cases this can prevent a precipitous and disastrous decision. When the decision to forgo life-sustaining treatment is a remote and abstract possibility, it is less likely to elicit the same protective responses that are provoked in family members and health care professionals when they are actually confronted with a human being whom they believe can lead a meaningful life but who chooses to die. Finally, advance directives are often made with certain implicit assumptions in mind about the expected condition of the patient when a treatment choice must be made. When the patient's actual condition is substantially different this calls into question the authority of the advance directive.

Once these four asymmetries are appreciated, we noted, it is clear that even if the competent patient has a virtually unlimited right to refuse life-sustaining treatment, it does not follow straightaway that a refusal of life-support ought always to be respected if it is expressed in an advance directive. We also noted, however, that in spite of these asymmetries the law and medical practice ought to regard valid advance directives as having nearly the same force as a competent patient's contemporaneous choice, because attempts to limit the authority of advance directives would in practice lead to their being ignored by paternalistic physicians or families, thus robbing them of their value.

III. LOSS OF PERSONAL IDENTITY

There is, however, a much deeper philosophical challenge to the moral authority of advance directives which remains intact even if one concludes that, all things considered, the asymmetries cited above do not provide sufficient grounds for limiting that authority. This is the objection that the very process that renders the individual incompetent and brings the advance directive into play can – and indeed often does – destroy the conditions necessary for his or her *personal identity* and thereby *undercut entirely* the moral authority of the directive. The remainder of this chapter is devoted to explicating and assessing the implications of this objection for the moral authority and practical value of advance directives.

The term "personal identity" is used in different senses in different contexts. In the sociological or psycho-social literature, "personal identity" often denotes an individual's *self-perception,* the individual's *identification with* a particular social grouping. That is not the sense of "personal identity" at issue here, however. Instead, the term "personal identity" as used here denotes those conditions which constitute an individual as the particular person he or she is and that make a person existing at one time, and a person existing at a later or earlier time, the same person. No assumption is made that an individual's identity and his or her self-perception or self-identification are always congruent. The philosopher John Perry clarifies the relevant sense of personal identity in this way:

> although a person is not commonly thought of as a process, we can think of his *life* or *personal history* as a process, a sequence of events, and the concept of a personal history is intimately associated with the concept of a person; someone could not be said to have mastered the concept of a person if he could not say, given the requisite information, whether two events belonged to *the history* of one person. . . . We will . . . introduce the notion of an "event belonging to a person" as shorthand for the familiar notion of an "event belonging to the personal history of a person."[1]

The philosopher's quest for an analysis of personal identity can be seen as an attempt to formulate a condition or set of conditions that constitute what Perry calls "the unity relation" for persons: two or more "person life-stages" are stages of the *same* person's life if and only if these conditions obtain. The criteria for personal identity, then, will be a set of *necessary and sufficient* conditions for this "unity relation," or, as we shall say, necessary and sufficient conditions for personal identity. In a nutshell, the objection to be examined is this: Advance directives only have moral authority if the person who issued the directive and the person to whom the directive would be applied are the same person; but the very circumstances which would bring an advance directive into play are often those in which one of the necessary conditions for personal identity is not present.

This challenge rests upon the assumption that whatever the correct theory of personal identity turns out to be it will include the claim that psychological continuity is (at least) a *necessary condition* for personal identity. In what follows this assumption is accepted for the sake of argu-

ment. Although we believe that it can be adequately defended, we shall not attempt to do so here. It is accurate to
say that this view about personal identity is already so
widely held and well-supported in the philosophical literature that the threat it appears to pose to advance directives
ought to be taken seriously.[2]

The notion of psychological continuity, of course, is
inherently vague, since the temporal continuity provided
by mental states (including memories, affective states, and
dispositions) admits of degrees. For example, a person
may have a great many or only a few memories now of his
experiences ten years ago, as well as many or few memories of experiences at intermediate times through that period. Thus the question arises: just how close must various
types of interconnections among such states and dispositions be to support an ascription of psychological continuity?

Nevertheless, the fact that there is a twilight does not
show that we cannot distinguish between noon and mid-
night. There are some cases in which human beings suffer
permanent neurological damage so severe that psychological continuity is utterly destroyed – cases in which there is
no psychological continuity regardless of how low we set
the standard of continuity necessary for the preservation of
personal identity. This is so because some neurological
damage causes the permanent extinction of all psychological properties and states, yet does so while stopping just
short of the point at which (according to the widely
accepted whole-brain version of the brain death criterion),
the individual ceases to live. An individual who is in a
persistent vegetative state, an irreversible deep coma, fits
this description, as do infants born with no cerebral cortex
(anencephalics). In such cases the being has no psychological states or properties, only "vegetative," that is, auto-
nomic, ones. For present purposes, such cases are wholly
unproblematic, because on the conception of personal
identity we are investigating, the psychological continuity

view, such patients have without question either never satisfied the conditions for personal identity (e.g., anancephalics) or have suffered a loss of personal identity (e.g., the permanently comatose). Difficulties arise, however, when irreversible neurological damage falls short of permanent unconsciousness but is nonetheless so severe as to call into question the persistence of enough psychological continuity to preserve personal identity.

The most unsettling sort of case might seem to be the following: Advanced Alzheimer's dementia has resulted in such extensive, permanent neurological damage that the patient's memory has been destroyed, his or her cognitive processes have been virtually obliterated, and all that remains is basic perceptual awareness. Unlike the persistently vegetative patient, the profoundly demented Alzheimer's patient can see and hear or at least has visual and auditory sensations (though this is not to say that the patient can distinguish conceptually and label appropriately what is seen or heard). In addition, the patient in question (again, unlike the permanently unconscious patient) is capable of pain and even of physical pleasure, although of fleeting and rudimentary sorts.

Such cases have seemed to some to rob advance directives of their moral authority.[3] Their argument may be reconstructed as follows:

(i) One person's advance directive has no moral authority to determine what is to happen to *another person*.

(ii) In some cases of severe and permanent neurological damage, for example, that due to advanced Alzheimer's dementia, psychological continuity is so disrupted that the person who issued the advance directive no longer exists.
(Therefore)

(iii) In such cases the advance directive has no moral authority to determine what is to happen to the individual who remains after neurological damage has

destroyed the person who issued the advance directive.

For dramatic emphasis, let us call this the slavery argument, since it portrays advance directives not as vehicles
for self-determination but as devices that can be used to
subjugate other persons.

The slavery argument, however, is invalid. Conclusion
iii does not follow from the conjuction of premises i and ii.
To make it valid, another premise must be added:

(ii') The individual who remains after neurological damage has destroyed the person who issued the advance
directive is a (different) *person*.[4]

Although the addition of premise ii' renders the argument
valid, it also makes it vulnerable to the charge that it is
unsound, because the truth of premise ii' can be challenged.

The key to appreciating the force of this challenge is
understanding what sort of judgment we are making when
we judge that the psychological continuity necessary for
personal identity no longer exists. Psychological continuity, as was already noted, admits of degrees, just as the
decision-making capacities that constitute competence are
a matter of degree. Further, just as, with competence,
where the threshold for competence is set is a matter of
choice, not a decision uniquely determined by the facts of
the case, so also a choice must be made as to what degree
of psychological continuity will be regarded as necessary
for personal identity and how much diminution of psychological continuity will count as the destruction of the
person. However, as with setting the threshold of decision-making capacity for competence, the choice of a
degree of psychological continuity necessary for preservation of the person (or a degree of psychological discontinuity sufficient for the loss of personal identity) need not be
arbitrary. There may be sufficient reasons for setting the

threshold at one level rather than another, just as there are sufficient reasons for setting the threshold of decision-making capacities required for competence at one level rather than another.

IV. HOW MUCH PSYCHOLOGICAL CONTINUITY IS ENOUGH?

It must be emphasized that the psychological continuity view does not itself answer the question "Just how much psychological continuity is necessary for the preservation of personal identity?" If the degree of psychological continuity necessary for preservation of personal identity is set rather *low* or, conversely, if the degree of diminution of psychological continuity compatible with the preservation of personal identity is set rather *high,* then *there will be very few if any real-world cases in which we would be justified in concluding that neurological damage has destroyed one person but left a living, different person.* For reasons that will soon become clear, a conception which sets the level of psychological continuity necessary for personal identity rather low may be called a *conservative* criterion of personal identity.

The crucial point is that if we adopt a conservative (low threshold) criterion of psychological continuity, then those cases in which we can confidently conclude that the person has ceased to exist because neurological damage has so severely diminished psychological continuity will be cases in which neurological damage is so catastrophic that we would be equally confident in concluding that the living being who remains is *not a person at all* and hence, *a fortiori,* not a *different* person.

Although there is dispute about precisely which properties are jointly necessary and sufficient for being a person, there is considerable consensus in the philosophical literature as to what at least some of the necessary conditions are.[5] Some of the strongest candidates for being included among the necessary conditions are the following cognitive capacities:

(a) The ability to be conscious of oneself as existing over time – as having a past and a future, as well as a present.
(b) The ability to appreciate reasons for or against acting; being (sometimes) able to inhibit impulses or inclinations when one judges that it would be better not to act on them.
(c) The ability to engage in purposive sequences of actions.

If any of these three, or anything even roughly similar to any of them, is at least a necessary condition of being a person, then it appears that the permanently and profoundly demented patient described above is not a person. It must be emphasized, however, that lack of personhood does not imply lack of moral status altogether. The very fact that a being can experience pleasure and pain may itself impose significant limitations on how we may act toward it. Thus, it is widely held to be wrong to cause gratuitous pain to animals that are, uncontroversially, not persons.

It might be objected that the immediately preceding line of reasoning is flawed by an equivocation on "person," because that term, as it occurs in debates about personal identity, embodies a *metaphysical* concept of a person, while the term "person" is used in a *moral* sense when it is said that features a through c are necessary conditions for being a person. Thus even though the living being that remains after neurological damage produces a drastic diminution of psychological continuity may not be a person in the moral sense, it does not follow that that being is not a person in the metaphysical sense and hence it does not follow that he or she is not a different person from the person who issued the advance directive. And if he or she is a different person, then the advance directive of another person has no moral authority concerning how he or she is to be treated.

There are two difficulties with this objection. The first is that it rests on the very dubious assumption that a metaphysical and a moral sense of "person," or a metaphysical and a moral concept of a person, can be neatly distinguished. The fact that philosophers typically appeal to our intuitions about responsibilities and commitments – that is, to basic *moral* concepts – in order to support their metaphysical theses about the criterion of identity for persons, casts serious doubt on this assumption. Second, and more important, unless the concept of a person implicated in the psychological continuity view is in some sense the concept of *moral* personality, it is difficult to see why showing that psychological continuity has not been so severely diminished as to result in a loss of personal identity would establish that an advance directive still has moral authority. In other words, if the concept of a person implicated in the psychological continuity view is a purely metaphysical, nonmoral concept, then it is hard to understand why certain marks on paper made by a person in *this* (metaphysical) sense should *ever* be thought to create obligations or confer authority, since obligations can be created and authority can be conferred only by persons in the moral sense.

Indeed, it is not surprising that it is difficult, if not impossible, to distinguish a purely metaphysical, nonmoral sense of "person," at least if we are looking for a criterion of personal identity that articulates or at least builds upon our ordinary, pretheoretical concept of personal identity. For surely our ordinary judgments typically, if not exclusively, are motivated by moral concerns – in particular, the ascription of responsibility, the recognition of rights and obligations, and the acknowledgement of commitments.

It was suggested earlier that if the degree of psychological continuity necessary for the preservation of personal identity is set rather low, the cases in which we should be most confident in declaring that neurological damage has destroyed personal identity (without causing death) will *not* be cases in which we would judge that one person (Jones) is replaced by another person (Jones II). Instead, our task will be that of deciding whether following a formerly existing person's instructions is compatible with discharging whatever obligations we may have toward a living being whose existence will probably be brief no matter what we do and whose mental capacities are much less sophisticated than that of a small child or of a nonhuman animal such as a dog, and who virtually always suffers debilitating and painful physical disabilities as well.[6] Should we follow the advance directive and terminate support for the surviving individual, or should we ignore the advance directive (now that its author no longer exists) and attend only to the interests of the surviving individual?

V. SURVIVING INTERESTS

Thus far, our discussion of the best interest principle (Chapter 2) has been concerned chiefly with the interests of various classes of incompetents *as such* – that is, the interests which beings in a particular state of impairment have only so far as they are considered as now being in that condition. But it is important to emphasize that some who are no longer self-determining once were and that the severely and permanently demented nonperson stands at the terminus of a process of increasing disability at whose commencement stood a person. This simple fact, when taken together with one other, greatly complicates the account of interests, rights, and moral status developed thus far. The additional fact is that the interests of persons can survive not only incompetence and the loss of personhood, but death itself.

Because of the values and preferences an individual now has, he or she may have an interest in the coming to be of certain states of affairs in the future. In some cases the state of affairs in question is not expected to come about until after death. Because of his or her commitments, a person may have an interest in his or her grandchildren getting a good higher education, in spite of the fact that whether that interest is satisfied or thwarted will depend upon events that will occur after his or her demise. Where at least some of a person's significant goals or commitments are of this sort, we must refrain from passing final judgment upon how good or successful the person's life was until the relevant interests are thwarted or satisfied. It was a saying among the Greeks that we should count no man happy while he lives, but we may go a step further and say that the assessment of a life may have to be deferred considerably longer than that.

If interests can survive death, then *a fortiori* they can survive permanent unconsciousness, loss of personal identity, and less extensive departures from competence. For this reason, we will sometimes be mistaken if we limit our consideration of the interests of an incompetent individual to those interests he or she has simply by virtue of his or her present disabled condition. A demented grandfather may now *take no interest* in the future education of his grandchildren because he has forgotten that he has grandchildren. Yet he may still *have* an interest in their future education by virtue of the fact that, prior to the onset of dementia, he took an interest in their education and made a commitment to it. But if this so, then in determining what is in the incompetent individual's interests we must look not only at the interests he or she has as a being in that disabled condition – in particular, his or her purely "experiential" interests in having pleasure and avoiding pain. We must also include among an individual's interests those whose formation presupposed capacities he or she no longer has but whose satisfaction or thwarting will depend upon events yet to transpire. Thus the application of the best interest principle in such cases requires consideration of both sets of interests – neither can be ignored.

Including under an individual's interest both the interests of the incompetent individual as such and his or her interests surviving from a condition prior to disability only makes sense, however, on the assumption that the imcompetent individual and the competent individual whose interests survive incompetence *are the same person*. Accordingly, in the case in which brain damage is so severe that personal identity is lost, there are two distinct sets of interests: the experiential interests of the severely and permanently demented individual and those surviving interests of the person who has ceased to be. There is no person whose interest is composed of those experiential and surviving interests.

Nevertheless, the surviving interests of the person who has ceased to be (and whose successor is a severely demented nonperson) may include an interest in what is done to or with the being who succeeds him or her and who "inhabits" his or her body after the individual has ceased to be. Such an interest is most likely to be derivative upon the formerly existing person's interest in the well-being of his or her loved ones. A person who cares about his or her family will have an interest in avoiding the financial ruin and emotional distress that family would suffer if expensive and intrusive life-support measures were applied after the point at which he or she regards the costs to exceed the benefits. Whether or not the interest in avoiding the burdens which futile treatment would impose on one's family is satisfied or thwarted will depend upon whether or not such treatment is administered, not upon whether or not the individual to whom it is administered is the same person whose interest it is.

VI. THE DISTINCTION BETWEEN THE SURVIVING INTERESTS OF A SELF THAT NO LONGER EXISTS AND SURVIVING INTERESTS IN THE PERSISTING SELF

Two cases need to be distinguished. In the first, a person or self survives the loss of the capacity for self-determination. Jones, when competent and self-determining, formed an interest in what treatment he would receive or not receive should he become so disabled as to lose the capacity for self-determination and hence for exercising a right of self-determination. However, the disease or trauma that robs Jones of his capacity now for exercising self-determination is not so severe as to destroy the conditions for the persistence of personal identity. Jones's self survives, not just his interest in what happens to him in his debilitated condition. Hence Jones's interest in avoiding what he considers to be futile treatment is the interest of an existing self in what happens to *that self.* Jones may seek to avoid futile prolongation of his life out of concern for the burdens it would impose on his family, or he may find the prospect of such an existence aesthetically repugnant.

The second case is different and the difference matters morally. Jones, when competent, formed an interest in avoiding what he considers to be a senseless prolongation of mere biological life should he become severely and permanently mentally disabled. This interest survives not only his loss of the capacity for exercising a right of self-determination; it survives the loss of personal identity that results from the most severe and permanent dementia. Jones no longer exists, yet his interest in avoiding the prolongation of the life of the body that was his survives him. But, unlike the first case, this surviving interest is not the interest of a self in what happens to that self. It is the (surviving) interest of a (no longer existing) self in what happens to something (a living, sensing body) that is not that self.

We noted in the discussion of self-determination in Chapter 1 that the importance or weight of a person's interest in making or controlling a particular choice or decision varies significantly depending on the nature of the choice or decision. In general, the self-determination interest of a self in what happens to that self deserves greater consideration, other things being equal, than the interest of a self in a thing that is not only not that self, but not a person at all. The right of self-determination concerning what is to happen to one's living, nonperson successor could perhaps best be conceived as something like a property right in an external object, and as such more easily limited or overridden than the right of self-determination concerning what happens to one's self.

However, it may be tempting to think that unless this aspect of self-determination, which might be called a "right of disposal," is accorded the same strength as the right of self-determination – the right to determine what happens to one's self – then some important surviving interests will be unacceptably vulnerable. If the right to determine what happens to one's nonperson successor is a limited, interior right, then the life of one's body might, contrary to one's wishes, be kept alive with the result that one's family would suffer great financial and emotional distress. This, however, would not follow. If the right to determine what happens to one's nonperson successor is viewed as a quasi-property right it would, like one's ordinary property rights, be dispositive in ordinary circumstances. It could only justifiably be overridden to secure some very important good or to avoid some important harm.

It is not difficult to think of such a case. Suppose that one's organs could be "harvested" and the lives of recipients would not only be saved but would be restored to their normal quality, but that to do so it would be necessary to keep one's nonperson successor alive longer than you, when competent, would have wanted. To prolong the life of your body long enough to do this great good would require thwarting your self-determination concerning your surviving interest in not having the life of your body sustained after you, the person that you are, have ceased to exist.

Our purpose here is not to argue that a policy of thwarting this sort of interest for this reason would be permissible, much less advisable. Our point, rather, is that in order to argue against such a policy it will not do to argue that the right of *self-determination* is so sacrosanct that proper respect for it precludes a policy of overriding this particular instance of it. To argue in this way would be to conflate the right of a self to determine what is to happen to something that is not that self (the aspect of self-determination we have called the right of disposal) with the right of a self to determine what happens to that self. To say that the right of disposal might be overridden by the interests of others is not to say, of course, that in cases in which it was overridden it would be permissable to require the family of the person whose body is sustained to bear the financial cost of doing so. Further, it would only be permissible to override the right of disposal in this way if reasonable steps were taken to shield the family from emotional distress by treating the living body of the person who has ceased to exist in a dignified and privacy-respecting manner.

The purpose of this brief discussion of the aspect of self-determination covered by the right of disposal is not to articulate the contours of that right. Rather, it has pursued two much more limited aims: (1) to make clear that not all instances of self-determination have equal weight or importance and so the right of self-determination need not always be a barrier to proposals for prolonging life for the purpose of taking organs for transplantation, and (2) to show that while a determination

of best interest must include surviving interests (as well as
the interests of the incompetent as such), not all surviving
interests are of equal weight.

The preceding argument only establishes that *if* the degree of psychological continuity necessary for the preservation of personal identity is set very low, then three
conclusions follow. First, adoption of the psychological
continuity view of personal identity does *not* undercut the
moral authority of advance directives because the slavery
argument is invalid and, if modified to achieve validity, is
unsound. Even if the person who issued the advance directive no longer exists, it does not follow that following
the advance directive is inflicting one person's will upon
another person. Second, as was argued in Chapter 2's analysis of the best interest principle, if the being that remains
after neurological damage undercuts personal identity is
not a person, but a being with radically truncated interests,
our obligations toward that being are quite limited.
Following an advance directive to achieve a painless termination of life-support for a being with such radically
truncated interests need not involve the violation of any
obligations toward that being. Third, whether neurological damage that results in diminution of psychological
continuity presents us with a conflict between following
one person's advance directive and preserving another person's life will depend upon what degree of psychological
continuity is required for the preservation of personal
identity.

This is an important result, for if faced with a choice
between following one person's wishes in an advance directive and saving another person's life we would have to
disregard the advance directive. To do otherwise would be
to give one person a wholly illegitimate, nonconsensual
power of life and death over another person. So if the
threshold for psychological continuity were set so high
that loss of personal identity was a frequent occurrence,
then the authority of advance directives would be fre-

quently undercut. If it is set quite low, such conflicts will only rarely, if ever, occur. However, nothing said so far supports the further claim that the degree of psychological continuity *ought* to be set so low.

VII. ATTEMPTS TO RAISE THE THRESHOLD FOR PSYCHOLOGICAL CONTINUITY

Some proponents of the psychological continuity view have adduced hypothetical examples calculated to convince us that we do or at least ought to set the threshold rather high – or, conversely, that we do or ought to consider some disruptions of psychological continuity far less drastic than those wrought by advanced Alzheimer's dementia to constitute a loss of personal identity. If they are correct, then the otherwise attractive strategy of advocating reliance on advance directives to ease the problems of decision making for incompetents must be abandoned. Consequently, to defend the moral authority of advance directives, we must show that these hypothetical examples do not adequately support a high threshold (i.e., radical, as opposed to conservative view).

The two examples that follow have been used to try to support the high threshold view in the following fashion. First, those who offer them surmise that most thoughtful and morally discerning people would respond to the cases in a certain way. Then they suggest that the explanation, or at least the best explanation, of these moral responses, or at least the best way to render them principled and consistent, is to acknowledge a concept of personal identity that sets the threshold of psychological continuity necessary for persistence of personal identity quite high.

The first case is that of a young nineteenth century Russian nobleman who is, he sincerely professes, committed to socialist ideals. Since he knows that later in life he will inherit vast wealth and may be tempted to abandon his socialist ideals, he extracts a promise from his young wife. If, after he inherits the fortune, he attempts to renege on his commitments to redistributing it to the poor (freeing his serfs, etc.), she is to prevent him from doing so. Those who employ this example first conclude that we think it proper for the woman to resist her middle-aged husband's attempts to keep the wealth for himself or that at the very least we recognize that she faces a serious conflict of moral obligations.[7] This first conclusion seems unexceptionable. However, they go on to contend that this moral assessment presupposes or at least is best explained by the judgment that we regard the young nobleman and the middle-aged husband to be *different persons,* for if they are not, then it would seem that the middle-aged husband could simply release her from the commitment she made to *him* when he was young.

This conclusion that they are different persons, however, is as unconvincing as it is gratuitous. To understand the wife's predicament we need only recognize that the obligations a person acquires through a promise made to another can sometimes conflict with other obligations she has toward *him* and that one may find it advisable to use a promise extracted from another to prevent *himself* in the future from abandoning his current commitments.

This is not to say that the wife would or should choose to honor the promissory obligation at the price of other values or obligations. She might, for example, conclude that her youthful husband had been deluded, brainwashed by leftist friends, and that his commitment had been formed under duress or at a time when he lacked competence to make it. (Similarly, we might conclude that a particular advance directive for medical treatment was invalid because issued under duress and hence fails to confer authority or create obligations.) If, on the other hand, the wife concluded that her youthful husband's commitment to socialist ideals and his decision to ask her to make the promise were ones he was competent to make and were substantially voluntary, then she might well conclude, with justification, that she should resist his current pleas. Clearly, one obvious condition for being released from a promise does not apply here: the wife cannot justify not acting on the promise on the grounds that the promisee failed to foresee the current situation and would not have wished the promise to be carried out in it. His whole point in asking her to make the promise, rather, was that he did foresee that he would be tempted to abandon his ideals.

Moreover, if we were to take literally the proposal that the man who extracted the promise no longer exists, we would get a dissolution, not an explanation, of the wife's serious *moral conflict*. For now her current husband is simply making the outrageous and immoral claim that he is entitled to her former husband's property. Though the "widow" may, for prudential reasons or out of love for her second husband, *prefer* to misuse the money her first husband entrusted to her, she can only view this as a conflict of *moral obligations* if she is either confused or self-deceiving. In sum, the first example does nothing to support the claim that the threshold of psychological continuity either is or should be set so high as to wreak havoc with the moral authority of advance directives.

There is another troubling feature of the Russian nobleman case, however, one whose appreciation does not require that we assume a loss of personal identity and which has a direct bearing on the status of advance directives. One might well ask: supposing that the idealistic youth and the conservative middle-aged man are the same person, what entitled the young man to bind himself to ideals he later rejects? Furthermore, why should the wife acknowledge any such attempt at self-binding? It is crucial to remember that the assumption is that the middle-aged conservative is competent, so the question is, why shouldn't a competent individual be free to repudiate his former ideals if he wishes?

It is worth pointing out that the current practice with respect to advance directives does *not* recognize the right of an individual to bind his or her *competent* self in the future. Advance directives, in all jurisdictions, are revocable at will by the competent individual. The fact that advance directives are so revocable may indeed signal a belief that the moral right of an individual to bind his or her future competent self is problematic. Indeed, most advance directive statutes can be read as going even further, allowing the revocation of the directive even at the behest of an *incompetent* principal. This feature, although it may be a well-intentioned effort to provide added safeguards, threatens to undercut the value of advance directives in some cases. Whether this threat is realized would depend upon whether the incompetent individual is given the opportunity to repudiate the directive and upon what is counted as evidence of repudiation. These issues are addressed in Chapter 6.

The second example is no more persuasive. It concerns an elderly, saintly man who is for good reason awarded the Nobel Peace Prize. After the prize is awarded it comes to light that some sixty years earlier a very young man – who not only bore the same name as the Nobel Laureate, but also had a body and brain identical with those of the Laureate – ferociously attacked and injured a policeman but went unpunished.[8] Purveyors of this example contend that it supports their claim that we do or at least should conclude that the young rowdy and the saintly Laureate are different persons, that the links of psychological continuity stretching from the former to the latter are sufficiently tenuous as to fall short of the appropriate degree of continuity necessary for the persistence of a single person.

This conclusion, as in the Russian nobleman case, is supposed to provide the best explanation of our moral responses to the case. Presumably the relevant moral response would be an unwillingness to punish the saintly, elderly Laureate for the crime of the rowdy youth. But it should be obvious that there is another way of explaining this response that is at least equally plausible as an explanation and that does *not* require us to embrace the radical conclusion that the young man and the Laureate are different persons.

We may, instead, conclude that *mercy* – which presupposes guilt and hence the preservation of identity – is appropriate in this case, for several reasons. First, in this case punishment would not serve at least two of the goals that are usually thought to justify it: it could neither *reform* the person on whom it would be inflicted (since he has already not only reformed himself, but become saintly), nor *deter* or *prevent* him from committing further crimes (since he is not now the sort of person who will ever commit any crime). Second, to the extent that we think of the criminal as having incurred through his crime a "debt to society," we may decide not to to punish him because we believe that through the extraordinary efforts that earned him the Nobel Peace Prize the Laureate has more than discharged that debt.

It might be objected that even if his debt to *society* has been discharged, the crime the young man committed wronged a *particular person,* the policeman, and that *this* debt has neither been paid to nor forgiven by that individual. To show mercy would be to fail to appreciate the nature of the criminal act – the fact that it was the wronging of a particular person. Consequently, we cannot explain the judgment that the Laureate should not be punished by saying that it is an appropriate exercise of mercy. Instead, we can only explain our judgment that he should not be punished – or at least we can only justify it – on the assumption that the Laureate and the youth are different persons.

This objection contains a grain of truth, but it is nonetheless spurious. All it establishes is that showing mercy by not punishing the Laureate is one thing, while deciding not to require him to render compensation for his wrong to the policeman is another. If, as seems appropriate, we view the crime both as a public and a private wrong, *we* may show mercy for the former, while acknowledging that it is up to the *victim* whether to forgive the latter.

Suppose the policeman has remained seriously incapacitated and wracked with pain since the injury. To the extent that we feel that the Laureate owes him compensation, this belief *supports* the conclusion that the youth and the Laureate are the same person. And, as we have seen, our feeling that the Laureate should not be punished does *not* presuppose that it is not one and the same person. So it seems that the second example, like the first, fails to provide solid support for the conclusion that we do or should set the threshold of psychological continuity sufficient for the preservation of personal identity quite high. Therefore, neither of these examples supports the claim that there will be a significant number of cases in which neurological damage is severe enough to undercut the moral authority of an advance directive by destroying its author while leaving in his or her place another *person*.

We have just seen that certain examples offered to support the claim that the threshold of psychological continuity required for the persistence of personal identity should be set rather high fail to do so. It also might be argued that a healthy and reasonable conservativism weighs heavily in favor of setting the threshold rather low. Some of our most important social practices and institutions – those dealing with contracts, promises, civil and criminal liability, and the assignment of moral praise and blame – apparently presuppose a view of personal indentity according to which a person can survive quite radical psychological changes and hence a high degree of psychological *discontinuity*. If this is so, then since these practices and institutions are so valuable, we would have to have extraordinarily weighty reasons for giving up the view of personal identity upon which they are founded. But as we have seen, examples like those of the Nobel Laureate and the Russian nobleman do not supply such reasons, since our responses to them can be explained quite well without assuming loss of personal identity. Nor, it should be recalled, does adoption of the psychological continuity view itself commit us to setting the threshold lower (or higher) than our social practices and institutions presuppose. That view is simply neutral as to what degree of psychological continuity is required for the persistence of the person. It appears, then, that since the value of preserving some of our most basic institutions and practices speaks in favor of setting the threshold of psychological continuity necessary for personal identity low, and since there is nothing of comparable weight on the other side of the balance, we clearly ought to set (or rather leave) the threshold low.

The issue may not be quite so clear-cut as this, however. Consider what would occur if a much higher threshold of psychological continuity necessary for the preservation of personal identity were *consistently* employed so that our expectations would adapt to it. Ponder, in particular, how such a change would affect the practice of issuing advance directives, and more generally our practices of caring for incompetents.

If people knew that the degree of psychological continuity that would be considered necessary for the preservation of personal identity would be rather high, and if they were confident that there would be reliable methods for ascertaining when such a degree of continuity had been lost, they would take this into account. One would know, for example, that after one becomes incompetent one might suffer sufficient neurological damage so that others would judge that one no longer existed, but without the damage (at least for a time) being so catastrophic that what remained was not a person at all. One would know that if this occurred, one would be declared dead and one's will would be read. The declaration of one's death might then have definite and predictable social, moral, and legal implications: for example, one's family might no longer be responsible (morally or legally) for the care of the different person who succeeded one after one ceased to exist.

There is another reason why raising the threshold of continuity required for the preservation of personal identity may not result in a severe disruption of basic social practices and institutions. On most versions of the psychological continuity view, not just memories, but also intentions, are important elements in the relations of connectedness that constitute psychological continuity. Moreover, social arrangements can foster a higher degree of psychological continuity by encouraging individuals to undertake long-range projects and the complex intentional connections that these require. In other words, the degree of psychological continuity is to an extent a matter of which sort of life an individual leads – a life of disconnected episodes or one of continuity, bound together by long-range plans and stable values – and social arrangements can significantly influence the choice between these modes of living. To that extent, social arrangements may not only be compatible with, but actively support, a higher threshold of psychological continuity.

It is a mistake, then, simply to assume that a significant raising of the threshold of psychological continuity necessary for the preservation of personal identity must be incompatible with some of our most valuable social practices and institutions. It is also a mistake to assume that such a shift must undermine the practice of issuing advance directives. Instead, what might occur would be a *revision* of those institutions and practices and a narrowing of the scope of the authority of advance directives. There would be no conflict between honoring one person's advance directive and preserving the life of the different person who succeeded him or her because the authority of the advance directive could be understood by all concerned to begin with the onset of incompetence and to terminate with the loss of personal identity.

Nevertheless, it is worth contemplating what the *cost* – both moral and financial – of such a shift would be. There would, of course, be *transition costs*. Greater or lesser degrees of confusion, lack of coordination, and anxiety might result, depending upon how the new conception of personal identity – along with the new legal definition of the death of a person it requires – were implemented. But even after the transition had been achieved there would be major social, legal, and moral problems to deal with.

The new system would result in the the "births" of large numbers of "new persons" who would, as it were, spring full-blown into the world and who would not, strictly speaking, be the sons, daughters, husbands, wives, or friends of anyone. Such "new persons" would have no financial assets (nor debts), nor would any individual or family be legally responsible for them. Of course, it might be possible to restructure our practices concerning family responsibility to include "quasi-obligations" of family members to the "successor-persons" of their deceased loved ones. Indeed we might fashion legal obligations of a limited sort and impute then to the "predecessor person" him- or herself. The price of setting the threshold for psychological continuity high is that doing so enormously complicates and magnifies the problem of in-tergenerational justice.

The strangeness and complexities of the arrangements needed to cope with the new problem of intergenerational justice – the potential for conflicts of obligations they generate – numb the mind. We gesture toward them here only to emphasize that those who have advocated adopt-ing a view of personal identity which significantly raises the threshold of psychological continuity necessary for the preservation of the person simply have not thought through the disturbing implications of their proposal. However, our reply is *not* that the Parfitian view ought to be rejected because adopting it would require significant disruptions of current arrangements. After all, sometimes such costs ought to be borne. Rather, the point is that proponents of that view have given us no good reasons for shouldering the burdens of undertaking such a radical revision of our practices, institutions, and ways of thinking of ourselves and our relationships to one another that taking their proposal seriously would require.

VIII. A COMPROMISE POSITION

We have argued that even if the psychological continuity view is accepted, it does not follow that we should recognize a high threshold of psychological continuity as necessary for personal identity. And from this it follows that we have no reason to fear that the moral authority of advance directives will dissolve with or soon after the onset of incompetence, thus rendering them useless.

Even if we are correct in this, however, there is another thesis which Parfit, the most prominent proponent of the psychological continuity view, holds and which remains unscathed by our criticisms thus far. According to Parfit, not only philosophers, but also ordinary people, have tended to assume that personal identity is or depends upon some deeper, metaphysical fact – for example, the fact that a soul or mental substance exists. This, he argues, is a mistake. Psychological continuity is all there is to personal identity. There is no deeper (or other) fact of the matter. Therefore we should attach less importance to personal identity to reflect the fact that there is no deeper fact. Moreover, psychological continuity is a matter of degree, not an all-or-nothing matter. Therefore, we should also acknowledge in our morality and in our social practices and institutions the implications of the fact that psychological continuity, not personal identity, is what matters, and that psychological continuity is a matter of degree.

We propose to understand this thesis as follows. In real-life situations, the judgment that A is the same person as B typically has moral implications. Once we see that personal identity depends only on psychological continuity (and not on any further or deeper fact) we should acknowledge that the character and force of the judgment that A is the same person as B *vary* with the degree of psychological continuity between the psychological states (or psychological properties) of A and those of B, and in general have less importance. For example, we ordinarily think that if A, the man we now see before us, is the same person as B, the cold-blooded killer who assassinated the President a year ago, then A is culpable for the killing. But, Parfit suggests, the less the degree of psychological continuity, the less the culpability. In a sense, it does not matter whether we *reconceive* of personal identity as being a matter of degree, thereby reducing the importance of personal identity judgments, or *replace* the concept of personal identity (understood as being an all-or-nothing notion) with the concept of psychological continuity (understood as being a matter of degree and of lesser importance).

The application of this general thesis to the case of advance directives is straightforward. First, all else being equal, the greater the degree of psychological continuity between A, the competent person who issued the advance directive, and B the (incompetent) individual whose body (and brain) are spatio-temporally continuous with A's, the greater the moral authority of the advance directive, i.e., the more *weight* A's wishes, as expressed in the advance directive, should be accorded in determining what is to be done to or for B. Second, since personal identity is nothing more than psychological continuity and so in general of less importance, then advance directives, whose force depends on personal identity, should in general be accorded less importance.

If taken at face value, this proposal does not represent a mere revision, even a radical revision, of our conception of personal identity. Rather, it is a proposal to do away with personal identity judgments as we ordinarily understand them and to replace them with judgments about differing degrees of psychological continuity and the differing moral weights that correspond to them. If we accept the psychological continuity view, the thesis that psychological continuity is necessary for personal identity, along with the seemingly unexceptionable claim that psychological continuity is a matter of degree, then the replacement of "all or nothing" moral judgments (e.g., A is responsible or he is not, or A's wishes should be dispositive or they should not count at all) with varying moral weight judgments may seem inescapable.

But this is not so. There are powerful pragmatic reasons for maintaining a social consensus according to which degrees of psychological continuity which meet or exceed a particular threshold are sufficient for an *unqualified* judgment of personal identity, a judgment which carries with it *maximal moral force*. And this is so even if the moral weights corresponding to degrees of psychological continuity below that threshold may vary, diminishing as the degree of psychological continuity decreases. Similarly, being a competent adult depends on a complex of skills and capacities that are always a matter of degree. Nevertheless, there may be decisive pragmatic reasons for recognizing a certain threshold of the relevant skills and capacities as necessary for maturity and for ascribing, in an *all-or-nothing* fashion, a distinctive social and legal status to persons whose skills and capacities fail to meet that threshold. So from the claim that the psychological continuity upon which personal identity depends is a matter of degree, it does *not* follow that personal identity judgments should be replaced by judgments about varying degrees of psychological continuity and corresponding moral judgments concerning the varying weights of rights and obligations.

What sorts of pragmatic considerations might count in favor of the social recognition of a threshold of psychological continuity and for using it to make all-or-nothing personal identity judgments? First of all, there are daunting epistemic constraints. Attempts to make numerous fine-grained judgments about degrees of psychological continuity would require far richer data than we ordinarily have or could acquire, even with great cost and effort. The various moral weights to be assigned to interests, rights, or obligations on the basis of these psychological continuity judgments would be correspondingly ill-founded and unreliable. Second, even if these epistemic difficulties could be surmounted, tailoring the ascriptions of rights and responsibilities to reflect such fine-grained distinctions would require institutions whose constituent rules would be so complex as to preclude most if not all people from mastering them well enough to achieve a stable framework for legitimate expectations and the efficient social coordination and cooperation which depend upon such a framework.

Again, an analogy may help. Being designated a mature person (or competent adult), as opposed to a minor, carries with it a fairly clear-cut bundle of legal rights and social privileges and responsibilities. Of course, it is theoretically possible to fragment this bundle by distinguishing different rights and obligations (and/or the same rights and obligations with different weights) and mapping them onto varying degrees of the several skills and capacities which together constitute maturity. But here, as in the case of attaching different moral weights to rights, obligations, or interests in such a way that the weights correspond to different degrees of psychological continuity, greater sensitivity may come at a prohibitive price: costly information-gathering that results nonetheless in inaccurate judgments and inefficiently complex institutions. One of the attractions of a system that designates thresholds as markers for ascriptions of status (such as that of "competent adult") and assigns bundles of rights (and obligations) indiscriminately to all who enjoy the status in question is that it facilitates coordination by sharply limiting the number and sensitivity of judgments upon which people must agree if their expectations are to be sufficiently congruent. It has long been noted that the social recognition of rights minimizes the need for com-

plex consequentialist reasoning (and the potential for disagreement, error, and lack of coordination which such
reasoning carries with it). Indeed, the appeal to rights
typically avoids consequentialist reasoning by declaring
consequences to be irrelevant. Similarly, the use of a
threshold of psychological continuity in the making of
personal identity judgments not only reduces the number
of estimates of degrees of psychological continuity, it also
simplifies the ascription of rights and obligations by
bundling them together, and avoids the problem of
recognizing different weights for rights and obligations
corresponding to different degrees of psychological continuity.

If, as we are suggesting, a strong pragmatic case can be
made for singling out a threshold of psychological continuity for personal identity judgments, there is nevertheless a way in which the (alleged) fact that personal identity
is *really* a matter of degree can still be accommodated. We
may attach full moral force to the rights and obligations
that we ascribe to those who clearly meet or exceed the
socially recognized threshold, while attaching diminishing
moral significance to those obligations and rights (or to the
interests that the rights serve) as we move "downward,"
further away from the threshold.

In the case of advance directives, this would amount to
the following procedure. So long as the degree of psychological continuity which we take to be necessary for the
preservation of personal identity is present, the advance
directive has full moral authority. (Recall, however, that
we argued early in this chapter that this "full authority"
may *not* be as robust as the authority of the competent
patient's contemporaneous decision.) As we move "downward" from this threshold, through lessening degrees of
psychological continuity, the moral authority or force of
the advance directive diminishes correspondingly. In other
words, for cases that fall *below* the threshold – and only for
those – the weaker the degree of psychological continuity,
the more readily the advance directive may be overriden

by competing moral considerations, including our concern for the well-being of the incompetent individual. Presumably, a point is eventually reached at which the degree of psychological continuity between the author of the advance directive and the incompetent individual is so small that the advance directive of the former has no authority at all over the latter, at least if the incompetent individual can be said to have interests of any morally significant sort.

Thus even where diminution of psychological continuity is great enough to lead us to conclude that the incompetent individual is not the person who issued the advance directive, we might nevertheless conclude that there is enough psychological continuity to give the wishes expressed in the advance directive *some weight* in our decision concerning the treatment of the incompetent individual. This would amount to recognizing as morally significant the especially intimate relationship which obtains between these individuals, while at the same time acknowledging that they are distinct individuals. It would also not differ significantly from giving less weight to future interests when only a nonperson survives.

The virtue of the compromise view is that it acknowledges both the value of our current institutions and practices, which to a large extent treat personal identity as an all-or-nothing affair, *and* the implications of the view that personal identity depends upon something (namely, psychological continuity), which admits of degree.

That such a strategy is coherent is again made clear by the analogy used earlier. We can (1) admit that maturity (i.e., being a competent adult) depends upon skills and capacities that admit of degree (and that there is no "deeper fact" about maturity), (2) single out a threshold level of these skills and capacities as necessary for maturity, (3) ascribe a bundle of moral rights and obligations only to those who meet or exceed the threshold level, and (4) ascribe successively more restricted (less weighty, more easily overridden) rights and obligations to those who fall further and further below the threshold. Thus nascent obligations and rights (or morally considerable interests) would ripen as the individual moves toward maturity. Whether or not the adoption of such a compromise position would be the best alternative is perhaps unclear. It is important to emphasize, however, that even if the compromise position is rejected, our basic response to Parfit remains intact: even if personal identity depends only upon something (namely, psychological continuity) that is a matter of degree, it does not follow that we ought to replace our usual all-or-nothing, threshold concept personal identity judgments with matter-of-degree judgments.

IX. CONCLUSIONS CONCERNING PERSONAL IDENTITY

The results of our investigation of the claim that a proper understanding of personal identity poses a serious challenge to the authority of advance directives can now be summarized. The thesis that psychological continuity is at least a necessary condition for personal identity is plausible and widely held. Yet on any reasonable interpretation of this thesis it is undeniable that there can be and indeed are some cases in which neurological damage results in loss of personal identity without being so complete as to result in death, as defined by the widely accepted whole brain-death criterion. Since those who are permanently unconscious have no *psychological* states or properties, there has been loss of personal identity in these cases, no matter how high or low we set the degree of psychological continuity necessary for the preservation of personal identity. Such cases, however, pose no radical challenge to the moral authority of advance directives for two reasons. First, they are not cases in which following one (formerly existing) person's advance directive will end another, different person's life, since the permanently unconscious are not persons at all. Second, we have argued that a person's prudential concern that is expressed in an advance directive can extend beyond the bounds of personal identity to the fate of the human body in which the person once "resided."

Nor do cases of *profound and permanent* dementia pose such a challenge, for in these cases neurological damage, although it falls short of permanent unconsciousness, destroys at least some of the necessary conditions for personhood. Here, too, as in the case of the permanently unconscious being, there is no conflict between the rights of one (formerly existing) person and those of another person. However, there is this important difference: the profoundly demented individual, although not a person, is by virtue of his or her capacity for pleasure and pain a being with morally considerable interests. For this reason a genuine conflict may arise – between implementing the advance directive and acting in morally appropriate ways toward the profoundly demented individual.

Here are two examples of such conflicts: A person while competent directs that all possible measures be taken to extend his or her life, but life now as a profoundly demented patient is dominated by suffering; a person while competent directs that all treatment should be stopped if he or she becomes profoundly demented, but now that he or she is profoundly demented palliative treatment is needed to relieve pain.

Such conflicts, however, are likely to be rare and are neither so fundamental nor so intractable as a conflict between the basic rights of two persons. Few if any persons would wish to have their lives extended or to be denied palliative care should they become profoundly demented. Moreover, the profoundly and permanently demented Alzheimer's patient is not like a happy and otherwise normal individual who has simply lost some of his or her cognitive functions. On the contrary, as we have already noted, the advanced Alzheimer's patient not only has truncated interests, but also has a very limited life-

expectancy and typically suffers a number of serious and
often painful physical ailments as well. Our obligations
toward such beings are to minimize their pain and to
provide comfort. The point has an important implication
for matters of distributive justice and cost containment:
granted the limits of our obligations toward such patients,
we are not required to seek to prolong their lives by costly
medical interventions.

The psychological continuity view of personal identity
does not itself provide an answer to the question: Where
should we set the threshold for psychological continuity –
what degree of psychological continuity is necessary for
the preservation of personal identity? If the threshold is set
high, then we will be forced to conclude that there will be
many cases in which neurological damage destroys the
person who issued an advance directive but leaves in his or
her place a different person, over whose fate the advance
directive can have no authority. If it is set low, the cases in
which we are confident that loss of personal identity has
occurred will be those in which what remains is not a
person and, *a fortiori,* not a different person.

Some philosophers have adduced hypothetical examples
to support the conclusion that we ought to set the
threshold very high. These examples do not succeed,
however, because our moral responses to them can be
explained just as well (or better) by alternative hypotheses
that do not presuppose loss of personal identity.

Setting the threshold high might not be incompatible
with the existence of some of our most valued social
practices and institutions (those involving commitment
and responsibility) nor even with a coherent practice of
implementing advance directives, for such institutions, as
well as the practice of advance directives, may be flexible
enough to adapt to a new conception of personal identity.
However, the moral and social costs of achieving the
restructuring of our practices and institutions that such a
shift in the threshold would mandate would be very high,

and as yet we have no good reasons to incur them. Thus the fact that neurological damage can destroy the psychological continuity necessary for personal identity does not, as some have argued, undermine the moral authority or value of advance directives as a basic tool for dealing with problems of decision making for those who are incompetent.

A quite different implication drawn by some advocates of the psychological continuity view is that the very attempt to locate a threshold of psychological continuity (whether high or low) reveals a failure to understand that personal identity judgments, understood as all-or-nothing claims, ought to be replaced with judgments concerning degrees of psychological continuity, along with corresponding judgments concerning the moral weight of rights, obligations, or interests – including the moral weight to be accorded to interests expressed in advance directives. We have seen, however, that the thesis that the psychological continuity upon which personal identity depends admits of degree does *not* entail that we should abandon the use of all-or-nothing personal identity judgments, any more than the fact that maturity depends upon skills and capacities that are a matter of degree entails that it is a mistake to designate as mature only those persons who possess the skills and capacities in question to a certain degree. There is nothing incoherent about designating a certain degree of psychological continuity as necessary for the persistence of personal identity *and* recognizing that psychological continuity is a matter of degree, *and* admitting that psychological continuity is all there is to personal identity.

Nor is there any inconsistency in combining the threshold approach with social practices and institutions that recognize the diminishing moral authority of an advance directive as the degree of psychological continuity decreases below the threshold. Moreover, we have indicated why such a way of thinking about personal ident-

ity – which we have labeled the compromise position –
might be thought to be a reasonable one. It would allow us
to preserve the core of some of our most valuable practices
and institutions, those which presuppose the use of all-or-
nothing personal identity judgments, while acknowledging in practice that personal identity is simply a matter of
psychological continuity and does not depend on some
deeper, metaphysical fact. This compromise approach
would allow us to make a significant place for advance
directives among our social institutions and practices without presupposing a dubious metaphysical theory of personal identity. For cases in which justified all-or-nothing
personal identity judgments can be made, valid advance
directives would have their full moral force. For cases in
which psychological continuity has diminished to points
below the threshold that grounds all-or-nothing personal
identity judgments, the moral force of advance directives
would be correspondingly weakened and might disappear
altogether.

None of this is to say, however, that advance directives
are never morally problematic. Perhaps the most troubling
case for according an advance directive absolute authority
would *not* be one in which we think that there has been a
loss of personal identity. Instead, it would be of the
following sort. An apparently valid advance directive
specifies that no life-sustaining treatments, including antibiotics, are to be used on the individual if he or she suffers
a serious loss of cognitive function. The patient does suffer
a serious loss of cognitive function due to a discrete neurological injury, such as a stroke. He or she is now a moderately mentally handicapped person, but clearly a person
– and indeed the same person – nonetheless. Moreover, the
patient is otherwise healthy, apparently quite happy, and
wants to live. Then the patient develops a life-threatening
pneumonia. Following the advance directive will result in
the easily avoidable death of a happy and reasonably
healthy, although mentally handicapped, person. Sup-

pose, also, that he or she is judged not to be competent to rescind the advance directive.[9] There is clearly a sense in which to ignore the advance directive would be to interfere with the patient's earlier autonomous choice.

Cases like this challenge the depth of the commitment to individual autonomy and with it the assumption that the moral authority of advance directives may never be limited on paternalistic grounds. We are not convinced that it is possible to provide a conclusive argument to show that paternalism is never in principle justified in any such case. However, our aim in this chapter is not to evaluate paternalistic challenges to advance directives but rather a more fundamental objection rooted in the problem of personal identity.

It is important to emphasize, however, that the combination of factors that make cases such as this so disturbing will probably be quite rare. And it is worth repeating that the challenge such cases pose to the authority of advance directives does not rest on the assumption that there has been a loss of personal identity. The fact that neurological damage can result in loss of personal identity without death is not, we have argued, a serious challenge to the moral authority of advance directives.

4. Distributive justice and the incompetent

I. THE NEED TO QUALIFY
THE PATIENT-CENTERED APPROACH

The courts, as well as most legal scholars and ethicists, have tended to assume that any explicit role for a consideration of the rights and interests of others in decisions concerning imcompetents should be strictly excluded. This reluctance to face up to the fact that others' rights and interests impose limits upon the moral authority of advance directives, the substituted judgment principle, and the best interest principle betokens an understandable and (up to a point) praiseworthy recognition of the extreme vulnerability of the incompetent individual. The key court cases from which these standards have developed and that have shaped the course of the debate have concerned the most momentous decisions – withdrawal or continuance of life-sustaining treatment. A reluctance to depart from a patient-centered approach and explicitly address questions of distributive justice, especially those relating directly to costs, is all the more understandable in cases of life-or-death decisions for incompetents.

There is another, less obvious, reason why these decisions – and hence the broader ethical debate whose assumptions they have fashioned – have not faced resource allocation issues head-on. The U.S. legal system operates on the "standing case rule," according to which courts are to respond only to actual cases brought by or on behalf of identified individuals. Yet it is in the case of the particular decisions that affect the welfare of identifiable individuals that there is the most discomfort about "rationing" scarce resources. Nevertheless, a sound ethical framework for decision making for incompetent individuals must reflect the fact that others have rights and interests as well, and that resources, including medical resources, are scarce.

It is far beyond the scope of this chapter to provide a comprehensive theory of distributive justice and apply it to decision making for incompetent individuals. Instead, we shall attempt to articulate the points of contact between such a theory and the patient-centered theory of decision making for incompetents we have advanced so far. Once again, the emphasis will be on articulating a framework for resolving the ethical issues rather than on providing fully developed solutions.

We can begin by taking stock of the implications for issues of distributive justice that already can be drawn from the ethical analysis presented thus far. Chapter 2's discussion of guidance principles for decision making for incompetent people already significantly limits the range of problems of distributive justice and provides some of the material required for solving them.

II. THE RELEVANCE OF GUIDANCE PRINCIPLES TO QUESTIONS OF DISTRIBUTIVE JUSTICE

In Chapter 2 it was argued that the moral authority of both advance directives and substituted judgment is based on but also limited by the right of a competent patient to refuse care or treatment at the time he or she is competent. This is, as we have also seen, a negative right, a right to be free from nonconsensual care or treatment by others. It is not a positive right, not a valid claim to services. (Whether there is a general positive right to health care and, if so, what it includes, is a much disputed question.) Consequently, neither advance directives nor substituted judgment create any *new* resource allocation issues peculiar to decisions concerning incompetents. An advance directive stipulating that "all" means of life-sustaining treatment are to be used regardless of the quality of the life that would be prolonged would not by itself create any obligation to commit social resources, nor would a similar decision reached through an appropriate exercise of substituted judgment. The effect of wider use of advance directives and of substituted judgment would, on the contrary, most likely be to withhold life-support more frequently by removing both the moral reservations and the paralyzing fear of legal liability that currently lead some physicians to "over-treatment." This would ease, rather than exacerbate, the strain on resources.

Nor does the best interest principle generate a right to resources. Instead, the best interest principle too is to be understood as operating *within* the constraints of distributive justice. If a right to health care can be ascribed correctly to the individual in question, then the best interest principle, where applicable, simply requires that whatever resources the individual is entitled to according to that right be employed for the maximal benefit of that individual, not for others, even if they could benefit more.

However, to say that for the most part the guidance principles that are appropriate for decision making for incompetent individuals do not themselves raise any *new* problems of distributive justice is not to deny that serious problems abound. Even if these principles do not endow the individual with any new positive rights – rights to be provided with services – three challenging questions remain: (1) What general rights to health care, if any, do people have? (2) Does incompetence in any way limit such rights, if they exist? (3) Even if incompetence *per se* does not limit or cancel an individual's rights grounded in distributive justice, are there certain circumstances or conditions that frequently cause or accompany incompetence which do so, and if so, how does this affect the application of the guidance principles? Our focus will be on the second and third questions, since it is not our aim to present a general theory of distributive justice in health care.

III. INCOMPETENCE, MORAL STATUS, AND RIGHTS OF DISTRIBUTIVE JUSTICE

The decision-specific analysis of competence developed in Chapter 1 makes it clear that incompetence *by itself* does not alter whatever claims an individual has according to valid principles of distributive justice. A decision-specific judgment that an individual is incompetent changes his or her moral status in one and only one, limited, way. It signals that, for this decision, the presumption of self-determination has been defeated and that limited paternalistic intervention is justified in principle. Nor does a judgment of general incompetence by itself entail any suspension of whatever valid distributive claims the individual may have. Instead, a determination of general incompetence only entails that the individual may be prevented, for his own good, from exercising a general right of self-determination because he has (perhaps only temporarily) lost the level of decision-making and agency capacities required for ascribing this general right.

While ascribing the general right of self-determination logically presupposes decision-making and agency capacities, ascriptions of rights of distributive justice do not. The latter logically presuppose only the capacity to benefit from receiving resources. Incompetence itself, then, neither dissolves nor limits an individual's distributive rights, and in that sense there is no separate theory of distributive justice for incompetents. The appropriate question, then, is whether there are certain classes of incompetents whose moral status, from the standpoint of distributive justice, is altered due to their conditions.

A. The permanently unconscious:
Minimal interests

As was argued earlier, a proper understanding of the limits of the best interest principle makes it clear that the continued support of permanently unconscious patients is *not* ethically required, and that withdrawal of support constitutes no injury to them. For even if, in subscribing to the whole-brain concept of death, one concludes that such patients are not dead, one can nonetheless exclude them as legitimate claimants for scarce resources because they do not, as permanently unconscious beings, have any experiential interests nor any reasonable prospects of regaining any. Thus, they lack interests of the sort that can compete for scarce resources with the claims of others who can genuinely benefit from the social resources in question. Yet it is important to recall, as we noted in Chapter 2, that the person who existed prior to the permanent loss of consciousness may have interests in what happens to his or her still living body after consciousness has permanently ceased. Some interests may survive the death of the person.

There is, however, as we have also already noted, an alternative route by which permanently unconscious patients as such may be excluded from the domain of problems of distributive justice. It is far from inconceivable that the process of conceptual change in response to technological advances that led from the cardiopulmonary concept of death to the whole-brain concept should eventually push us to a higher-brain function concept of death. If this change – which has already been advocated by a number of ethicists – does occur, then permanently unconscious individuals will be declared dead and thus as such will no longer be viewed as having claims on social resources.

The only remaining questions of distributive justice concerning this class of individuals would then be much less fundamental and much more tractable. For example, if a person while competent issued an advance directive stating that he or she was to be sustained indefinitely in a persistent vegetative state, this document would have no more legal or moral authority than an ordinary will would have if it stipulated that a brain-dead individual was to be maintained indefinitely on a heart-lung machine or that the body of the deceased was to be kept frozen in perpetuity just in case science eventually develops a technique for reviving him or her. People have a right to have their mortal remains treated with dignity, but not a right to be forever frozen or infused with blood and oxygen – at least not if society is helping to pay the bill. If, on the other hand, an individual provided sufficient resources (after deductions for estate taxes, etc.) for such measures, there is nothing inherently more suspect about such a will than many actual wills that are currently recognized to be legally valid, including those that establish trust funds for beloved goldfish or that found philanthropic institutions for idiosyncratic causes.

There is considerable anectdotal evidence, however, that some permanently unconscious patients are sustained longer than is required to confirm the prognosis, not in order to implement the patient's advance directive using his or her own resources, but for the sake of loved ones who have not come to terms with the fact that the patient is totally and permanently bereft of awareness. (In the case of brain dead individuals, there is a clear professional and public consensus, reflected in the law, that continuing treatment measures for these reasons is acceptable only for a very short term – hours or, at most, a few days.) This way of responding to the family's denial uses public resources or insurance funds that spread the cost socially.

Although such a practice is understandable as an expression of concern for the family, its rationality and propriety are highly questionable. If it could be clearly shown that resources used on the permanently unconscious patient were thereby denied to a patient who could genuinely benefit from them, then the use of social resources to continue life-support simply for the family's sake would be extremely difficult to defend morally. However, in the current U.S. health care system – or some might say, nonsystem – withholding resources from one class of patients does not ensure that those resources will be used on others who can benefit more.[1] There is no fixed, overall budget and no allocation system such that individual physicians can systematically divert resources from less to more efficacious uses. Nevertheless, use of social resources to sustain the permanently unconscious is irrational and, it could be argued, poor medical practice as well, if there are other, less costly ways of dealing humanely with the family's denial. The most obvious alternative is to counsel the family during the recommended period of two- to three-week waiting period in which the prognosis of persistent vegetative state is confirmed, utilizing the expertise of social workers, psychologists, psychiatrists, or chaplains, if necessary, to enable the family to come to terms with the fate of their loved one.

B. The severely and permanently demented: Truncated interests

These patients, who were described in some detail in Chapter 3, are unlike the permanently unconscious in one morally crucial respect: they are capable of pain and simple pleasures. Unlike the permanently unconscious, they have an interest in experiencing pleasure and in avoiding pain. It was also seen, however, that at least the most severely brain-damaged members of this group lack one or more of those cognitive capacities that are widely thought to be the necessary conditions for personhood. Finally, we also noted that even if it can be said that these beings have an interest in a continued existence that includes a favorable balance of pleasure over pain, any obligation we might be said to have to use social resources to continue such an existence is of lesser weight than our important obligations to persons. The same would appear to hold true for whatever obligations we might be thought to have to provide pleasure to sentient nonpersons. In other words, if a conflict occurred between an obligation to give pleasure to a nonperson (or to continue a nonperson's on-balance pleasurable existence) and important obligations toward persons, we could forego the former in order to fulfill the latter, without injustice. Indeed, it is only because these nonpersons were once persons, embedded in relationships with others, that it is plausible to argue that there is *any* significant obligation to continue a pleasurable existence for them. Other nonpersons, such as many animals, are not commonly believed to have claims on social resources to continue their pleasurable lives, though it remains wrong to cause them gratuitous suffering.

It is plausible to hold that a severely demented individual in whom the psychological continuity necessary for personhood has been destroyed has no current, as opposed to surviving, interest in life-sustaining treatment. He or she does, however, have a current interest while alive in palliative care to relieve pain or suffering and to produce pleasure.

To see why such severely demented individuals have interests in pleasure and in minimizing pain and suffering, but no interest as such in continued life, it may help to consider how we would or should regard beings that *never* had advanced beyond the mental life of the severely demented. While wishing not to offend those who care deeply for those who have now become severely demented, we believe the comparison with some animals is instructive. It is widely agreed, for example, that mice and chickens are not persons. Presumably, this is not simply because they are not members of the human species, since it is at least possible that there are nonhuman persons, but because they lack some important properties or capacities that humans normally possess. Animals such as dogs and horses surely are sentient beings – they are conscious and capable of experiencing pleasure and pain, and in particular they can be made to suffer. What they presumably lack is the capacity for or experience of *self*-consciousness, a conception of themselves as, and experience of being, a single self-conscious individual who persists through time. Thus, while they can experience pain and suffer here and now in the present, and can be conditioned to associate pain and suffering with experiences not themselves painful, they lack capacities for hopes and fears, dreads and longings for their futures, and more generally the capacity to form plans for their future. For this, they would require what it is commonly believed they lack, a belief that they themselves are beings that persist through time with a continuity of self-consciousness over time.

This may go some way toward explaining what otherwise appears an anomalous feature of many persons' moral views about the treatment of animals. Many persons hold that causing gratuitous pain or suffering to animals such as mice and chickens is seriously wrong, although painlessly killing such animals is not wrong. The apparent anomaly is that with persons it is commonly believed that killing them against their will is one of the, if not the, most serious wrongs that can be done to them, and specifically is a more serious wrong than causing them pain or suffering. Why then for animals is the more serious wrong of killing commonly held not to be a wrong at all, while causing them pain or suffering remains a wrong? We believe the explanation lies in the difference between humans and animals just noted – while each can be caused pain, which is immediately experienced as unpleasant and unwanted, only humans but not animals can have plans and desires about their future, and indeed have desires to have or experience that possible future, which can all be frustrated, or at least left unsatisfied, by being killed. It is this capacity to envisage and desire a future for oneself that best explains why killing a normal adult human wrongs that person.

The severely demented, while of course remaining members of the human species, approach more closely the condition of animals than normal adult humans in their psychological capacities. In some respects the severely demented are even worse off than animals such as dogs and horses, which have a capacity for integrated and goal-directed behavior that the severely demented substantially lack. The severe dementia that destroys memory undermines the individual's psychological capacities to forge links across time that establish a sense of personal identity across time, and for this reason robs him or her of personhood. This means in turn that such individuals lose the fundamental basis for persons' interest in continued life and in measures which sustain life – that their future life is a necessary condition for satisfying all of a person's desires about and plans for the future.

The priority of interests of persons has significant implications for problems of distributive justice. It implies that in choosing public policies that will ration health care by withholding life-support resources from the severely and permanently demented in order to fulfill our obligations to persons who can benefit from those resources we would not be failing to honor any legitimate distributive claims of the severely and permanently demented. This way of understanding our obligations to the severely and permanently demented who are nonpersons captures and renders coherent two strong elements of commonsense morality. The first is the belief that the distinction between persons and nonpersons marks a fundamental difference between two kinds of moral status. The second is that those nonpersons who have the capacity for pain and pleasure have some rights, although these rights are limited due to the inferior moral status of nonpersons.

Commonsense morality, at least upon reflection, generally resists attempts to introduce any *further* distinction of basic moral status *within* the class of persons. It is, of course, true that we do not ascribe a general right of self-determination (or more specific agency rights such as the right to enter into legal contracts or the right to refuse medical care or treatment) to those persons whose mental disabilities prevent them from meeting the appropriate threshold of competence. But the withholding of *these* rights does not affect the moral weight of those rights we *do* ascribe to such beings.

IV. RATIONING HEALTH CARE: THE ROLE OF PHYSICIANS AND SURROGATES DECIDING FOR INCOMPETENTS

Probably no other issue has received more attention in public and policymaking discussions of health care in recent years than the need to control relentlessly increasing health care costs. This issue concerns costs throughout the health care system, of course, and not only health care for incompetents. Nevertheless, it has special importance for incompetent persons for at least three reasons. First, fueled by data showing that they use a disproportionately large amount of health care resources, much attention has focused on limiting use of care for patients near the end of life, when a large proportion of patients experience some period of incompetence. Second, many of the paradigm cases in which care is delivered that is widely believed not to provide benefits warranting its costs are incompetent patients such as the severely demented and patients in a persistent vegetative state. And these are cases in which the strongest pressures are often felt by physicians and surrogates for the incompetent patient to limit care because of its costs. Third, some proposals to control health care costs are explicitly age-related, arguing that the elderly have less claim than do younger persons on social resources to provide health care.[2] Once again, the elderly who would be affected by such proposals include disproportionately large numbers of incompetent persons. Thus, the general issue of controlling increasing health care costs has special importance for incompetent persons.

We cannot systematically address here the nature, basis and extent of the social responsibility to provide health care to those otherwise unable to secure it, including those persons who are incompetent. To do so would require developing a general theory of distributive justice in health care.[3] Moreover, there is no widespread consensus to which we might appeal either on theories of distributive justice in general or on theories of just health care in particular. This lack of consensus in theory is reflected as well in a lack of consensus in public debate and social policy. At the same time, faced with this lack of agreement, it is not plausible to hold that economic considerations about cost should never in any way affect the utilization of health care. It would be irrational to provide all care to patients of any possible medical benefit to them, no matter how uncertain and small the benefit and no matter how great the cost of the care. Physicians and surrogates must now make decisions about treatment for incompetent patients while recognizing simultaneously both the clear relevance to those decisions of some economic concerns about limiting the costs of care, and the lack of any social consensus as to the nature and extent of the care that justice requires be provided. In this context, to what extent should health care professionals, and especially physicians, allow economic concerns about the cost of care to influence health care treatment decision making?

There *is* wide agreement that it is ethically permissible for a competent patient to decide to forego any care, including life-sustaining care, that he or she judges to be unduly burdensome. One of the burdens of care is the financial cost it imposes on the patient or others about whom the patient cares. Patient resources used for health care will not be available for other uses. Thus, a patient might freely choose not to undergo some forms of even life-sustaining treatment in order, for example, to preserve an inheritance for his or her family. Few would find such a choice inherently ethically objectionable.

Likewise, an incompetent patient may have left an advance directive with essentially the same instructions to forego certain expensive care. In the absence of an advance directive, surrogates must use the substituted judgment principle where applicable. If there is clear and compelling evidence that the patient would not have wanted a particular treatment, in part because of its expense, respecting the patient's self-determination strongly supports the patient's surrogate deciding against the costly care. Thus, there is nothing intrinsically unethical in either patients or their surrogates sometimes deciding to forego treatment because of its cost.

Nevertheless, especially in the case of incompetent patients who are both unable to express their own wishes about care and whose debilitation limits the benefits they can receive from care, there is potential for the costs of care to loom large in decision making. Do constraints of distributive justice at the present time nevertheless justify physicians or surrogates deciding to limit a patient's care on grounds of its costs to others – whether family members, other participants in insurance pools, or society generally – when the patient has not indicated any wish to do so?

There are several important reasons why they generally should not. First, the patient may have obtained health insurance in order to cover the costs of the care in question. While this does not obligate the physician to offer whatever care the surrogate might demand for the patient, it would appear to obligate the physician not to deny the patient care covered by the patient's insurance on grounds of its cost. The patient's insurance in effect creates both an entitlement and a legitimate expectation that any medically appropriate care covered by the policy will be paid for by the insurance. While the insurance payments for the patient's care will come from the pooled funds largely of others, all members of a private insurance pool join together to combine their resources precisely in order to fund members' entitlements to reimbursement for health care costs. Even if the insurance comes from a government program funded by general tax revenues, that program would have the same democratic legitimacy as would other government spending programs and the entitlements the program establishes should be honored, not surreptitiously undermined by a patient's physicians.

Institutions such as the government, employers, and health insurers all have an interest in holding down their bill for health care. But they should not expect or pressure physicians, however, to deny care to patients in circumstances in which patients have an entitlement to be reimbursed for the financial costs of care. That would be to put the physicians in an ethically unacceptable position.

It is ethically acceptable for physicians to help patients or their surrogates weigh the true costs of care against its benefits when the patients or surrogates wish to do so. It is also ethically acceptable and indeed desirable for the incentive structures of reimbursement systems to encourage patients or surrogates to weigh the true costs of care against its benefits more accurately than is now common, so long as that does not result in denying patients an adequate level of care. The main reason this is notoriously difficult to do is that health care insurance, the means of reimbursement for most health care in our country today, reduces or eliminates out-of-pocket costs to the patient for care utilized, and in turn the patient's economic incentive to consider or even learn the true costs of care. Yet the unpredictability and great variability in the amount and cost of health care that an individual may need provide powerful reasons to have insurance for health care costs.

A second important reason why physicians should not

take it upon themselves to decide whether their patients' care is not worth it to the other members of their insurance pools is that they lack any social, moral, or legal authorization to do so. If there is to be a serious public debate in this country about limiting utilization of noncostworthy care (care whose benefits are insufficient to warrant its costs), particularly if that is life-sustaining care, then we are now only in the early stages of that debate. Yet any authorization for physicians to act as health care rationers with their individual patients should come as a *result* of such a debate, and not merely from the pressures from third party payers to reduce their health care outlays. These pressures would be likely to fall most heavily on the vulnerable and powerless incompetent elderly.

When cost containment measures are openly adopted in financially closed health care systems like HMO's, then both physicians and patients can have a reasonable assurance that cost savings will be passed on in the form of lower rates, improved quality of care, or new available forms of care to the members who have foregone certain forms of care to produce the savings. In such settings, it is possible for patients and physicians to cooperate with the shared goal of providing good-quality health care while limiting health care costs. When physicians instead only reduce "society's" overall health care costs by denying care that may benefit or be wanted by their patients, their justification cannot be that the savings are returned to those denied the care for them to spend in alternative and more desirable ways.[4]

A third serious concern about physicians assuming the role of health care rationers with imcompetent patients is whether denials of noncostworthy care would be equitably or fairly applied to different patients. If physicians are left to determine without further guidance what care is costworthy for individual patients at the bedside, then almost certainly the effects of these attempts to control health care costs will *not* be equitable. This is because physicians, in the absence of clear standards of costworthy care, would inevitably reach markedly different conclusions about what care is costworthy and would also be susceptible to allowing ethically irrelevant factors, such as the social worth of the patient, subtly influence their judgments. Relatively vulnerable and powerless incompetent patients could be expected to suffer a disproportionate share of the effects of such rationing.

A fourth major concern about physicians becoming "bedside rationers" with the incompetent is that this will create new conflicts of interest between patients and their physicians and so be likely to undermine the trust necessary for well-functioning physician/patient relationships. If physicians increasingly come to think of themselves primarily as trustees responsible for ensuring that society's resources are prudently spent, patients' trust that their physicians' treatment recommendations and decisions are guided first and foremost by concern for their patients' well-being will quite justifiably erode. It is this concern that lies behind the common view of physicians that they should remain unconstrained advocates for their patients and that someone else should decide when treatment is too costly to provide.

These various worries about physicians becoming bedside rationers do not imply that economic considerations should never play any role in decisions about utilization of treatment. We have already argued that this would – and does – lead to an overutilization of noncostworthy care. Instead, these worries support the conclusion that standards and/or procedures for identifying care that will not be provided to patients, whether competent or incompetent, because it is not costworthy, should satisfy these conditions:

(1) They are arrived at through public processes that allow substantial input to those who will be affected by the decisions made.
(2) Health care institutions limiting access to noncostworthy care inform current and potential patients and members of these limitations.

(3) There are effective procedures to monitor the application of limitations on provision of noncostworthy care to insure that it is done equitably and without denying patients access to at least an adequate level of health care.

The appropriate decision-making bodies for defining limitations on noncostworthy care will vary depending on the context. For example, in an HMO these issues might be addressed in a committee within the HMO with substantial patient member representation. For government insurance programs, open debate at relevant points in the political process such as legislatures, public hearings, and so forth, would be appropriate. In other cases, participant input might be fostered by employers and health insurers providing their employees and insurees with a greater range of alternative insurance plans that vary in the extent they attempt to define and limit reimbursement for noncostworthy care. There is no single institutional mechanism or group of persons that should address and make decisions about what care is costworthy. Nor, in our view, is there any single correct definition of costworthy care, or any ethical necessity for societal uniformity in the definitions to be employed. What is needed now is a public dialogue and debate about how to define and when to limit noncostworthy care, as well as about what physicians' roles should be in any rationing processes.

There is no reason to believe, however, that incompetents should be singled out as such for any special limitations of care. At most, only other conditions that often, but by no means always, accompany incompetence and limit the benefits that care can provide should serve as grounds for limiting costly care to incompetent patients.

The rejection of a fundamental distinction between competents and incompetents regarding their moral status from the standpoint of distributive justice does not imply, however, that there are no common differences between competents and incompetents that affect their interest in and just claims to health care treatment. The point is only that persons do not, simply by virtue of their incompetence, have lesser claims to care and concern on grounds of justice. Particularly when the determination of a person's incompetence is based on severe and permanent decision-making incapacities, these same incapacities will commonly affect what treatments may be in the patient's interests and the nature and degree of benefit treatment can provide.

Although there is no commonlaw, statutory, or Constitutional general legal right to health care in this country, there is broad agreement that certain basic health care services, a so-called adequate level or decent minimum, ought to be guaranteed for all. It is clear that any rational and just determination of the adequate level or decent minimum of health care will exclude some care of medical benefit to the patient when the benefit is too small to justify its cost. Thus, when the incapacities that result in incompetence also reduce the benefits an incompetent patient can obtain from a given treatment, care may not be warranted that would be provided to competent patients as a matter of entitlement of individual right.

V. THE MORAL RESPONSIBILITY OF FAMILIES TOWARD ELDERLY INCOMPETENT INDIVIDUALS

As noted earlier, each of the guidance principles for making particular care or treatment decisions for incompetent individuals is exclusively patient-centered, and none of them makes any explicit reference to constraints on the use of scarce resources. Since none confers any positive right to services and the resources they require, the guidance principles must be understood as operating within a framework that specifies the scope and limits of morally justified legal entitlements to services. Yet it is highly probable that any system of legal entitlements to health care likely to exist in this country in the foreseeable future will be far from comprehensive, and that consequently families will frequently bear a significant share of the financial burden.

There are, however, limits on the burdens it is reasonable to expect family members to bear, and these limits must be kept in mind by courts and protective agencies in their efforts to see that decisions concerning care and treatment are being appropriately made by family members. For example, even though the family ought to be guided by the patient's best interests (in cases in which there is no advance directive and substituted judgment cannot be exercised), the family has no moral or legal obligation to provide the *very best* care if doing so imposes excessive burdens on them or deprives them of resources needed to fulfill important obligations to other family members (such as their own children). For this reason the fact that a family decides to place an elderly incapacitated parent in an adequate nursing home, rather than in the best facility their money could buy, would itself not be a reasonable basis for guilt on their part, much less for justified intervention by the courts or protective agencies in the name of protecting the elderly person's rights.

Although there is no hard and fast general formula for determining when the burdens of caring for an incapacitated family member become excessive, it does seem clear that the degree of responsibility is stronger or weaker depending upon the *nature* of the relationship, not simply its biological or legal "closeness." In particular, it is plausible to hold that the obligations of grown offspring toward their aged parents are less extensive than those of parents toward their minor children or of spouses toward one another.[5] There are two main reasons for this.

First, and perhaps of lesser importance, although children have had no opportunity to make provisions for their own welfare, most normal adults have had the chance to make some provision for their own care during old age. The greater a parent's opportunity for doing so, the less the obligation of their offspring to incur serious financial burdens if the parent failed to take responsibility for him- or herself.

Second, although children (usually) have benefitted from their parents during the long period of dependency characteristic of human development, they did not ask to be put in this relationship of dependency. Instead, at least where effective and available birth control makes parenthood substantially a voluntary matter, parents can reasonably be viewed as having assumed an obligation to care for their offspring until they are fit to care for themselves. Similarly, in the absence of premarital agreements to the contrary, a person voluntarily assumes special responsibilities for his or her spouse. Children do owe special gratitude and support to parents who have chosen to make special sacrifices, those that go beyond what we think parents ordinarily owe their children. It is a common feature of otherwise divergent moral views that the strongest positive duties to provide care for others arise from responsibilities freely and knowingly assumed. Because there was no freely assumed assumption of responsibility, children do not, as a matter of *justice,* owe their parents as much as spouses usually owe each other.

This is not to say, however, that a reciprocal practice over generations, in which parents care for their dependent children and are in turn cared for by their grown children when elderly, could generate no obligations to care for one's elderly parents. Such obligations based on a principle of reciprocity might be part of a broader theory of distributive justice. Or these obligations might be part of a shared understanding of intergenerational responsibilities within a particular community. But for such a practice to be viewed as fair, at least two conditions should be satisfied. First, such a practice must in fact be established in the community. To the extent that the government, through such programs as Social Security and Medicare, has increasingly assumed major responsibilities for the elderly, adults now have reasonable expectations that the government will bear a major share of responsibility in the future for their parents. That is, *our* ongoing practice is *not* the full-bodied reciprocal one in which adult children are recognized as having *principal* responsibilities for the financial and medical well-being of their parents. Moreover, there are good reasons for this governmental role, among them that the government can level out the shared burdens which would otherwise be very unequally distributed because of the great differences in needs for care of the elderly. Also, many elderly adults simply do not have any children who might bear responsibility for their care. Second, such a reciprocal practice of intergenerational care, to be fair, would have to impose roughly proportional burdens on different generations when they come to assume the role of adult caretakers of their elderly parents. The burdens such a practice could fairly impose on one generation of adult caretakers are limited in part by the level of burdens previous generations of caretakers before them have borne.

An interview in a recent television documentary on the problem of caring for elderly parents with Alzheimer's disease is illustrative.[6] An elderly woman whose eighty-eight-year-old demented mother was in need of care and supervision twenty-four hours a day complained bitterly that her entire adult life would be spent caring for others, with "no time" for herself. Her early and middle adult years had been spent as a mother, taking primary responsibility for raising her own children. Now her remaining active years would be devoted to caring for her severely demented but far from terminally ill mother. By the time her mother dies and she is free from the onerous responsibilities that rob her of friends and enjoyable activities, she will herself be old and likely incapacitated or in ill health. This case shows how unevenly the burdens of caring for elderly family members may be distributed.

This problem is becoming more common because modern medicine has become more successful in preserving the bodies of the very elderly than it has in preserving their minds or their capacities to lead independent lives. In the past, life expectancy was shorter, and terminal illness and severe loss of competence went more closely hand-in-hand – and fewer middle-aged and elderly people faced the prospect of years of caring for their aged parents.

As already noted, in our society at the present time neither the law nor social custom clearly and unambiguously assigns primary, much less exclusive, responsibility to grown children for the care of their elderly parents. To do so under current conditions would certainly exacerbate existing inequalities in the distribution of wealth. Moreover, it might actually worsen the problem of access to care. Since poverty and ill-health are positively correlated, and since poor parents are more likely to have poor children, requiring grown children to shoulder full or major responsibility for the care of their elderly parents would not only result in many cases in substandard care for parents but would reduce the resources available to the grown children for their own care and for the needs of their minor children. Thus, quite apart from whether it would be politically feasible or Constitutional to assign strong legal responsibilities to grown children for the care of their elderly parents, there are strong moral reasons against doing so in a society such as ours. It follows that any attempt to "privatize" these issues of distributive justice and thus avoid the need for explicit public responses to the problem of providing resources for the care of the elderly incompetent is unacceptable.

Part two
APPLICATION

5. Minors

This chapter develops for the case of minors the implications of the general analytical framework set out in earlier chapters. At the same time, this application will elucidate the framework itself and confirm its usefulness. The greater part of the investigation will focus on older minors, not on infants, for two reasons. First, and most importantly, some of the most difficult and complex issues arise in the case of minors who are sufficiently mature that it is implausible to exclude them from the decision-making process altogether, but whose competence to make certain important decisions is questionable. Second, in the scholarly literature and in the popular press there has been an extraordinary preoccupation with decisions concerning infants, in part as a result of much publicity concerning a very few sensational cases, and in part because of highly controversial administrative policies (the "Baby Does Regs") of the Federal government. Without denigrating the ethical and political significance of decision making for disabled newborns, it is important to avoid a narrow preoccupation with this one (extremely limited) class of minors. Nevertheless, a fairly extensive discussion of problems concerning disabled newborns is included.

I. NONINFANT MINORS

A. The current legal presumption of incompetence

What role should children play in decision making about their health care? The doctrine of informed consent requires that medical treatment only be given to adults with their competent, informed and voluntary consent. The law as well as common medical practice presumes that adults are competent to decide about their medical treatment, although this presumption can be rebutted in particular instances. On the other hand, the law presumes that minors, who in most states are defined as persons below the age of eighteen years, are *not* competent to decide about their medical care, although with some exceptions to be noted below. For minors, the law generally holds that others, usually parents or guardians, are to make decisions about their medical treatment. However, physicians, as we shall see, have often involved minors in decision making about their care to a greater extent than the law seems to require.

One purpose of Part I of this chapter is to ascertain whether the general policy presumption of minors' incompetence for health care decision making is sound, or whether it ought to be revised. Questions about the competence of both adult and minor patients arise not just at the level of general legal policy, however, but also in concrete circumstances concerning a particular patient's decision for or against a specific treatment. Hence the second broad purpose of Part I of this chapter is to clarify the nature of judgments about the competence of a minor to make a particular treatment decision. Clarity on the nature and basis of competence judgments is important both for assessing whether current legal policy concerning minors' competence to make health care decisions is sound or ought to be revised, and for responding adequately to medical situations in which current legal policy already permits a case-by-case assessment of a minor's competence.

We note here that our concern throughout Part I of this chapter is with minors' competence to decide about their medical treatment or care, and not with their competence to participate in research. While much of the analysis presented here could be applied to it, research raises some distinct issues of its own that we do not address in this volume.[1]

Questions of children's competence raise conceptual issues about competence and incompetence, as well as empirical issues about the degree to which children at particular ages possess the various decision-making capacities that conceptual analysis shows to be necessary for competence. It is not unfair to say that much current legal and medical practice displays both considerable confusion about the conceptual issues concerning competence determinations, whether of children or adults, and an inadequate appreciation of the empirical evidence from developmental psychology about children's capacities. Our discussion in this chapter will be structured around the conceptual issues, integrating the relevant empirical data into the analysis at appropriate points. The argument and analysis are complex, and we forego drawing implications for legal policy and medical practice until the investigation is completed. Readers who want a preview of these conclusions before setting out should consult the final section, Section L, of Part I of the chapter.

B. The concept of competence

For children as well as adults, competence is relative to a specific decision, and an adolescent's competence may vary over time with changes in his or her condition and so may be intermittent or fluctuating. Over longer time frames, children's competence will vary with developmental growth and changes. As was noted in Chapter 1, different health care decisions vary in the demands they make on the decision-maker – for example, in the complexity of the information that must be understood or the balancing of risks and benefits of different alternatives that must be weighed. Where a number of closely competing and complex alternative treatments exist for a condition such as bone cancer, the understanding and reasoning required may be much greater than when there is only one standard, relatively simple, low-risk, and clearly beneficial treatment for a less serious condition. Competence determinations, therefore, involve matching the capacities of a particular minor at a particular time and under particular conditions with the demands of a particular decision-making task.

Throughout this chapter, when we speak of children's decision-making competence, we do not mean, of course, their capacity to make decisions on their own without the collaboration of health care professionals and parents. What is in question, just as with adults, is their capacity, with the help of their physician, other members of the health care team, and family, to understand the nature and consequences of alternative treatments sufficiently to be able to give or withhold informed consent to a recommended treatment alternative.

C. The developmental evidence about children's decision-making capacities

Chapter 1 distinguished three broad sorts of capacities necessary for decision-making competence: capacities for communication and understanding of information, capacities for reasoning and deliberation, and capacity to have and apply a set of values or conception of the good. As philosophers, and as neither developmental psychologists nor empirical researchers, we have no new or original data to offer on children's decision-making capacities.

What we shall do instead is to summarize very briefly some results from child development studies and theory that are relevant to general assessments of these capacities in children.[2] Though we will assign age ranges to the development of a number of capacities, it should be emphasized at the outset that these are only rough generalizations and that there is considerable variation among children, including variation outside the specified ranges, in the ages at which they reach particular stages in the development of the capacities needed for decision making.

The capacities for understanding and for reasoning can be considered together since the relevant empirical evidence and theory often do not distinguish clearly between them. At a minimum, the capacity for communication and understanding requires sufficient linguistic and conceptual development to enable the child to understand the semantic content of the information relevant to a particular treatment decision. As Grisso and Vierling conclude in their excellent review from a development perspective of minors' capacities to consent, "we have practically no systematic information regarding children's understanding of the meanings of terms likely to arise in situations in which consent to treatment is sought."[3]

Physicians and other health care professionals often use terms and concepts in decision-making contexts that are difficult or even impossible for many patients, whether children or adults, to understand. However, the question is whether it is possible to put information relevant to patients' treatment decisions in terms that children can understand. The principal understanding children need for most treatment decisions is not of technical medical data, but of the impact that treatment alternatives will have on their lives. While systematic data on this is lacking, there is little reason to hold that children who otherwise have the capacities to consent are barred from doing so by inadequate semantic understandings of necessary information. Even for difficult concepts like "death" there is probably an adequate understanding by early adolescence.

The major issues lie in the capacities lumped under reasoning and deliberation. As Grisso and Vierling note, among the capacities that may be needed for the reasoning process are the ability to sustain "one's attention to the task, ability to delay response in the process of reflecting on the issues, ability to think in a sufficiently differentiated manner to weigh more than one treatment alternative and set of risks simultaneously (i.e., cognitive complexity), ability to abstract or hypothesize as yet nonexistent risks and alternatives, and ability to employ inductive and deductive forms of reasoning."[4] Developmental theorists also hold that the degree to which children perceive the locus of control in a particular area as internal and subject to their decision, or external and a matter of fate, will affect their attentiveness to the decision, their awareness of its details, and the effort they will exert to gather information about it. Children below the ages of twelve to thirteen are significantly more prone than older children or adults to see the locus of control as external to them. Lewis found that children in the six to nine age range often did not perceive themselves as deciding even when they were doing so.[5] Role-taking skills are also thought to be necessary to enable a child to consider as potentially valid both a position presented to him or her by the physician and his or her own, different position, so that the alternatives can be weighed against each other. These skills are undergoing substantial development in the eight to eleven age period, and are often quite well developed by twelve to fourteen.

Perhaps most important for reasoning are several capacities Piaget identified in what he called the formal operations stage of cognitive development.[6] As characterized by Grisso and Vierling, "this stage includes the development of an increased cognitive capacity to bring certain operations to bear on abstract concepts in problem-solving situations."[7] Included is the ability to "perform inductive and deductive operations or hypothetical reasoning at a level of abstraction that would be represented by many consent situations involving treatment alternatives and risks."[8] These capacities are related to children's understandings of the causation of disease and illness, which also appear to follow a developmental pattern.

Beginning with quite magical views of causation of disease at around age five, it is not until around age twelve to thirteen that most children begin to understand "that there are multiple causes of illness, that the body may respond variably to any combination of agents, and that host factors within the body interact with the agent to cause and cure the illness."[9] Further, "emergence of the formal operations stage allows a child to become sufficiently flexible in thinking . . . to attend to more than one aspect of a problem at once – for example, to entertain alternative treatments and risks simultaneously."[10] In the formal operations stage, children's general problem-solving abilities increase markedly, as does their ability to consider novel data and to use logic in the solution of problems. With the usual qualifications about the variability with which different children reach a particular developmental stage, it is generally in the eleven to thirteen age period that the various skills and capacities of the formal operations stage appear in children.

In addition, children's decision-making capacities are limited by their values and conception of the good. An important issue is the extent to which children's values adequately reflect their future interests. While children in the seven to thirteen age range have largely left the earlier magical stage of thinking and now view the world in concrete, naturalistic terms, they can have great difficulty anticipating their future.[11] This can lead to two important problems: children may give inadequate weight to the effects of decisions on their future interests, and also fail to anticipate future changes in their values that may be predictable by others. A related problem is the instability in children's values in this period, particularly as they concern the child's future goals, and due in part simply to limitations in their experience, especially with adult roles. (Some features of this category of capacities for competence overlap with the reasoning category, since limits in anticipating the future will result in irrational decisions if present effects receive disproportionate weight in comparison with future effects.) All of these factors underly the widespread concern about relying fully on the values or life plans of children below the age of fourteen. To reiterate: (1) The presence and magnitude of these factors varies significantly among children of the same age. (2) other things being equal, these limitations become progressively more prominent the younger the child. (3) Their impact can vary greatly depending on the nature of the treatment choice before the child.

Adolescents above the age of thirteen tend to be more concerned about their physical appearance than do adults or children at earlier stages of development, and this concern can have a substantial effect on treatment choices.[12] It is important to avoid the mistake of judging such values mistaken or distorted simply because they differ from those of adults. Children's distinctive values may be quite appropriate to the extent that they reflect their current stages of development. Thus the effects of a treatment on the physical appearance of an adolescent may properly be given more weight than they might be given by an adult because being perceived as unattractive by one's peers may be a greater detraction from happiness in a youth than in an older person whose acceptance in his or her peer group and self-esteem depend less on appearance than on other characteristics. The adolescent's incapacity may reside only in his or her failure to appreciate how the importance of that effect may be expected to recede later as an adult.

As a very broad generalization, the developmental evidence briefly summarized here supports the conclusion that children by age fourteen or fifteen usually have developed the various capacities necessary for competence in health care decision making to a level roughly comparable to that attained by most adults. The policy implications of this conclusion are developed in Section L of Part I of this chapter.

There is an additional factor besides competence in decision making that is necessary for valid informed consent: consent must be voluntary. Therefore, children's capacities to give voluntary consent also bear on whether they should have decisional authority about their treatment, and there is significant developmental evidence about these capacities as well. We have already noted above that whether children perceive the locus of control on a matter as internal to themselves or external in the environment affects their capacities for understanding and reasoning. This perception is relevant to voluntariness as well: If children believe that the choice is not really theirs to make, they will not resist attempts by others to impose those others' choices on them. A related point is that "children (particularly young children) are unlikely to perceive of themselves as having rights . . . children learn that they should 'obey thy father and mother – and anyone else bigger than they are.' "[13] More generally, development theorists have observed that children below the age of fourteen or fifteen do not assert themselves well against authority figures, and of course the other parties typically involved in the consent process – parents and physicians – are likely to be perceived as strong authority figures. Indeed, children in the eleven to thirteen age range have been found to be more conforming in their behavior than younger children of ages seven to nine. On the other hand, for children in strong oppositional stages during later adolescence, the voluntariness of their *dissent* to the treatment recommendations of authority figures is in question. Grisso and Vierling conclude that below the age of fifteen there is at least significant question about children's capacities to give voluntary consent.

D. Determining a standard of competence

As we have seen, in children even more commonly than in adults, the capacities necessary for competence in health care decision making are possessed by different individuals, as well as by the same individual at different times and stages of development, in varying degrees across a broad continuum. Nevertheless, because of the role the competence determination plays in the law, and in turn in medical practice, we should resist the notion that a person's competence to make a particular health care decision is a matter of degree, of more or less. The function of the competence determination can only be fully understood within the broader doctrine of informed consent of which it is a part. The doctrine of informed consent mandates that health care treatment only be given to a competent patient with that patient's voluntary and informed consent. The ideal underlying the informed consent doctrine is that of patients deciding, together with their physicians, what treatment, if any, will best serve their particular needs and aims.

Within this very broad understanding of the informed consent doctrine, what more specifically is the function of the competence determination for children, and does it differ from its function with respect to adults? For adults, who are presumed to be competent, the question is whether they should be declared incompetent for the decision at hand. The central consequence of the competence determination for adults, as we have seen, is to sort them into two classes: (1) those whose informed and voluntary decisions about their health care treatment must be respected and accepted by others, and (2) those whose decisions may be set aside and for whom others will be designated as surrogate decision-makers. This sorting function amounts to an "all or nothing" classification of persons regarding whether they are to be accorded a right to make a particular treatment decision for themselves.

Although *based on* matter of degree findings about a person's decision-making capacities and skills as brought to bear in a particular decision, competence *itself* is not a matter of degree. For this reason, we have said that competence is a threshold concept, not a comparative one.

Understood as a threshold concept performing this sorting function, the crucial question is *where* or at what *level* of decision-making abilities and performance on a particular decision this threshold separating the competent from the incompetent should be set. For adults, this is a question of how defective their decision-making capacities must be in a particular decision for the presumption of their competence to be overcome or rebutted, for them in turn to be found incompetent, and for another to be designated as surrogate decision-maker for them. For children, given the law's presumption of incompetence, the question is how good their decision-making abilities and performance must be on a particular decision to overcome or rebut the presumption of their incompetence and for them to be found competent to decide for themselves. But how can the level of decision-making capacity required for competence be set in a nonarbitrary manner? Our answer has been that the appropriate level represents a balancing of the major values at stake in the decision whether to permit a person to decide for him- or herself about his or her own care or treatment.

E. The values at stake in the competence determination

As we will show shortly, both *how a child's well-being is determined* and *the nature of a child's interest in self-determination* differ from the case of adults. Nevertheless, both self-determination and well-being are the chief values at stake for both children and adults. In each case it is the *patient's* self-determination and well-being that are at stake in the determination of whether the patient will decide about his or her own treatment. These values will be discussed further below, but note first that the reason the competence determination can serve to sort adult patients into two groups – those whose decisions must be accepted as binding and those for whom others must decide – is that the patient's self-determination and well-being are the overriding values generally accepted to be at stake. In the case of adults there are typically no substantial other-regarding values, which are thought to be decisive for the question of whether the patient is to be permitted to make his or her own decision.

In decisions about health care treatment for children, however, a *third substantial value* is commonly recognized: the interest of *parents* in making important decisions about the welfare of their minor children. In our view, the determination of whether a child is to be accorded decision-making authority must take account of this third value. Thus, the determination of *competence,* which involves only the patient-centered values of self-determination and well-being, cannot by itself resolve the issue of the child's *decisional* authority. This is an important difference in the nature and role of the competence determination in children, as opposed to adults, that has not been sufficiently appreciated in either the literature on informed consent and competence or in health care practice. We shall examine briefly the two principal values at stake in setting a standard of competence for either children or adults, and then turn to the third value relevant to the allocation of decisional authority for the treatment of children, the parents' interest in making important decisions about the welfare of their children.

F. The child's well-being

There is a long tradition in medicine that the physician's first and foremost commitment should be to serve the well-being of the patient, and no less so when the patient is a child rather than an adult. However, because children's treatment choices, like those of adults, may sometimes fail to serve their own good or well-being, the protection and promotion of their well-being sometimes requires them to be protected from the harmful consequences of their own choices.

Besides the factors which often diminish the health care decision-making abilities of all patients, adults as well as children, there are the more general developmental limitations discussed above in children's decision-making abilities. Thus, other things being equal, and even in the best conditions for making decisions, the younger a minor is, the less weight we give to their expressed preferences, and to their views about their own good, in our judgment of what is best for them. We generally accept normal adults' settled aims and values as being ultimately determinative of their good or well-being (the theoretical and practical reasons supporting this were developed in Chapter 1, Section IV.A.), and so accept their choices as best for them except when their decision making is defective in ways that result in their choices being incompatible with their settled aims and values. The greater the limitations of judgment and experience in children and adolescents, the less weight is given to their expressed aims and values as ultimately determinative of their good. Thus, for example, a choice by a mature adult, based on an unusual but considered and settled conviction, such as a Jehovah's Witness's rejection of a blood transfusion, may be accepted as consistent with that person's overall well-being. A similar decision by a nine-year-old child, on the other hand, may not be considered consistent with the child's well-being because the child's aims, values, and commitments have not yet developed and endured to the point where we are prepared to accept them as the ultimate determinants of his or her well-being.

A child's good is more fully determined by the developmental needs of children generally at that age than by

his or her current but predictably transient goals and preferences. These developmental needs are based in significant part on the aim of preparing the child with the
opportunities and capacities for judgment and choice
necessary for exercising self-determination as an adult.
Consequently, efforts to promote children's well-being
focus prominently on fostering these abilities and opportunities so that as adults they will be able to choose, revise
over time, and pursue their own particular plans of life, or
aims and values, now suited to the adults they have become.

So in any particular society children need to develop
certain general abilities and traits in order to be able, as
adults, to enjoy a reasonable range of opportunities from
among which to choose their own particular aims, pur-
suits, and life paths. This is why, for example, it is reasonable to require that all children receive some minimal level
of education, as state laws generally do. This is also why it
would not be reasonable, however, to require that all
persons pursue postgraduate education, since that is only
necessary for the pursuit of a small subset of available
alternative life plans. Likewise, it may be reasonable to
allow adults to assume a risk to health or even life because
doing so is necessary to the particular life plan they have
chosen for themselves. That may be life within a particular
religion, as when a Jehovah's Witness rejects blood transfusions, or life within a particular occupation as in the case
of a professional athlete who rejects the standard treatment
of amputation for bone cancer in the hopes of saving both
limb and career, or life defined by a particular social role,
as when a woman with rheumatoid arthritis opts for long-
term steroid therapy and its damaging side-effects in order
to continue functioning in her homemaking role.

The general point is that children's well-being depends
less on their current individual preferences and more on
the objective conditions necessary to foster their development and opportunities than does the well-being of adults.

One of the principal reasons for involving adults in decision making about their health care is to recognize this sense in which they are sovereign in the determination of their good. In the case of children, while this basis for involving them in decision making is not absent entirely, it is substantially less important than with adults.

One final point about how children's well-being is at stake in decisions whether to permit them to participate in choices of their own medical care ought not to be overlooked. Involving patients, whether children or adults, in decisions about their treatment often promotes their well-being by increasing their level of compliance in co-operating with the care-giver, thereby enhancing the effectiveness of the treatment.

G. The child's self-determination

The value of self-determination too constitutes a weaker basis for children's involvement in decision making than it does for adults. The interest in self-determination, as we have seen, is people's interest in making important decisions about their lives for themselves according to their own values and aims. It involves the capacities to form, revise over time, and pursue a plan of life or conception of the good. Having a conception of the good is more than merely having a set of desires, which young children and even infants possess as much as adults. Persons have a capacity for reflective self-evaluation, for considering what kinds of desires and character they want to have, what kinds of persons they want to be. There are, of course, biological and environmental limits to the extent to which persons can determine their desires and character, but within these limits we adopt particular values and create a unique self. In these ways people are capable of shaping their character and of taking responsibility for the kind of person they are and will become. It is through the ongoing exercise of the capacity for self-determination that persons become and are active as responsible agents, shaping their lives and controlling their destinies.

From early childhood well into adolescence, children are in the process both of developing the various capacities necessary for the exercise of self-determination and of beginning to exercise their imperfect capacities for it. An important developmental task of adolescence is the process of psychological separation from one's parents and the establishment of a sense of identity with some consistency and stability.[14] Moreover, the development of a conception of the good and of the capacity for responsible choice requires being allowed a certain freedom to choose for oneself. And this freedom must include some freedom to choose badly, as the old adage that we learn best from our mistakes bears out. Nevertheless, the less well-developed the capacities for deliberation and choice required by self-determination, the weaker is both children's interest in self-determination and the case for respecting either their desire to choose for themselves or the choices that they make.

In many cases children desire as strongly as adults to choose their medical treatment and to have the treatment they choose. Yet the case for letting them decide and abiding by their decision is weaker than for adults. Besides the respects in which serious illness may limit all patients' decision-making capacities, the developmental limitations in children's decision-making capacities discussed above mean that their choices are less likely to serve their well-being than are the choices of adults.

The value many people ascribe to self-determination rests not just on the fact that persons generally tend to choose what is good for them, but also on a particular ideal of the person. We value being, and being recognized by others as, the kind of person who is able to determine and take responsibility for his or her own destiny. There is a dignity and integrity in being self-determining that is lost in even a satisfying subservience. Children who are in the process of acquiring rights of self-determination are often acutely sensitive to this point. It is this ideal of the person that is often expressed in patients' desires to make significant decisions about their lives for themselves, even if others (for example, physicians, parents, or even computers) might be able to decide for them at least as well if not better than they themselves could. Nevertheless, the plausibility of this ideal of the self-determining person assumes at least some minimal development of the various capacities necessary to its exercise.[15] When these capacities for self-determination are possessed in substantially reduced degrees, as they are with developing children and adolescents, the value of their choosing for themselves is likewise diminished. More accurately, children are less able to realize the ideal and so the value it represents.

The importance of self-determination also depends upon the nature of the decision being made. For a particular person, whether child or adult, some decisions may bear directly on centrally important aspects of his or her life; some choices, for example, may force changes in a career path or violate strong religious commitments. Other decisions may have only minor or peripheral effects on the person's goals and values, whatever choice is made. The value or importance of one's self-determination being respected varies directly with how centrally and pervasively one's life plan will be affected by the choice being made.

An important part of children's and adolescents' interest in self-determination is not their interest *qua* children in making decisions for themselves, but their interest in developing the capacities to be self-determining adults. This was already noted in discussing the application of the concept of well-being to children and adolescents. Looked at from this perspective, self-determination is principally, or at least significantly, to be achieved in the future by children and adolescents rather than exercised while still children and adolescents. At the same time, the process of developing capacities for self-determination requires that children's opportunities for decision making be continually expanded.

We have now seen that although both the same values of well-being and self-determination are at stake in determination of a standard of competence for children and for adults, those values take different shape and importance with children. The very same trade-off for adults recurs with children – protecting their well-being from the harmful consequences of their choices when their decision-making capacities are defective must be balanced against respecting their interest in deciding for themselves when they are able. But what best serves children's well-being is determined less by their own preferences than for adults, while the value of the exercise of self-determination for children is also less than for adults. This means that, other things being equal, we will sometimes be justified in setting aside a child's or adolescent's choice for the sake of a conception of well-being that differs from his or her own, when doing so in the case of an adult would be impermissible.

H. The parents' interest in making decisions concerning their children

A third important value commonly asserted in determinations of the decision-making authority to be accorded to children is the interest of parents in making important decisions about their children's welfare. This, too, marks a significant difference between children and adults. Two questions must be answered: (1) What is the precise nature of this purported interest? (2) To what extent should it be a factor in determining whether a child ought to be allowed to decide for him- or herself?

Several strains of reasoning can be identified as an answer to the first question.[16] One strain simply bases parents' decision-making role on the incapacity of children to decide for themselves, and a presumption that parents will usually do a better job of deciding than anyone else who could, as a general practice, be substituted for them. Because in most cases parents both care deeply about the welfare of their children and know them and their needs better than others do, they will be more concerned as well as better able than anyone else to ensure that the decisions made will serve their children's welfare. This argument accords to parents *no* independent interest or right to decide for their children and to enforce their choice when the choice may *not* best serve their children's welfare. Instead, it makes the parents' claim to decide wholly dependent on their tendency to decide more closely in accordance with their children's welfare.

A second line of argument appeals to the fact that parents must bear the consequences of treatment choices for their dependent children and so should have at least some control of those choices. Parents are held financially responsible for the costs of treatment, and bear as well some of the longer-term consequences, financial and otherwise, of the particular choice made. As a result, it may be unfair to force them to bear the consequences of the treatment choice while denying them any input into it. Even if this argument is accepted, it would establish only an interest of the parents in having *some* input into and control over the treatment choice, but certainly not unlimited discretion. The child, in nearly all instances, bears the principal consequences of the choice, and so on this line of reasoning the child's interest should principally determine the choice.

A third line of argument claims a right of parents, at least within limits, to raise their children according to the parents' own standards and values and to seek to transmit those standards and values to their children. Virtually no one today believes that children are simply their parents' property, to be done with as the parents wish. Rather, proponents of this line of argument claim that children begin life as a tabula rasa and only through a process of socialization and development will they acquire values, goals and standards, together with sufficient experience and powers of judgment to warrant our respecting their choices. For this reason, the case for parents' discretion in treatment choices for their children who have not yet acquired stable and mature values of their own is more persuasive than the analogous case for family members deciding for now incompetent, but once competent, adults. Previously competent adults, unlike children, once did have their own values and goals which can now guide others' choices for them. Someone must inevitably shape children's goals and values, however, and since we assign child-rearing responsibilities in our society largely to the family, it seems reasonable to accord to the family as well some significant discretion in imparting its values to the children within it.

A related but distinct fourth line of argument appeals to various respects in which the family is a valuable social institution, in particular its role in fostering intimacy. It can be argued that in our society the family provides the most significant source of intimacy for many adults, as well as the context in which children's own capacities for intimacy are developed. The family must have some significant freedom from oversight, control, and intrusion to achieve intimacy, and one aspect of this freedom or privacy is the right, at least within limits, to make important decisions about the welfare of its incompetent members.

I. Children's competence and children's decisional authority

These various arguments for an independent right of parents to make health care treatment decisions for their children raise large and complex issues that cannot be pursued further here. Although these arguments do not directly bear on children's decision-making competence, they do

bear directly on the issue of children's appropriate decisional authority. For if parents do have a legitimate interest in making decisions for their minor child, then
determining that (1) the child is competent to decide and
that (2) his or her decision is informed and voluntary in the
narrow sense (not coerced or made under duress) cannot
fully settle the issue of the child's right to decide. This is an
important and inadequately appreciated difference in the
function or role of the competence determination in children and adults.

The child's competence will be even less decisive for
settling the question of decisional authority if, as some
commentators maintain, there are, in addition to the parents' interest, legitimate third-party interests, such as the
state's interest in a healthy citizenry.[17] We assume,
although we shall not argue the point here, that the interests of the child's well-being and self-determination,
together with the interest of parental authority, form the
predominant interests for virtually all cases concerning
children's decisional authority about their medical care.

J. The legitimate interests of parents and the best interest principle

In Chapter 2 it was noted that the courts have required that
parents' decisions concerning medical treatment for their
minor children should be guided by the best interest principle. There we endorsed this legal position as ethically
correct, although with three important qualifications.
First, the best interest principle applies only to those incompetents who have morally considerable interests, and
this excludes those minors (for example, anencephalic infants) who are permanently unconscious. Second, utilizing
our distinction between guidance principles and intervention principles, we noted that – except perhaps where the
most basic interests of the child are at issue – a mere failure
on the part of the parents to *optimize* the child's interest is

not sufficient to trigger justified intervention by third parties, or even a challenge to the parent's decision-making authority. Third, we observed that even as a guidance principle, the best interest principle is to serve only as a regulative ideal, not as a strict and literal requirement, because parents' obligations toward their other children as well as their own legitimate self-interests can conflict with doing what *maximizes* the child's well-being, and sometimes may take precedence over it. While parents are rightly expected to make sacrifices for their children, they are not obligated to thwart their own most important interests whenever doing so would achieve some additional increment of benefit for their child, no matter how small, no matter at what price, and regardless of how well-off the child already is.

One perceptive analyst of children's rights, Ferdinand Schoeman, offers the following explanation of the implausibility of the claim that the best interest principle should strictly guide parents' decision concerning their minor children.

> . . . the family is to be thought of as an intimate arrangement with *its own goals and purposes* . . . it is [therefore] inappropriate to impose upon that arrangement . . . abstract liberal principles.[18]

Schoeman goes on to note what he takes to be a common failure to recognize the legitimacy of "the familial perspective" and "familial objectives."

However, to speak of the family as having its own goals and purposes and to speak of the familial perspective and familial objectives is to engage in dangerous reification. The case for legitimate departures from the best interest principle as a guidance principle in decision making for children depends exclusively upon the fact that optimizing for the sick child may conflict with the legitimate interests of other *individuals* within the family. Acknowledging this simple fact requires no appeal to the sort of supraindividual interests suggested by talk about "familial objectives," etc. On the contrary, talk about group interests is in general warranted only under two circumstances, neither of which obtains in the case at hand: (1) The group has expressed some preference through a collective decision-making process (e.g., voting) or (2) there is something that is in the interest of all members of the group individually. Given the very great inequality of power between parents and children, reference to the family's interest or "familial objectives" is all too likely to serve as a cover for the parents' interests precisely in those cases in which the latter conflict with those of the child. It is far more conducive to clear thinking and sound moral judgment to recognize that there can be conflicts of *individuals'* interests within the family, and thus be in a position to ask which individuals' interests should prevail.

On this point, however, our analysis and Schoeman's are in complete agreement: not only should the best interest principle as a guidance principle for parents' decisions not be understood as requiring literal *optimization* of the child's interest in all cases, but also suitable *intervention* principles will allow parents considerable leeway – tolerating departures from what would be best for the child – in order to protect the family from intrusions that would violate the privacy which it requires if it is to thrive as an intimate union whose value to those who participate in it depends in great part upon its intimacy.

K. The variable standard of competence

Our discussion of the values at stake in competence determinations aims at clarifying the proper standard of competence. (Strictly, as noted in Section I, it is the standard for children's decisional authority, not competence, that is in question. However, we shall follow common practice in the literature and speak of the standard of competence for children.) If in setting a standard of competence at least the three values of protecting the child's well-being, respecting his or her self-determination, and honoring legitimate parental authority are all at stake, and must often be balanced against each other, then the central conclusions supporting a variable standard of competence for adults will follow for children as well.[19] First, there is no reason to believe there is one and only one objectively correct trade-off to be struck between these competing values, even for a particular decision under specified circumstances. Determining the proper trade-off goes beyond an empirical investigation of the child's decision-making capacities and is not simply a scientific or factual matter, but a value choice. The proper standard is thus an essentially controversial matter concerning the proper weight to be accorded these different values.

Second, while there may be no single, objectively correct balancing of these values, the polar extreme standards of competence that we rejected for adults as failing to represent a reasonable balancing of the values are inadequate for children as well. The minimally paternalistic standard requiring only that the child be able to express a preference for some alternative fails either to provide any protection of the child's well-being against the harmful consequences of his or her decision-making incapacities or to give any weight to the parents' interest in deciding.

At the other extreme, standards that look simply to the content or outcome of the decision and then apply some "objective" measure of the correct decision fail to give any weight to the child's own emerging and distinctive conception of the good and capacities for self-determination. In contrast to adults, there is more room in an account of children's good for appeal to the objective conditions necessary for the development and preservation of the abilities and opportunities that will enable them later, as adults, to be self-determining agents with choices from among a reasonable array of life plans. Other things being equal, the younger the child, the stronger the basis for discounting his or her expressed values and substituting an opportunity-based, objective conception of well-being. To the extent that children's good is defined in terms of developing the capacities and opportunities for determining the course of their own life as adults, their good also cannot be determined by the particular values and goals that their parents have chosen for themselves and might wish to apply to them.

As with adults, an appropriate standard of children's competence should focus on the *process* of their reasoning. The central features of the variable standard of competence for adults noted in Chapter 2 also apply to children's competence. Here, we repeat only the main conclusions regarding the variable standard. No single answer is adequate to the threshold question of how defective a child's decision making should be on a particular occasion for the child to be judged incompetent to make that decision. This is simply because both the effects on the child's well-being, as well as the importance of his or her exercise of self-determination, can vary greatly depending on the choice the child has made. The most important variable is the expected consequences of the choice for the child's well-being which may vary from clearly and substantially beneficial (for example, preventing serious, irreversible disability or loss of life) through trivial or negligible, to seriously harmful (for example, causing serious, irreversible disability or loss of life). The more adverse the expected consequences to the child of accepting his or her choice, the more reasonable it is to require both a higher level of decision-making capacity and a greater certainty that this level is attained. As with adults, the appropriate level of decision-making capacity required for a particular choice can vary along a full range from low/minimal to high/maximal.

Finally, just as with adults, the fact that a child is competent to consent to a treatment does *not* imply that he or she is competent to refuse it *and vice versa*. For example,

consent to a low-risk, life-saving procedure by an otherwise healthy child should require a minimal level of competence, while refusal of that same procedure by the child
should require the very highest level of competence.

L. Implications for medical practice and legal policy regarding children's competence

Our principle concern up to this point has been with the
nature of the competence determination, with the relevant
data, largely from developmental studies, concerning children's possession of the various capacities on which that
determination should be based, and on how to determine
an appropriate level of competence required in a particular
decision-making situation. We shall now consider some
issues of general legal and medical policy regarding children's competence.[20] However, before doing so it is important to note that our concern is with the standards for
competence in particular cases and the general policy for
children's competence to decide about their health care
when they wish to do so. Nothing in our analysis above or
the policy implications discussed below implies that children should be forced, pressured, or even encouraged to
decide about health care for themselves when they do not
wish to do so. If a child, for example, does not feel emotionally prepared to take responsibility for a difficult
treatment decision, then even if his or her other decision-making capacities appear well-developed it could be
harmful to the child to have to take responsibility for
the decision. Waiver by competent adults of their right
to give informed consent and their transfer of that right to
others is well recognized in medical practice, medical
ethics, and the law, and deserves to be equally honored for
competent minors.[21]

As noted at the outset of this chapter, in most states the
law presumes that minors (in most states, persons below

the age of eighteen) are incompetent to give informed consent for their own health care. Most states also have statutes enabling children of specified ages, usually ranging between twelve and seventeen years, to give informed consent for treatment for specific medical conditions. The conditions covered by such specialized consent statutes include alcoholism, drug abuse, emotional disturbance, mental illness, pregnancy, rape, sexual assault, organ transplantation, blood donation, and sexually transmitted diseases. Which of these conditions are covered by specialized consent statutes varies from state to state, as does the age at which consent by a minor is permitted. These reductions in the age of consent, however, usually do not seem to be based principally on assumptions about the minor's competence. Instead, their usual rationale seems to be to permit minors to seek and obtain treatment when requiring parental consent and/or notification for treatment would likely discourage many minors from seeking treatment important to their own and/or others' well-being.

Many states also have statutes specifying conditions in which minors are considered emancipated from their parents or guardians for the purposes of giving informed consent to all forms of medical treatment. The emancipating conditions specified by such statutes include marriage, pregnancy, self-management, self-support, being a parent, military service, and being a high school graduate. The conditions establishing emancipation vary considerably from state to state. Some states also have what have been called subjective rules permitting consent by a minor of two general sorts: "1) Conditional Minor – a minor may consent if he will be in serious danger unless health care services are provided; 2) Mature Minor – a minor may give consent if he understands the nature and purposes of the proposed treatment."[22] The conditional minor rule may be intended to be restricted to emergency or quasi-emergency conditions, and in any event in Alexander Cap-ron's 1982 survey of state laws it had been adopted in only two states.[23]

The mature minor rule also has been adopted in statu-tory law in only a small minority of states, although it probably has a broader basis in other states in case law.[24] It retains the presumption that minors are incompetent to consent to their own treatment, and requires that their "maturity," that is, their understanding of the nature and purposes of the proposed treatment, be demonstrated in any particular instance to rebut this presumption. Moreover, the application of the mature minor rule has generally been restricted to minors very close to the age of majority, usually not less than fifteen, independent of the particular minor's general capacities to decide. Despite these limitations, the mature minor rule does come closest to rejecting the general legal policy that minors are not permitted to give informed consent to their own treat-ment. Does our analysis of competence and the available empirical data concerning children's decision-making capacities support further revision in legal policy and/or in medical practice, insofar as the latter is guided by legal policy?

Two limitations in the implications to be drawn below from our analysis for medical practice and legal policy need to be underlined. First, because we have not at-tempted to assess fully the merits of the various strands of argument identified earlier as commonly offered in sup-port of parental authority to make treatment decisions for minor children, we address the policy question about chil-dren's competence *independently* of the claims and value of parental authority. Second, we make no attempt here to assess fully the potential effects and side-effects of the changes in the law discussed below regarding children's competence. To do so would require a detailed legal analy-sis that we have not provided, as well as an assessment of possible legal and institutional practices that might serve to limit undesirable effects of these changes. Nonetheless, we shall at least attempt to sketch an answer to this question: If we employ our analysis of competence together with the relevant evidence about children's capacities, and then seek to balance children's interests in having their well-being protected and in having their emerging self-determination respected, what ought legal and medical policy be?

One relatively clear implication of our analysis of the nature of the competence determination together both with empirical studies of children's decision-making capacities and with development theory is that the general presumption that all minors are incompetent for health care decision making is very difficult to defend.[25] As we saw above, there seem to be no significant differences between adults and children of roughly ages fifteen (some would say fourteen) to seventeen years in the general capacities that are needed for health care treatment decision making. This suggests that the presumption of competence for health care decision making that holds for adults should be extended to minors in this age range as well. The most direct way of doing this would be through statutes that explicitly lower the age of majority for medical decision making. At the time of Capron's 1982 survey, three states had enacted such statutes: Alabama, age of majority for medical decision-making set at fourteen; Oregon at fifteen; South Carolina at sixteen, with restrictions on consent for operations. It bears emphasis that a presumption of competence extended to fifteen- to seventeen-year-olds would be, just as with adults, *only a presumption* and so rebuttable in any particular case by evidence concerning the child's decision making in that case. This presumption of competence would cover both consenting to treatment without the need for parental consent, and refusing treatment to which the child's parents might or might not be prepared to consent.

Below age fifteen, there seems good reason to maintain

the current presumption of incompetence because of the extent to which various general decision-making capacities then are usually still undergoing significant development and are appreciably more limited than for most adults. Nevertheless, in the nine to fourteen age period some children will demonstrate sufficient capacities to make particular decisions to be deemed competent to make them. Since the younger the child within this age period the less often is competence likely to be demonstrated, the presumption of children's incompetence for medical decision making in the nine to fourteen age range should be understood to be increasingly strong the younger the child. Grisso and Vierling go somewhat further in concluding that "there may be no circumstances that would justify sanctioning independent consent by minors under eleven years of age, given the developmental psychological evidence for their diminished psychological capacities."[26] While this would be correct for the vast majority of cases, the very great variability among children of this age in decision-making capacities, as well as the very great variability in the demands made by different decisions, justifies allowing for the possibility that the very strong presumption that nine- and ten-year-olds are incompetent to decide about treatment for themselves might on occasion be rebutted.

The fact that children in this nine to fourteen age range sometimes demonstrate competence may have greater implications for medical practice rather than for legal policy. Physicians treating children in this age group should always explore treatment alternatives with children, as well as with their parents, in an effort to determine the children's preferences regarding treatment, to understand the reasoning on which their preferences are based, and to assess their competence for decisions. If parent and child are in agreement with the physician's treatment recommendation and the parent's competence is not itself in question, then the physician will have both the parent's consent and the child's assent and can proceed with treatment. We speak of the parents' *consent* to signify their retention of decision-making authority, and the child's *assent* to signify his or her agreement with the treatment choice although lacking decision authority.

If the child is in disagreement with the physician's recommendation and/or the parents' choice, the first response, as always, should be to seek to resolve that disagreement through further discussion. When disagreement cannot be resolved, whether the child's disagreement is with the physician, the parents, or both, the physician should seek to assess the child's competence in this decision-making situation. If the physician judges the child to be competent, it should be his or her responsibility to accede to the child's wishes if the parents are also in agreement with the child, or to serve as the patient's – the child's – advocate in pursuing further steps to enable the child's wishes to be heard and respected. Such a practice would insure that treatment of children in this age range would never proceed without their consent, if competent, and if incompetent, without either the child's assent to the treatment or an evaluation by the physician of the child's reasoning in the case in question that affirmed the presumption of the child's incompetence to refuse the treatment.

While the preceding suggestions concern medical practice, they would require some changes in the law in virtually all states. What is needed is clearer authority, and in turn legal procedures, for rebutting the presumption of incompetence of children in this age group and for establishing their competence. We have no special suggestions about what those mechanisms should be, but, plainly, if they are desirable, it would not be impossible to develop them.

For children below the age of nine it is probably reasonable to maintain the practice of treating the presumption of their incompetence as unrebuttable. Despite the significant variation in different children's decision-making capacities at any particular age, it is hard to imagine the circumstances in which so young a child's refusal of a treatment or request for treatment should be honored in the face of the united opposition of the parents and the physician. However, just as with incompetent adult patients, such children should always have their treatment explained to them, before they receive it, in a manner appropriate to their abilities to understand. This is a way of respecting their dignity appropriate to their limited decision-making capacities.

II. NEWBORNS

Thus far this chapter has concentrated on older minors, for whom questions of competence greatly complicate the decision-making process. This section focuses on disabled newborns, a class of minors who are clearly incompetent to make any decisions whatsoever. The aim is to show how the general analysis developed in preceding chapters illuminates special features of decision making concerning infants, while at the same time using reflections on this area of application to refine the general analysis and make it more concrete.

A. The correct guidance principle: Best interest, not substituted judgment

In Chapter 2 we argued that, despite several confused court rulings, the substituted judgment principle is not to be applied to individuals who were never competent or at least who never even came close to being competent. For such individuals, including newborns, the best interest principle is the only appropriate guidance principle. Difficulties arise, however, because of (1) the complex nature of the infant's interests, (2) the difficulty of ascertaining what is in the infant's best interest due to severe limitations in the infant's ability to communicate and to uncertainties regarding prognosis, and (3) the limitations which the legitimate interests of others, usually the parents and siblings, place on the parents' obligation to act in the infant's best interest. At a more fundamental level, troubling questions arise concerning the moral status of all infants and hence the extent of our obligations toward them, whether disabled or normal, if certain assumptions are made concerning the necessary conditions for personhood. Each of these issures will be examined in turn.

B. The nature of the infant's interests

Like adults and older minors, infants have two types of interests: current interests and future-oriented or forward-looking interests. The current interests of infants are exclusively experiential and functional: They are interests in achieving pleasure and in avoiding pain and discomfort, as well as interests in maintaining organic functions. What may be called *developmental interests* are especially prominent among the forward-looking interests of the infant. Developmental interests are of several sorts, the most important being what may be called (1) agency development interests, (2) opportunity interests, and (3) human relationship interests. Given that human thriving, the success of a human life, includes the exercise of agency capacities (rather than merely passive satisfactions), the infant who is capable of developing the capacities necessary for being an agent has an interest in developing those capacities and a derivative interest in the conditions required for this development to occur. Since exercising agency capacities requires not only the capacities themselves but also objective conditions for their exercise, the infant's interest in becoming an agent also implies an interest in having opportunities. For this reason, Joel Feinberg, in emphasizing the need for special protections for these opportunity interests, has spoken of "the child's right to an open future."[27]

Further, to the extent that human thriving requires personal relationships – friendship, love, intimacy, ties of loyalty and caring – the infant has an interest in developing the capacities for such relationships and in the objective conditions for exercising them. All of these interests are forward-looking in that whether or not they are thwarted or adequately or fully satisfied depends upon future states of affairs. Yet the infant has these interests while he or she is still an infant. In addition, the infant also has future-oriented interests of a purely experiential sort. The infant (now) has an interest, for example, in avoiding pain which it will suffer in the future and, derivatively, in that which will prevent the pain from occurring.

Normal newborns, in part because they lack conceptual abilities that develop only as language is acquired, do not have the ability to conceive of themselves as subjects that persist through time, that have a future and a past as well as a present. Yet it seems that unless we ascribe to the infant the future-oriented interests described above we have missed something of profound importance. If this is so – if it *does* make sense to ascribe to infants forward-looking interests such as the interest in becoming an agent – then one thesis about interests which some philosophers have advanced cannot be correct. This is the thesis that an individual, A, can at time t have an interest in some future state of affairs, S, which will exist at time t+n, only if A at time t can conceive of himself or herself as continuing to exist at time t+n. In a sense, the implausibility of this thesis should come as no surprise, given our earlier analysis of surviving interests.

Whether or not one has an interest in the higher education of one's grandchildren, for example, depends upon what one values, not upon one's ability or inability to think of oneself as continuing to exist up until the time one's grandchildren complete or fail to complete college. It is true that only a being who can and does conceive of him- or herself as a subject persisting over time can have this particular future-oriented interest, but this does not imply that an individual cannot have any future-oriented interests unless he or she can conceive of him- or herself as a persisting subject.

At least for infants who will, with appropriate care and treatment, have a good chance of becoming agents and of participating in personal relationships, developmental interests are especially important, since they influence the infant's prospects throughout the remainder of life. Consequently, an infant's forward-looking interests might be thought to outweigh his or her current experiential interests in avoiding pain. Thus a parent might conclude that acting in a disabled infant's best interest requires consenting to aggressive treatment, even if this treatment is extremely painful, for the sake of removing obstacles to the infant's development in the future. To this extent, application of the best interest principle to a disabled infant might allow us to justify current pain and suffering which would not be justifiable in applying the same principle to an elderly individual who lacks developmental interests and whose life expectancy even with treatment is short.

There is, however, another distinctive feature of infants which weighs *against* discounting current pain and suffering in order to further developmental or other important forward-looking interests. This is the fact that the infant is unable to understand that his or her current pain is the price to be paid for future benefits, and unable to console him- or herself with the thought that the pain is temporary. The Massachusetts Supreme Judicial Court in the *Saikewicz* case quite rightly emphasized this point in its attempt to determine whether painful and debilitating chemotherapy treatments would be in the best interests of a man who had the mental development of an infant.[28]

So any attempt to justify acting contrary to the infant's

current experiential interests for the sake of his or her developmental interests must avoid the error of failing to take seriously the full extent of the infant's current pain and suffering by projecting onto the uncomprehending infant our own belief in its "therapeutic necessity." The latter term, of course, simply begs the question as to what really is in the infant's best interest. The relative poverty of scientific studies concerning the pain sensitivity of infants, as well as the medical profession's rather questionable practice of not anesthetizing infants during painful surgical procedures, from circumcision to open-heart surgery, at least suggest that there is a real danger that the pain and suffering of infants is inappropriately discounted in the pursuit of therapeutic goals.

An unbiased weighing of the infant's experiential interest in avoiding current pain and suffering requires information about the infant's ability to experience pain and about the intensity and duration of the pain it will suffer if various causes of action are chosen. Even for normal infants, scientific knowledge in this area is relatively undeveloped and, of course, the infant's inability to communicate verbally makes techniques used in the study of pain in older patients inapplicable. The problem is exacerbated in cases in which it is difficult to determine whether an impaired infant's neurological damage has affected the ability to experience pain. So even if we had much better information than is now available concerning the development of pain sensitivity in normal infants, there would still be unanswered questions about impaired infants.

Some disabled newborns are described by physicians and nurses as being "unconsolable" – they writhe and cry incessantly, and do not become calm or cling when handled affectionately. There can be no doubt that they are not thriving and that they are in extreme discomfort, but whether they are in severe pain or what the felt quality of their existence is like may be very difficult, if not impossible, to ascertain.

In addition, the problem of determining the best treatment choice for an infant, when treatment inevitably involves significant pain and discomfort, is severely exacerbated by the prevalence not only of *risk* but also of *uncertainty*. Formal decision theory distinguishes two types of conditions of ignorance in decision-making situations. In decision making under *risk* the decision-maker knows what the consequences (outcomes) of the various options under consideration are, but can only assign probabilities (of less than one) to each of those outcomes. According to orthodox decision theory the rational chooser under conditions of risk will maximize expected utility. The expected utility for each option is the expected benefit (probability of benefit times magnitude of benefit) minus the cost or harm (the probability of cost or harm times the magnitude of the cost or harm). To maximize expected utility is to choose that option with the greatest expected (net) benefit or smallest expected (net) harm.

In decision making under *uncertainty,* ignorance is more profound. the chooser cannot even assign probabilities to the benefits and costs (harms) of the outcomes. For decision making under risk there is a single, relatively uncontroversial rule (namely, maximize expected utility), but there is no single decision rule whose appropriateness for all cases of decision making under uncertainty is acknowledged. Instead, decision theorists have generally conceded that (1) whether a given rule for decision making under uncertainly is appropriate for a decision-maker to use in a given choice situation may depend upon what that decision-maker's attitude toward risk is (whether he or she is risk averse, risk neutral, or not risk averse), that (2) there can be a range of attitudes toward risk, none of which is uniquely rational, and that (3) different kinds of decisions may call for different decision rules.

Even where the choice of whether to employ or withhold treatment intended to extend life is to be made under
conditions of risk rather than uncertainty, there may still
often be no uniquely rational choice. For even if the probabilities of the occurrence of the various possible outcomes of each option are accurately known, there may be
no uniquely rational estimate of the relative value or importance of the harms and benefits. Perfectly rational
choosers as well as imperfectly rational but reasonable
persons may disagree, for example, as to whether the pain
and suffering of multiple surgeries, the social isolation of
an infancy spent in an intensive care unit, and the life-long
physical and social handicaps of partially corrected neurological damage from spinal bifida are outweighed by the
pleasures and activities of a life that would have ended
quickly had aggressive treatment not been undertaken.
Indeed, even to speak of different persons reasonably *dis-
agreeing* about the importance of harms and benefits in
some of the more difficult cases is to assume more *objectivity* in these matters than is warranted. At the very most,
one may be able to say that *for oneself* an extension of life
would be worth the pain, suffering, and social isolation
that aggressive treatment involves.

Yet the question that the decision-maker is supposed to
be answering is *not* what would be best for *him or her* under
such conditions, but what would be best for the *infant*.
Moreover, in those cases in which we think there is an
answer to the question of whether the benefits of prolonged life would outweigh the harms, whether in our
own case or that of another, it is because we can relate the
alternate outcomes to the individual's "value history" – his
or her stable preferences, commitments, and characteristic
ways of responding to life's exigencies. The element of
subjectivity is therefore irreducible. No advances in prognostic skills, physiology, or even in individual psychology
can be expected to eliminate it.

Nevertheless, there may be some cases in which reasonable people would agree that the balance of harms over benefits is clear – cases in which we have sufficient reason to conclude, with great reluctance and grief, that the infant's life is not worth prolonging for the infant. If one thinks of this judgment as resting on a comparison of the harms and benefits of existence with the harms and benefits of nonexistence, one is liable to succumb to a metaphysical anxiety attack. For since in nonexistence there is no subject who can be harmed or benefitted, it would seem that no such comparison can be made or even sensibly attempted.

This metaphysical barrier to judging whether a life is worth living vanishes, however, if we recast the question as follows: Would a rational (or reasonable) person prefer to terminate such a life in order to end its pain and suffering even though this means the end of all pleasures and projects as well?

The latter question is a sensible one, even though, as we have seen, it may be extremely difficult to answer. It is the question a competent adult *does* answer in deciding whether to forgo life-sustaining treatment. There are at least two classes of disabled infants which include some members for whom the answer to it may be "yes"" those with Lesh-Nyan syndrome and those with Tay-Sachs disease. The former appear to be souls in torment, engaging in ultimately lethal self-mutilation unless constantly restrained. Even with aggressive treatment, the latter live at most a few years, suffering increasingly severe pain and disability. There may be other infants as well whose particular conditions and disabilities may support the conclusion that life-sustaining treatment is not in the infant's interest.

The importance of fixing firmly on the admittedly difficult task of estimating what is in the infant's best interest is clearly illustrated by two famous or, rather, notorious cases involving Down's syndrome infants who were allowed to die from dehydration and starvation because their parents elected not to authorize surgery routinely used for mentally normal infants. The first occurred at Johns Hopkins University Medical Center over fifteen years ago, the second, the case of "Baby Doe," in Bloomington, Indiana in 1982. Though there is still some controversy about the facts of these cases (especially the second, since the judge ordered the court records sealed), there is reason to believe that in both the decision to withhold life support was *not* guided exclusively or even primarily by a reasonable application of the best interest principle.

In the first case the interests of others may have been controlling in the decision-making process, and the most fundamental interests of the infant may have been disregarded entirely or given too little weight. In the latter case it is possible that the parents, relying on their physician's incorrect statement that Down's individuals are little more than vegetables, may have applied the best interest principle, but erroneously concluded that the infant's life was not worth living. What these cases have in common, however, is that they both vividly illustrate the danger of undertreatment.

Another well-known and in some ways more disturbing case is that of Baby Andrew, an apparent victim of over-treatment.

> The sad list of Andrew's afflictions, almost all of which were iatrogenic [treatment-caused], reveals how disastrous this hospitalization was. Andrew had a months-long, unresolved case of bronchopulmonary dysplasia, sometimes referred to as "respirator lung syndrome." He was "saved" by the respirator to endure countless episodes of bradycardia and cyanosis, countless suctionings and tube insertions and

blood samplings and blood transfusions, "saved" to develop retrolental fibroplasia, numerous infections, demineralized and fractured bones, an iatrogenic cleft palate, and finally, as his lungs became irreparably diseased, pulmonary artery hypertension and seizures of the brain. He was, in effect "saved" by the respirator to die five long, painful, and expensive months later of the respirator's side effects.[29]

If, as appears to have been the case, this infant's prospects for survival even with the most aggressive treatment were extremely poor, and if, as also seems likely, the severe iatrogenic damage he suffered was known to be highly probable at the outset, then a decision that focused at least primarily if not exclusively on the infant's best interest would not have allowed treatment to continue so long.

The Baby Andrew case and others like it invite a number of mutually compatible hypotheses to explain how they could occur. One of the most widely offered of these has already been discussed above: Physicians may have a tendency to discount too sharply the infant's current pain and suffering when balancing them against possible (though highly improbable) future gains for the infant. Another plausible explanation is that some physicians exhibit an over-optimistic attitude toward the efficacy of their skills and are unwilling to "let a patient go," because, although perhaps only subconsiously, they view their patient's death as a personal defeat.

To counterbalance these tendencies and to try to minimize the occurrence of overtreatment and the suffering it entails not only for the patient but also for the patient's family, one might be tempted to retreat to an ancient principle of medical ethics: First, do no harm. This principle seems singularly plausible in the case of neonatology because profound uncertainty concerning prognosis is relatively common in this specialty. However, it should be noted that this principle was introduced at a time when medicine's capacity to benefit was virtually nonexistent, although not its potential for harm. (Recall the Hippocratic Oath's admonition to physicians "not to cut for the [kidney] stone" – no matter how severe the patient's agony.) To observe strictly the prohibition on harming at a time when medicine can confer genuine benefits would be unconscionable.

Instead, we might view the "First, do no harm" principle as a dramatic expression of a more plausible idea for our time. In order to correct the tendencies to discount unduly the infant's current experiential interests and for professional biases toward over-treatment of noncommunicating patients in conditions of great risk or profound uncertainty, one might assign extra weight to iatrogeric harms and benefits when one applies the best interest principle.

Under conditions in which bias is especially strong and other safeguards against bias are lacking, such a procedure of deliberately overestimating the magnitude of expected iatrogeric harms may be a rational response to cope with the irrationality which such biases would otherwise produce. There is always the danger, of course, that the same strong psychic needs that have led to biases toward over-treatment may lead the physician to cancel the extra weight he or she assigns to iatrogenic harms by over-estimating the magnitude or the probability of the gains which treatment may bring.

Nevertheless, the physician's reliance on the "do no harm" principle as a counterweight against his or her own professional bias may be a good deal better than nothing. Indeed, it might be the only plausible safeguard that could be had if physicians worked in a vacuum, independently, rather than within an institutional context.

However, especially in neonatology, physicians and parents are in fact embedded within a complex institutional structure. Given that this is so, it seems more prudent to rely more heavily on institutional mechanisms – consultations, prognosis review, and review by ethics committees – than on the physician's ability to apply the "do no harm" principle as an internal corrective to his or her own biases. This is merely one illustration of a much more general point: The most rational thing to do, for an agent who wishes to choose rationally but who is aware of his or her own tendency toward irrationality, is often to initiate or help support external mechanisms that will limit this irrationality. For if the factors that lead to irrational choices in the first place are sufficiently internal to the agent – as is the case with professional biases toward overtreatment – then purely internal checks on them may be too easily subverted.

An analogy may help. The alcoholic may find it more effective to arrange to have a friend restrain him or her from having more than two drinks than to try to apply the rule "Only have two drinks" to him- or herself, especially after having had two drinks. Here, and in the medical context as well, reliance or an external mechanism can be an exercise of autonomy, not a violation or abdication of it.

Our strategy throughout this book rests on a recognition that good decision making not only requires a knowledge of the appropriate guidance principles but also depends upon appropriate institutional structures within which decision-makers will have the right incentives to enable them to apply these principles appropriately. This is nowhere more important than in the case of decision making for disabled and critically ill newborns. In the final subsection of this chapter we shall suggest some basic institutional safeguards designed to enhance the probability that morally acceptable decisions will be made concerning life-or-death decisions for disabled newborns.

Taken by itself, the "do no harm" principle, like other medical ethical principles addressed directly to individual physicians, represents, as we have just seen, an attempt to imporove decision making in cases of great risk or uncertainty, *without relying upon institutional mechanisms.* A prominent psychologist and medical ethicist, Dr. Joseph Goldstein, has offered another noninstitutional (or nonprocedural) response to the problems of risk and uncertainty in decisions for disabled newborns. We single out Dr. Goldstein's view here not only because of his considerable influence, but also because we believe it is widely held and, unfortunately, quite incorrect. Sensitive to the prognostic and moral uncertainties that can make life-or-death decisions for disabled newborns so trying, Goldstein opts for a very wide range of parental discretion to refuse life-sustaining treatment. His chief reason is this: Where there is no right answer, the parents cannot be criticized for choosing the wrong answer.[30]

This inference, however, is invalid, for two distinct but equally important reasons. First, from the fact that there is no right answer in the sense of a single, uniquely correct solution, it does not follow that one answer is as good as the next nor that some answers are not wrong. When it comes to hard moral choices the best that we can do – and the least that we should demand – is often simply that we identify a *range of reasonable solutions.* This is usually achieved largely by eliminating unreasonable solutions. Second, especially in circumstances in which reasonable persons do not converge on a single answer, we can often best discharge our responsibility by ensuring that the *process* of decision making was reasonably fair and provides reasonable assurance that relevant factors have been given due consideration. In the case of life-or-death decision making for disabled newborns, there is no plausible alternative to procedural safeguards built into the structure of the institutions in which decision making occurs. Perhaps the single most promising example of such mechanisms is the institutional ethics committee, whose functions were examined in Chapter 3.

C. The interests of others

Our analysis of the best interest principle emphasized that there is a sense in which that principle is not to be taken literally, as requiring that we always do what is *optimal* for the individual to whom it properly applies. To treat the best interest principle as a literal and absolute commandment, rather than as a *guidance* principle, would be to impose morally excessive and indeed impossible demands upon any decision-maker who recognizes that persons other than the imcompetent patient, including the decision-maker herself, have legitimate interests. A parent cannot be expected to choose what is optimal (as opposed to good or acceptable) treatment for a disabled newborn if doing so requires expending resources – emotional or financial – which will destroy his or her marriage and thwart basic interests of his or her other children. Even within special relationships, which generate especially stringent obligations, we still can and ought to distinguish between duty and supererogation.

From this we should not conclude, however, that parents may refuse life-sustaining treatment for a disabled infant whenever such conflicts of interests arise. It is one thing to say that parents may *responsibly* divest themselves of the duty to care for their infant in order to insure that they can pursue their own legitimate interests or those of their other children. It is quite another to say that they may disregard the infant's basic interests while refusing to divest themselves of decision-making authority, terminating the infant's life *in order* to terminate their obligations. In the case of the Down's syndrome baby at Johns Hopkins, there is reason to believe that this distinction was overlooked or willfully ignored. The parents refused to sign the operation permit, citing as their reason for refusal that they were unable to care for a disabled child while preserving the existing family unit. If the parents chose, as they apparently did, not to be guided even primarily by the infant's best interest, then they should have divested themselves of responsibility. The right to terminate one's responsibility as a parent is not the right to decide for one's child while disregarding that child's fundamental interests.

None of this is to deny, however, that there may be cases in which the death of an infant may be better for the infant than the alternative of abandoning him or her to a short life of misery, neglect, and impersonal custodial care in an institution that merely "warehouses" living human beings. Nothing in the Johns Hopkins case, however, indicates that these were the only alternatives or that the best interest of the infant even played a central role in the decision.

D. The fundamental moral status of infants: A radical challenge to the decision-making framework

Thus far we have proceeded on the orthodox assumption, embedded in both commonsense morality and the law, that *normal* infants are *persons* – full-fledged members of the primary moral community, beings whose moral status is in no way inferior to that of older children or adults. This assumption is seriously challenged, however, by the view that personhood and the basic rights we ascribe to persons require certain minimal *cognitive capacities* which even normal infants lack. As noted earlier (in Chapter 4), these are usually said to include (1) the ability to be conscious of oneself as existing over time, (2) the ability to appreciate reasons for or against acting, and (3) the ability to engage in purposive action. If any one of these capacities (or anything approximating their cognitive sophistication) is a necessary condition for being a person in the primary moral status sense, then not just profoundly demented adults and severely brain-damaged infants, but *normal* newborns and young infants as well fail to qualify as persons.

Despite its disturbing implications for the orthodox view of the status of normal infants, the radical postion cannot easily be dismissed. In large part it draws its plausibility from its power to explain our intuitions about the difference in moral status between human beings and nonhuman animals and about hypothetical extraterrestrial, nonhuman, intelligent beings.

When asked to provide an informative *explanation* of why we believe human beings ought to be treated differently from animals such as pigs and chickens, one quite naturally responds that the former are human beings while the latter are not. Simply to say that human beings have a higher moral status than nonhuman because the former as humans and the latter are not, however, is sheer speciesism. Like the racist's steadfast declaration that blacks are inferior to whites because they are black, speciesism is *arbitrary* discrimination – treating different classes of beings differently without providing a morally relevant reason for doing so.

Simply to say that we may treat nonhuman animals differently from humans because humans are *persons* and nonhuman animals are not does not rebut the charge of speciesism unless content can be given to the notion of personhood, and in such a way as to make it clear that nonhuman animals are not persons. Yet if there is any morally relevant basis for treating nonhuman animals differently than humans – for according them an inferior moral status – it seems to be their lact of the cognitive capacities listed earlier. Given that this is so, we are then led to conclude that these cognitive capacities are necessary for personhood. Thus it appears that the explanation we are forced to give to avoid the charge of speciesism pushes us toward the radical position, since some human beings, including normal infants, lack the cognitive capacities which we believe to be distinctive of persons.

The plausibility of the view that certain cognitive capacities are necessary for personhood and that *being a person* and *being human* are quite distinct properties is reinforced by our intuitions about the moral status of hypothetical nonhuman, extraterrestrial, intelligent beings. Suppose humankind encountered a radically different form of life in its exploration of the galaxy. What seems relevant to determining the moral status of such a profoundly alien being is certainly not whether it is a human being, which clearly it would not be, differing as it would from members of our species both morphologically and genetically. Instead, to determine its status we would try to ascertain – perhaps with great difficulty – whether it was capable of purposive action, whether it had a conception of itself as a persisting subject, etc.

Reflection on the hypothetical case of an encounter with a clearly nonhuman but indubitably intelligent alien being leads us to conclude that being human is not a *necessary* condition of personhood. An informative explanation of why we may treat nonhuman animals as having an inferior moral status leads us to conclude that being human is not *sufficient* for personhood either. We need not look to science fiction, however. As we saw in Chapter 4, some living members of our own species – namely, permanently unconscious individuals and the profoundly and permanently demented – lack the cognitive capacities necessary for personhood. At this point the radical position, as disturbing as it may be, seems unavoidable: only some human beings are persons, and normal infants are not among them.

In what some might characterize as a desperate attempt to stave off this conclusion, some have advanced the potentiality principle:

> P: A being that now is not a person, but has the potential to become a person (a being who will, under normal circumstances, develop the capacities necessary (and sufficient) for personhood) should be accorded now the moral status (the rights) of a person.[31]

Given P, we can conclude that normal human infants (unlike pigs or chickens) ought to be treated as persons.

A number of writers have been quick to point out the implausibility of P as an account of the logic of moral rights through the use of counterexamples. Suppose, for example, that Jones is potentially president of the U.S. (he has won the election but not yet taken office) and that being president confers certain rights. It does not follow from this that Jones now has any of the rights of a president.[32] Such counterexamples may not be decisive, however, since it is open to the defender of the potentiality principle to argue that its scope is restricted only to the right not to be killed. In addition to its inconsistency with the logic of other moral rights, the potentiality principle has another liability, at least for those who wish to utilize what is clearly the most powerful argument to justify abortion. That argument relies on the premise,

F: Fetuses lack the moral status of persons.

But (normal) fetuses have the potential for personhood and if the potentiality principle is true then F must be false. It is not our purpose here, however, to enter the familiar controversies concerning abortion.

Quite apart from whether the fetus as such has moral rights, the *futurity of interests* discussed earlier in Chapter 3 provides limited although significant resources for responding to the radical view without adopting anything so implausible as the potentiality principle. It is true that infants have future-oriented interests, most prominently what we have called the developmental interests in becoming an autonomous agent and in participating in the personal relationships generally necessary for living well. But such interests are most plausibility understood as being *conditional*. The infant has them only on the assumption that he or she is likely to survive to the point in the future at which they will earlier be thwarted or could have been satisfied.

If a decision is made to sustain an infant's life and if it is expected that the infant will live long enough that his or her potential for becoming an autonomous agent will be realized, then respect for the future-oriented interests the infant now has provides a firm basis for according him or her the same moral status as a person, even though he or she currently lacks the capacities necessary for personhood. However, if the infant's future-oriented interests are *conditional,* then they *only* provide a basis for treating the infant as a person *if* the infant is expected to live long enough for those interests to be satisfied. This condition will not be met, of course, if a decision is made to allow the infant to die or even to kill it. So it follows that no appeal to the infant's future-oriented interests can serve as a basis for according him or her a moral status that would preclude active or passive termination of its life.

Appeals to the infant's current experiential interests would be relevant, but could provide no protection against the infant's being painlessly killed, and would fall far short of grounding the claim that the infant is to be accorded the same moral status as other persons. Even if, as seems doubtful, it could plausibly be held that the infant's current experiential interests include an interest in *continuing to experience pleasure,* any obligation we have to provide a continuation of pleasurable existence for him or her must surely be one that can be overriden by conflicting obligations to secure the important interests of persons or of those infants whom we choose to allow to become persons. Proper consideration for the infant's current experiential interests would also, of course, require that if we choose to kill the infant or to allow him or her to die, we must make sure that his or her demise is painless. But these two ways in which infants' current experiential interests place moral constraints on our treatment of normal infants, neither singly nor in combination, amount to according them the full moral status of persons. So the radical challenge to the commonsense legal framework and to the analysis we have developed in this book thus far is not fully answered.

There are, however, some additional considerations of a pragmatic sort that speak in favor of according full moral status to all infants, except those whose disability results in the absence of interests or in severely truncated interests, and consequently for not allowing them to be killed or allowed to die for any reasons that would not equally justify the same treatment for a normal adult. The chief pragmatic concern is this: to design and implement a reliable institutional framework that would allow the painless termination of the lives of normal infants, while at the same time scrupulously protecting the developmental and experiential interests of those infants who are allowed to live, would be extremely difficult. To sustain in ourselves the set of attitudes, dispositions, and attachments required for doing the latter while at the same time achieving the psychological disengagement required for the former would if anything be more difficult still. Thus an appreciation of the need to be the kinds of persons who can protect and nurture those infants who do become persons may in the end provide the best response to the radical challenge.

Furthermore, it is a fact about us – and a far from superficial one, being reflected as it is in our most fundamental legal institutions – that we tend to regard infants who are likely to develop the cognitive capacities of persons as at least more closely approximating the moral status of persons than that of nonpersons. Consequently, any theoretical view which utterly denies the rights of moral personhood to normal human infants, no matter how strong its philosophical arguments, is in our society at present and for the foreseeable future not likely to be adopted.

Nevertheless, while the pragmatic considerations sketched above cast doubt on the policy implications of the radical position they do not refute it decisively.[33] And there is considerable evidence that even if we accord a

higher moral status to newborns than to nonhuman beings, there is a tendency in popular opinion and perhaps
even in isolated cases in the legal system to weigh the
rights of newborns somewhat less heavily than those of
older individuals when the former conflict with the latter.
Whether this ambivalence about the moral status of very
young infants will persist is hard to know.

6. The elderly

This chapter describes and explains in greater detail both formal and informal practices of decision making for incompetent and questionably competent elderly people, and the institutional and legal framework within which these practices occur. Its purpose is not restricted to description and explanation, however. Current practices are evaluated by applying the analysis of competence set out in Chapter 1 and the primary ethical framework developed in Chapter 2.

I. THE MAGNITUDE OF THE PROBLEM

The issue of decision making for incompetent or questionably competent elderly people touches us all – as individuals who have or will have friends or family members who are elderly and incompetent, as persons who are ourselves likely to be in this situation at some point during our last years, and as concerned citizens.

Incompetence may be limited or complete, chronic or intermittent, and it may be due to one or more of a diverse group of medical disorders (although for most of these disorders, only some, not all, persons afflicted with them are incompetent), including: (1) degenerative neurological disorders such as Alzheimer's disease and Parkinson's disease, (2) single or multiple cerebrovascular accidents (stroke), (3) severe acute or chronic depression that impairs cognitive function, (4) temporary or permanent coma, (5) mental retardation, (6) psychosis, or (7) severe personality disorders.

The problem is especially grave for the elderly, not because advanced age itself is to be equated with loss of competence, and not simply because some forms of dementia are more common among the elderly, but chiefly because the incidence of chronic illness is higher among them and because under the conditions of modern medicine many patients in the last stages of chronic illness are incompetent. Especially in the tertiary care setting, medicine contributes to the magnitude of the problem, in part because it has been so successful. Through the use of sophisticated life-sustaining technology such as ventilators, as well as much simpler devices such as the gastrostomy feeding tube, medicine can prolong life – sometimes for many years – even when disease or trauma have impaired or obliterated the patient's cognitive functions.

Medical technology also plays a role in the problem in another way: Some medical interventions themselves diminish the patient's competence. Steroids and other highly toxic drugs used in cancer therapy can seriously impair mental function, and dosages of narcotics sufficient for effective relief of pain can prevent an otherwise competent patient from communicating preferences, or from contradicting the presumption of incompetence.

The scope of the problem is enormous. The elderly as a group are increasing rapidly, both in absolute numbers and as a percentage of the overall population. In 1975, for instance, there were 22 million people aged sixty-five or older; by the year 2000, there will be 30 million.[1] Table 6.1 indicates for selected years the percentage of the population that is elderly.

It is not simply that there are more people over sixty-four than ever before; there is also a remarkable increase in those over seventy-four, as well as those over eighty-four. In 1950, for example, 29 percent of the elderly were seventy-five or older; by 1975, the number had increased to 38

Table 6.1. *Share of U.S. population over 64 years of age,*
1900, 1940, 1960, 1975, and 2000

Year	Percent
1900	4.0
1940	6.5
1960	9.0
1975	10.5
2000	11.5

Source: National Institute on Aging (1977). *Our future selves: A research toward understanding aging.* Washington, DC: National Institutes of Health.

percent; by 2000, an estimated 45 percent of the elderly population will be at least seventy-five years old. Table 6.2 outlines this growth.

By the year 2000, even if there are no improvements in mortality rates, it is estimated that there will be 12 million very old (seventy-five or older) people. If mortality rates decline, this figure may reach 16 to 18 million.

Since the incidence of the two most prevalent forms of dementia – Alzheimer's disease and multi-infarct (or cerebrovascular) dementia – increases with age, these demographic changes will greatly enlarge the class of

Table 6.2. *Distribution of U.S. elderly population by age-group,*
1950, 1975, and 2000

Age-groups	Percent of Total Elderly		
	1950	1975	2000
65–74	71	62	54
75–84	25	30	34
85 or older	4	8	11

Source: National Institute of Aging, *ibid.*

incompetent individuals unless significant progress is made in the treatment of these diseases. It has been estimated that between 10 and 18 percent of all persons aged sixty-five or older suffer from some form of dementia, and that between 15 and 20 percent of those eighty or older fall into this category.[2] These figures have led many experts to conclude, with Sir Martin Roth, a world-renowned expert on dementia, that dementia among the elderly is "the largest and most pressing single problem facing present day health [science] and social science in different parts of the world."[3]

The problem is daunting not simply in terms of the numbers of elderly individuals who are or will be incompetent, but also with regard to the types of decisions that must be made and the different sorts of settings in which those choices must be faced. Decisions often must be made about (1) medical care, (2) placement in nursing homes, mental institutions, hospice, or residential homes for the elderly, (3) the financial details of estate management, and (4) whether the incompetent individual is to participate as a subject in medical or social science research.

This chapter concentrates primarily on decisions concerning medical care. Placement and financial decisions will also be discussed (although in much less detail), not only because they can have a great impact on the life of an elderly incompetent person, but also because they both influence and are influenced by decisions about medical care. For example, a decision to undertake a vigorous course of chemotherapy for an elderly patient may entail removing that person from the family home for hospitalization, whereas placement in a nursing home that lacks sophisticated emergency life-sustaining technology will limit a patient's medical options. Relatives may decide to place an elderly person in a hospital or nursing home because they lack the financial or emotional resources to provide home care. This change may be so traumatic that the elderly individual suffers a diminution of competence and a decline in health.

No attempt is made here to address the important and complex ethical issues concerning medical or social science research involving those elderly individuals who are incompetent or of questionable competence.

II. HOW INCOMPETENCE IS DETERMINED, FORMALLY AND INFORMALLY, AND BY WHOM, IN VARIOUS SETTINGS

It must be emphasized that data are scarce here because comprehensive, empirical studies are presently lacking. It is generally agreed, however, that by far the majority of all determinations of incompetence in the elderly are made informally. In many cases, other people – spouses, family members, nursing home personnel, physicians, family attorneys, or neighbors – simply decide that an elderly person is no longer able to make his or her own medical decisions or to manage financial affairs, without any formal procedure and without any explicit declaration of incompetence being made, even to the elderly individual him- or herself.

Even when the elderly individual lodges no protest, it is not safe to conclude that he or she has freely delegated decision-making authority to others, or freely acquiesces in their implicit judgment that he or she is no longer competent. An eighty-year-old widower who is almost entirely dependent upon his grown daughter for emotional support – and who lives with her because he is physically frail – may find it impossible to resist her efforts to take complete control of his assets. This financial dependence may itself contribute to a decline in his mental capacity, simply because it deprives him of opportunities to keep his faculties intact by exercising them, and leads to a lowering of self-esteem, attended by depression.

A. Determining competence
to make medical decisions

In Chapter 1 it was noted that competence determinations in medical contexts are usually made without court involvement of any kind. In general this is not a failing, it was argued, because reliance on formal guardianship hearings is often unproductive and unnecessary. What is disturbing about this informality in the medical setting is *not* that competence determinations are made without court involvement, but that there is no assurance of consistency and reliability. There are often no clear and accepted criteria that: (1) articulate standards and operational criteria for such determinations, (2) fix responsibility on someone in the institution for establishing whether a given person is competent or incompetent to make certain decisions, (3) include effective safeguards against abuse or error, and (4) provide guidance as to when court involvement is appropriate.

The failure to develop and monitor compliance with policies that meet these minimal requirements can perhaps best be illustrated by focusing upon a growing body of evidence concerning the ways in which "No Code" orders ("Do Not Resuscitate" or DNR orders) are issued. It is true that DNR orders are not written exclusively for the elderly, but their occurrence is most frequent in this group. Although it would be imprudent to make sweeping generalizations about other medical decisions based simply on DNR orders, the way in which an institution handles this one type of decision can provide something of a litmus test for other decisions. For accreditation, all hospitals are now required to have explicit policies regarding DNR decisions. If an institution's practices concerning DNR decisions are seriously deficient, it is likely that it will not have sound policies for less highly visible and less dramatic types of decisions.

Perhaps the most shocking revelation of deficiencies in

DNR orders was the so-called Purple Dot Affair, which came to light because of a lawsuit against a large hospital in New York State.[4] A patient went into cardiac arrest in his hospital room during a visit by several members of his family. The resuscitation unit rushed into the room, but stopped short, then retreated, after one member of the team remarked that this patient was a "No Code." The outraged family, who apparently had not been consulted, demanded to know how this could be, since there was no DNR order in the patient's chart. It soon became known that a DNR order was marked in the patient's chart by affixing a purple dot to the chart, that nurses did this, and that purple dots were available in the hospital gift shop, where anyone could purchase them.

In another institution, instead of a purple dot, a red circle on the hospital room door next to the room number served as a secret code for "No Code" status – known only to hospital personnel, not to patients or their families.[5] The utter disregard for the rights of patients and families, and the enormous potential for gross abuses (including murder) that such "policies" carry are obvious.

One hopes that such egregious deficiencies are rare. There is, however, mounting evidence that many, perhaps most, hospitals either lack an adequate DNR policy or have an announced policy with which few physicians comply. A 1984 study of three teaching hospitals that lacked any official DNR policy concluded that DNR orders are currently not fulfilling their major goals of promoting patient autonomy and facilitating decision making prior to a crisis, where possible.[6]

Another recent study at a large teaching hospital involved 82 private physicians, 75 residents, and 154 resuscitations.[7] This study indicated that only 19 percent of the patients had discussed resuscitation prior to its being administered, although 86 percent of the total group were competent. Further, only 33 percent of the families were consulted about whether resuscitation was to be used. And although the vast majority of physicians – 151 out of 157 – said they believed in discussing resuscitation with patients, only 15 actually did so. In spite of this lack of communication, the physicians in 68 percent of the cases believed that they knew their patients' attitudes toward resuscitation. This study dramatically illustrates the hazards of others assuming that they can know a patient's wishes about resuscitation in the absence of explicit discussion of the question with the patient. Eight out of twenty-five competent patients who survived resuscitation said they had not desired it, and fifteen out of the sixteen physicians treating those eight patients incorrectly believed that the patient wished to be resuscitated. Moreover, the percentage of cases in which the physician discussed resuscitation with the patient did not vary significantly between competent and incompetent patients. Yet another study observed that ". . . attending physicians, who have legal responsibility for patient care, were involved in decisions to withhold cardiopulmonary resuscitation (CPR) in only 30 percent of cases. . . . In the majority of cases, residents and interns made the decisions."[8]

If these studies are representative, then many physicians and health care institutions fail grievously in five respects. (1) They do not clearly and effectively assign responsibility for seeing that DNR decisions are made in an appropriate way to one individual, namely the attending physicians, the person ultimately responsible for the patient's care. (2) They do not have adequate policies and procedures in place to encourage discussing resuscitation with the competent patient or the incompetent patient's surrogate well ahead of the need for this intervention. The need for such policies and procedures is all the greater to counteract the natural tendency to be reluctant to discuss such a disquieting possibility. (3) They fail to ensure that, when competent, the patient, and not merely the patient's family, will be consulted about his or her wishes concerning resuscitation. (4) They do not take seriously the crucial task of determining whether the patient is competent to decide. (5) If the patient is determined to be incompetent, they fail to proceed on the assumption that the family is to serve as surrogate (in the absence of evidence that they are not qualified to do so). Finally, it is important to emphasize that the hospital studied by Bedell and DelBanco (Beth Israel of Boston), unlike those in the first study, has for many years had an announced DNR policy that affirms the importance of patient and family participation. Existence of a written policy is one thing, compliance quite another. At a minimum, adoption of a DNR policy needs to be coupled with ongoing educational efforts to inform staff of the policy and to secure its implementation.

The following case, reported by an experienced internist at a large university hospital, provides insight into why, in institutions that lack coherent policies, physicians often fail to make a careful determination of incompetence before identifying a surrogate and bypassing the patient as a decision maker altogether. The patient was terminally ill, suffering from cancer, with extensive metastases to the chest, abdomen, and brain. The disease was unresponsive to chemotherapy and radiation. The patient was brought to the hospital by her family, who said that she was confused and euphoric. The internist, who was primarily responsible for her care, did not interview the patient for purposes of evaluating her competence. Instead, he conferred privately with the patient's family, and recommended that a DNR order be entered in the chart and that no other aggressive treatment be undertaken. In retrospect, the physician says that he is confident that the decision to terminate treatment was correct, but he criticizes himself for not attempting to talk to the patient and determine if she was competent. He stated that he failed to do so because he found it psychologically easier to deal with the family than to confront the patient explicitly with the fact that nothing more could be done to retard the progress of her disease.[9]

Still more basic issues regarding competence to make medical decisions in general, and decisions concerning resuscitation in particular, arise in the nursing home context, although the issues have received far less attention than the cases that occur in hospitals. Many nursing homes do not possess equipment or trained personnel for mechanical cardiopulmonary resuscitation (CPR); some do not call for paramedics to perform CPR, and they transfer patients to a hospital when they have a cardiac arrest. A director of a midwestern nursing home explained that at his facility, if during the nightly bedcheck it is discovered that a patient is not breathing, nothing will be done to resuscitate the individual.[10] His explanation was that elderly people come to the nursing home to die, and that everyone was aware of that.

Such a policy is unacceptable for several reasons. First, not all residents of nursing homes are old, much less so old and afflicted with illness that attempting to prolong their lives through resuscitation never makes sense. Second, it would only be permissible to have such a blanket policy if it were clearly announced *in advance* of admission to all patients and their families, and if appropriate measures were taken to ensure that the patient when competent (or the appropriate surrogate when the patient is not competent) freely chooses to forego this form of life support. Yet the director of the nursing home made it clear that the policy was not announced at the time of admission (nor subsequently, for that matter), and that there was no procedure for ascertaining whether particular patients were competent to decide about resuscitation. Although such fundamentally flawed policies may not be common in nursing homes, they raise serious ethical concerns where they do occur.

This criticism of some existing practices does not rest on the erroneous assumption that CPR is appropriate for all patients, much less for all or even most elderly patients. In many cases, resuscitation is a traumatic and futile invasion to which an individual ought not be submitted. Although CPR has higher success rates for the exceptional case of an otherwise healthy person who suffers cardiopulmonary arrest following surgery or near-drowning, success, especially successful resuscitation that allows the patient to survive to leave the hospital, is low when CPR is used on the general hospital population, and rare in elderly patients with one or more serious chronic illnesses.[11] Nevertheless, broad statistical generalizations do not justify disregarding the preferences of a competent patient or excluding the family from participating in the decision-making process when a patient is incompetent.

A policy for DNR orders is only one aspect of planning for crisis. Especially in the nursing home context, the same kinds of ethical considerations that speak in favor of issuing a "do not resuscitate" order may also in some cases justify a "do not hospitalize," or a "do not feed by tube," or a "do not administer antibiotics" order. Investing a surrogate with the authority to make these decisions is acceptable only within the framework of safeguards provided by a carefully thought-out and conscientiously monitored institutional policy. The analysis developed in earlier chapters was used to develop the following principles to guide the development of an institutional DNR policy, which we offer to help avoid some of the errors and abuses discussed above. Actual policies themselves will have to take account of particular differences between institutions.

We use the example of DNR decisions and policies only to illustrate the kind of institutional policies and practices appropriate for surrogate decision making more generally. The example is important because of the importance of resuscitation decisions themselves and their often especially troubling nature for those involved in making them. The example of DNR may be especially useful because most hospitals now have explicit DNR policies which can be evaluated in light of our proposed principles and in the hope that reevaluation of institutional DNR policies may stimulate development of policies for other aspects of surrogate decision making.

Principles to guide formulation of an institutional DNR policy

It should be the accepted policy of the institution to provide an environment within which patients may exercise full freedom of informed choice in regard to treatment, to allow medical professionals freedom in the exercise of their professional judgment, and to respect and protect human life. To that end, the following principles should be incorporated in the institution's DNR policy.

(1) The attending physician is responsible for ensuring that patients who are competent to decide whether or not they are to be resuscitated are distinguished from those who are not, in order to protect the right of the competent patient to accept or refuse resuscitation and to initiate appropriate decision-making processes for those who are not competent.

(2) The attending physician is responsible for seeing that possible future resuscitation decisions are discussed and documented with those competent patients who are at significant risk for cardiac or respiratory arrest or for whom there is reason to believe they would not want resuscitation (or with families or guardians of such patients if the patients are incompetent). The existence of an advance directive or discussion with family members should not substitute for direct involvement of a competent patient.

(3) In cases of formerly competent patients who are now deemed incompetent, the attending physician should be responsible for seeing that a reasonable effort is made to ascertain the patient's former wishes, so that they may guide decisions concerning resuscitation. In particular, inquiry should be made as to the existence

of a living will, durable power of attorney, or other advance directive.

(4) When the patient is incompetent and there is no advance directive, the attending physician is responsible for seeing that a reasonable attempt is made to identify a suitable surrogate decision-maker and for ensuring that the surrogate is adequately informed about facts relevant to the decision concerning resuscitation. Normally, neither a relative or relatives with whom other close relatives disagree, a remote relative, nor the physician should serve as a surrogate decision-maker. When no relative or close friend is available to serve as an appropriate surrogate, the institution should identify a decision-making procedure that adequately safeguards the incompetent patient's interests. For example, this might involve consultation with an ethics committee or the Chief of Service, or the formal appointment of a guardian by a court.

(5) A written "Do Not Resuscitate" order only applies to full cardiopulmonary resuscitation. Decisions concerning other forms or levels of intervention are to be considered independently and documented accordingly. The existence of a DNR order should never result in a diminution of appropriate medical and nursing care for the patient.

(6) The attending physician is responsible for documenting in the medical record discussion or decisions concerning resuscitation with the patient or the patient's family or guardian.

(7) Regular review of the appropriateness of a DNR order (for example, daily) should be required and documented in the patient's medical record.

(8) Full cardiopulmonary resuscitation for all inpatients who suffer cardiac or respiratory arrest should be a standing order in the institution unless there is a writ-

ten "Do Not Resuscitate" order. In the event that the circumstances of a particular case provide an appropriate exception to this standing order, the attending physician must enter in the medical record a full explanation of why resuscitation was not attempted.

Implementation of a DNR policy that includes these elements along with the minimal guidelines for the determination of competence presented in Chapter 1 (Section XV) would do much to avoid the errors and abuses discussed thus far in this chapter. The elderly as a class would benefit significantly from such a policy.

B. Formal determinations of incompetence for decisions concerning finances and places of residence

Again, although systematic data are scarce, there is considerable anecdotal evidence of widespread confusion, error, and abuse in the procedures by which elderly individuals are determined to be incompetent to manage their own affairs and by which surrogate decision-makers for them are identified. Two especially serious and apparently pervasive errors stem from a failure to appreciate two fundamental points: Incompetence is often intermittent, not permanent, and competence is decision-relative.

The first error is that a diagnosis is confused with a determination of competence, and the role of medical judgment in determining incompetence is thus misunderstood. For example, courts typically rely on affidavits from physicians in declaring an individual incompetent for purposes of appointing a guardian or conservator. In some cases, the affidavit will simply state that the individual is "incompetent" or "unable to manage his or her own affairs" due to "organic brain syndrome" or "cerebral arteriosclerosis." Aside from the fact that the diagnosis itself may be inaccurate, the diagnosis may be taken – by the physician and the judge – as entailing a global judgment of incompetence. This, however, is a mistake. A person may suffer from cerebral arteriosclerosis, from Alzheimer's disease or other dementias, or from psychosis, and yet still be competent to make some decisions – at least at certain times, in certain environments. To make a judgment that an individual is competent or incompetent is to make a judgment about the adequacy of the person's decision-making capabilities to the task at hand. As such, it cannot be reduced to a medical judgment concerning diagnosis.

The second error lies in mistakenly believing that a determination of incompetence always justifies "plenary powers" for the court-appointed surrogate, even when the evidence of incapacity only supports a more limited role for the surrogate. A judicial finding of incompetence can result in a radical change in the individual's moral and legal status. There can be a total takeover by others, when in some cases a more circumscribed sphere of decision-making authority for the surrogate would have provided adequate protection both for the incompetent and for those in whom the person's financial undertakings create legitimate expectations.

Both of these common failings are graphically illustrated by the "Dirty Sally" case in California, which received a great deal of publicity a few years ago.[12] Through a joint but highly uncoordinated effort of city officials and county administrators, an elderly woman who lived alone was deprived of her home, lost all her belongings and her pets, and was grossly deceived. This occurred even though the weight of evidence indicated that she was not in fact incompetent and posed no danger to herself or others.

After complaints from her neighbors that her yard was filled with old furniture, and expressions of concern on their part that her house might be so unclean as to endanger her health, city officials first issued nuisance citations to "Dirty Sally." When this action proved largely ineffective, the matter was turned over to the office of the county public administrator (apparently in part out of fear that the public would react adversely to putting an elderly woman in jail for having a messy yard). A county worker arrived at the woman's house, told her she was just being taken for "a little ride," and delivered her to a nursing home instead. When she arrived at the nursing home – with only her purse and the clothes on her back – she was refused permission to use the telephone. Her house was sold, along with all of her personal possessions. One of her dogs was sold for experimentation, the other sent to the pound.

Nothing like a determination of competence occurred, and no effort was made to ensure that the intervention took the path of the least restrictive alternative, which would have limited surrogate decision making to those areas in which it was necessary. Indeed, subsequent examination – after press coverage triggered a public outcry – revealed that the woman in question was healthy, that she regularly paid her bills, and that she appeared quite capable of managing her own affairs without significant risk to herself.

Apparently the only evidence of her incompetence – aside from her cluttered yard – was an affidavit supplied by the county and merely signed by her physician, which read as follows:

> In my opinion, the proposed conservatee is not able to manage her own affairs and is suffering from chronic brain syndrome associated with cerebral arteriosclerosis.[13]

The affidavit also stated that the woman would not be able to attend the hearing in which her fate was to be decided "by reason of risk of increasing mental disability."

Granted the importance of being able to respond in person to those who wish to take control of one's life, the right to appear at a guardianship or conservatorship hearing is a fundamental safeguard that ought to be waived for an individual by others only when there is strong evidence that exercising it would seriously and directly endanger the individual's physical or mental well-being. In the "Dirty Sally" case, this basic right was disregarded in the most cavalier fashion, as the physician apparently signed the affidavit without investigating whether an appearance at a hearing would in fact endanger the woman's health. The physician later testified that he would not have signed the affidavit had he known that she was to be put in a nursing home.

This case also illustrates a third feature of "formal" determinations of incompetence in guardianship and conservatorship proceedings: the characteristic vagueness of the statutory definition of incompetence. Guardianship and conservatorship statutory definitions vary from state to state, but the most common definition of "incompetence" (sometimes called "incapacity") is that a person is "unable to manage his own affairs," or "unable to care for himself."[14] The former is often illustrated by references to an ability to resist fraud or undue influence, as in the California Probate Code.[15] And the latter is often illustrated by references to health, food, clothing, or shelter.[16] These standards, it must be acknowledged, represent a significant improvement over previous statutes, which included such characteristics as "old age" as indicative of incompetence.

However, this latest generation of criteria remains vague. It is crucial to understand that such definitions do not themselves indicate, much less constitute, clearly applicable and consistent standards for determining incompetence. At most they imply what is obvious – namely, that individuals who are totally unable to make decisions (e.g., the profoundly retarded, the comatose, the severely demented) are incompetent. But since, as indicated in "Chapter 1, decision-making abilities may be present to a greater or lesser extent, individuals may be more or less "unable" to care for themselves or manage their affairs. Consequently, a statutory definition of the common sort indicates nothing about *how defective* the ability to make decisions must be before an individual is considered incompetent. And it is important to keep in mind that everyone's decision-making abilities – even those who are uncontroversially competent – are to some extent imperfect or defective (that is, no one is a perfectly rational decision-maker in all contexts).

It is not difficult to see how these three conditions – the vagueness of statutory definitions, the failure to recognize the decision-relative nature of competence, and the confusion of a diagnosis of mental illness or neurological disease with a determination of incompetence – encourage the abuses so vividly illustrated by the "Dirty Sally" case. Nevertheless, it does not follow that the appropriate remedy is to try to specify more concretely the statutory definition of incompetence. Although a cautionary statement in the statute to the effect that a diagnosis of mental illness or neurological disease does not itself entail incompetence would be helpful, some vagueness in the definition of incompetence seems unavoidable.

What is needed is a clearer statutory articulation of appropriate standards of incompetence, with emphasis on the factors examined in Chapter 1. This would include, above all, reference to the complexity of information required for the particular decision and the risk involved. Greater clarity on the need for different standards for different decisions is not enough, however. More rigorous procedural safeguards than are presently available in many jurisdictions are needed as well. To help remedy these defects, procedures such as the following might be instituted in all jurisdictions where they are not already present:

- The subject of a guardianship or conservatorship hearing must be notified of the hearing and of the right to appear.

- Hearings are not to proceed without the presence of the individual whose competence is in question unless the individual has submitted a notarized statement waiving the right to appear, or there is well-documented, strong evidence from two or more independent medical or psychiatric experts either that the individual is unable to attend because of the potential of serious harm to him- or herself, or that the individual's attendance would be futile because of his or her level of incapacity. These statements by the physicians should be made under penalty of perjury and should include the last date on which the physician visited the patient.

- For all proposed wards or conservatees who are not represented by counsel, an independent investigation is to be conducted by trained professionals. The report resulting from this investigation – which would include personal, health care, and financial information – must be submitted to the decision-maker and made available to all interested parties.

- Those who petition for a determination of incompetence are to bear the burden of proof that the least restrictive alternative is being taken (subject to appropriate resource constraints) and that the sphere of surrogate authority is as limited as is incompatible with protecting the individual and the legitimate expectations of others.

- Reasonable efforts must be made to restore or enhance competence where possible (e.g., through better medical treatment, nutrition, psychotherapy, or medication to relieve pseudodementia due to depression and other conditions that may be remedied or alleviated).

- Evidence of lack of appropriate decision-making ability must be provided from sources not likely to be biased by conflicts of interest. At the same time, corroborating evidence from those closest to the person is to be given due (though cautious) weight.

- Ongoing surrogate decision making for financial management must be supervised or reviewed periodically (by requiring, for instance, accounting reports from a conservator of the estate at regular intervals, at least where expenditures exceeding some specified level are involved).

These procedural safeguards are not offered here as final formulations of statutory requirements, but rather as a stimulus for further reflection. The specific form that such requirements take will of course be influenced by the particular provisions of existing statutes, and these vary from state to state.

The need for embedding inherently vague definitions of incompetence in a framework of more rigorous safeguards is due in part to the reinforcing effect that pervasive attitudes have on tendencies to subordinate an elderly individual's interests to those who are his or her potential heirs. The following case demonstrates vividly how standards of decision-making ability are sometimes applied in an invidiously discriminatory way to elders, and in so doing promote the financial interests of relatives at the expense of the elderly person's autonomy.

The relatives of an elderly single man petitioned to have him declared incompetent on the grounds that he was making irrational financial decisions.[17] It emerged that the gentleman's "irrationality" consisted of his propensity to send gifts to strangers who had done him some relatively minor service. For example, on more than one occasion he had send roses to a telephone operator who had been especially helpful and courteous. Apparently, the man took great pleasure in such gallantries, and they were very important to him.

It is extremely doubtful that the issue of competence would ever have arisen had the individual in question not been elderly, with the prospect of leaving his assets to his relatives in the not-too-distant future. Here, and in many other cases, behavior that in a younger person would at most be considered quaint or somewhat eccentric (if not charming and generous) is branded irrational – in part because of the prejudice that equates being old with being mentally deficient.

Further, and perhaps more importantly, another erroneous assumption about the appropriate standard of decision-making capacity may be at work in this case – the tendency to impose on the elderly the standards for rational resource allocation that are generally appropriate for younger individuals, but that may in fact be *irrational* for the elderly. It is generally thought that the appropriate pattern of resource allocation decisions for a young or middle-aged adult is one that emphasizes a rather high ratio of savings to current consumption. This is, of course, quite reasonable, granted the crucial assumption that the individual has many years and many opportunities for enjoyment ahead. However, according to the standard economic model of rationality, what is rational for a young or middle-aged person may be irrational for an older one. In principle, perfectly rational elderly people might choose to spend their last penny as they draw their last breath.

It is a sad irony that in some cases the elderly are judged to be incompetent simply because they are behaving rationally. So long as the elderly individual does not squander his or her resources in such a way as to become a financial burden on others or to renege on obligations to his or her family, the fact that the person's consumption pattern differs from that characteristic of younger rational individuals is no reason whatever for challenging competence.

The relative lack of due process and procedural safeguards that often characterize "formal" determinations of incompetence is especially striking when contrasted with the elaborate protections available in two other legal methods for curtailing an individual's basic civil and political rights: criminal prosecution and involuntary civil commitment proceedings. In the recent past, safeguards for involuntary civil commitment were often grossly deficient, but legal reforms and changes in attitudes toward "mental illness" have done much to improve the situation. On the face of it, it is somewhat puzzling that comparatively little attention has been paid to the problems of error and abuse in guardianship and conservatorship, once it is recognized that the deprivation of freedom that results is sometimes almost as great as in criminal incarceration or internment in a mental hospital.

A standard explanation of the traditional lack of adequate safeguards in guardianship and conservatorship proceedings is that all involved have acted on the assumption that rigorous safeguards are not necessary because everything that is done is for the benefit of the alleged incompetent. The assumption of benevolent intentions, it is said, allows those in roles of authority – including judges and agents of public protective agencies – to view guardianship and conservatorship proceedings as essentially cooperative enterprises in which the adversarial approach (which is found in its most extreme form in criminal proceedings) is unnecessary. There are problems, however, both with the assumption itself and with appealing to it as an explanation of current practices.

The assumption that rigorous safeguards are not needed because everything is directed toward the best interest of the alleged incompetent is too facile. As has been noted earlier, appeals to the needs to protect that individual are often nothing more than smokescreens for the conflicting interests of others, especially their financial interests. But perhaps almost as important is the fact that even genuinely benevolent intentions can lead to disastrous results when the would-be benefactor is mistaken about what would be best for the individual the benefactor sincerely hopes to help.

Moreover, the "beneficient intentions" explanation does not fully explain why safeguards for involuntary civil commitments in general have recently been strengthened, while those for guardianship and conservatorship have not received as much attention – since it is generally assumed that a chief purpose of involuntary civil commitment is to protect (and, where possible, to benefit) the "mentally ill." It seems more likely that one reason why reforms in guardianship and conservatorship have lagged behind is that abuses are less publicly visible, more widely dispersed, and, in some cases, more subtle.

III. HOW SURROGATES ACTUALLY DECIDE FOR THOSE ELDERLY INDIVIDUALS WHO ARE CONSIDERED TO BE INCOMPETENT

Both the enormous diversity of types of decisions made by surrogates for elderly persons who are deemed incompetent and the current dearth of empirical studies of surrogate behavior make it impossible to offer systematic generalizations about how surrogates actually make decisions. This chapter will have achieved a salutory result if it succeeds in calling attention to the need for further empirical research.

One area in which a picture of the behavior of surrogate decision-makers has emerged is that of medical care, largely because decisions concerning the use of life-sustaining treatment elicit more public attention than "merely financial" decisions. Information is also more likely to be available because of the institutional context in which medical decisions are made.

The data that do exist in this area suggest that health care professionals often fail to recognize and facilitate the family's presumptive role as surrogate. First, there is direct evidence (presented earlier in this chapter) that physicians frequently make critical decisions – in particular, those concerning resuscitation – without significant participation by the family of the incompetent patient. Second, as was noted earlier, a number of studies of the behavior of physicians toward competent patients, as well as several recent court cases and the "Do Not Resuscitate" studies, indicate that many physicians still behave as if the requirement of informed consent is a hollow legalistic ritual.[18] Such physicians do not, in fact, adequately recognize the competent patient's right of self-determination. Indeed, two of the most careful and comprehensive studies of informed consent now available concur in how far practice is from the doctrine's ideal:

> Nowhere in the hospital did we see decision-making and communication patterns that looked very much the way they were supposed to look under the ethical doctrine of informed consent.[19]
>
> It is not unduly harsh to conclude that current informed consent policy has been a dismal failure in the settings we studied, at least when measured against the loftier goals of the doctrine.[20]

To a large extent, this disregard of the competent patient's rights is rooted in a paternalist attitude, according to which the physician is supposed to be the principal decision-maker. Indeed, the evidence suggests that physicians often take it upon themselves to act as surrogates for incompetent patients, even when family members are available and qualified to play that role.

IV. SOME IMPORTANT TRENDS IN RECENT CASE LAW

Evolving case law also provides indications of how surrogates actually decide for elderly patients, although it would be naive to assume that compliance with the law is perfect. Current trends in case law are important not only because the perception about legal permissibility of certain ways of making decisions can influence a surrogate's behavior, but also because new legal developments frequently serve as a kind of official recognition of the acceptability of practices that have already become widespread. With the exception of *Quinlan* (1976) all the cases cited below involved elderly patients, and the *Quinlan* ruling itself laid down general principles that are applied most frequently to the elderly.

No attempt will be made here to expand the analysis already presented in Chapter 2 to provide a comprehensive survey of recent doctrine as it affects the substance of surrogate decision making. Instead, it will suffice to highlight what appear to be the most significant recent developments as they bear on the subject of this chapter. Although the judicial rulings considered in the highly selective discussion that follows all involve decisions about medical care or treatment, their import is much broader. In part, this is because they rely upon the guidance principles set out in Chapter 2, and these are so general as to cover the whole range of decisions, both medical and nonmedical.

Three developments in influential recent court rulings are especially significant:

- There is a growing recognition of the right of an appropriate surrogate to refuse life-sustaining treatment or care for an incompetent, even in the absence of an advance directive authorizing refusal.
- Courts are rejecting the view that forgoing the use of sophisticated life-sustaining devices such as respirators is sometimes permissible but that withholding other procedures such as artificial feeding is never permissible. They seem to be moving toward acceptance of the fact that any sort of life-support may sometimes justifiably be withheld or withdrawn.
- Courts are showing an increasing awareness that substituted judgment is an appropriate guidance principle

only for incompetents who previously were competent, not for all incompetents.

It is too early to say with confidence that each of these
three elements will become firmly entrenched in the law in
all or even in most jurisdictions.

Four recent rulings exhibit the growing recognition of
the legal right of a surrogate to refuse treatment for an
incompetent in the absence of an advance directive. The
New Jersey Supreme Court's extremely influential 1976
ruling in *In re Quinlan* has received such wide attention
that it is not necessary to present its details here.[21] For
present purposes, *Quinlan's* chief significance is its affirma-
tion of the right of the family or other legal guardian to
serve as surrogates, and recognition of their right to refuse
life-prolonging treatment through the exercise of substituted judgment in the absence of an advance directive.
Perhaps just as important, this ruling also recognized that
if such awesome decision-making authority is to be
accorded the family or other legal guardian, then the incompetent's interests must be protected by impartial institutional safeguards in the form of review of the family's
decision by a "hospital ethics committee" although in fact
the Court only asked for a confirmation of the patient's
prognosis from the Ethics Committee). The significance
of this second element of the *Quinlan* ruling is that it
marked the beginning of an attempt to develop new institutional arrangements to enhance the quality of decision
making. It represents an effort to remedy the defects of
purely private decision making without taking decisions
out of the hands of those closest to the patient and turning
them over to judges who are often ill equipped to make
them.

In the more recent Brother Fox case, the New York
Supreme Court also affirmed the right of a surrogate to
request removal of a respirator as an exercise of substituted
judgment.[22] The court accepted evidence from the

patient's guardian and long-time friend that Brother Fox, an elderly Catholic priest who became permanently comatose after suffering a stroke during surgery to repair a hernia, had, when competent, clearly expressed a desire not to be sustained in such a condition.

In *Severns v. Wilmington Medical Center* (1980), the husband of a woman who became permanently comatose due to injuries received in an automobile accident petitioned to be appointed guardian of her person with authorization to request removal of "all medical supportive measures that were keeping [her] alive."[23] Chancery Court granted the husband's request, and the Deleware Supreme Court upheld the ruling. Both courts affirmed that an appropriate surrogate (in this case, the spouse) can refuse life-sustaining measures through an exercise of substituted judgment.

In its decision the Delaware Supreme Court interpreted "medical supportive measures" as including the use of a respirator, the administering of antibiotics to combat infection, and the surgical insertion of a feeding tube. It also stated that no order requiring cardiopulmonary resuscitation was to be written in the woman's chart. Although the husband had also explicitly requested the removal of a nonsurgically inserted nasogastric feeding tube, the court omitted this form of nutrition from the list of "medical supportive measures."

As noted in Chapter 2, such a distinction between different methods of feeding as such is ethically arbitrary. In fact, the reasons the Delaware Supreme Court gave for allowing the withholding of a respirator and a surgically inserted feeding tube apply with equal force to the nasogastric tube as well, although the court failed to draw this implication. Although the language was not as clear as it might have been, the court held that "medical support" could be withheld if it gave no reasonable prospect of providing benefit to the patient without disproportional harm. If consistently applied, this ruling can also justify withholding forms of treatment or care that the Delaware court did not include under the rubric of "medical support."

The ruling of the New Jersey Supreme Court in *In re Conroy* (1983) also affirmed the principle that the surrogate can refuse life-sustaining measures for an incompetent patient, but it went further in two respects.[24] First, unlike *Severns, Conroy* did not distinguish between surgical and nonsurgical insertion of a feeding tube, and the court very forcefully held that there is no distinction to be drawn between withholding use of a respirator and withholding feeding by intravenous line or nasogastric tube. Although *Conroy* stopped short of explicitly affirming that any form of care, including "natural" feeding (by spoon), may also be withheld when doing so is required by substituted judgment or the best interest principle, apparently this form of support was not at issue in the case (since the patient could not swallow, and so could not be fed in this way). Even more clearly than in *Severns,* the New Jersey Supreme Court's reasons for allowing withholding of "artificial" feeding support the withholding of natural feeding as well. Drawing on the report of the President's Commission, *Deciding to Forgo Life-Sustaining Treatment,* the New Jersey Supreme Court argued convincingly that the appropriate question is whether feeding, like any other life-support measure, accords with what the patient would want if competent or, where this is not or cannot be known, whether it provides the patient with a balance of benefits over burdens. The decision-relative concept of competence was also explicitly acknowledged by *Conroy*.[25]

Conroy and *In re Storar* (1980) both clearly affirm the limitations of substituted judgment as a guidance principle for surrogate decision making.[26] Reversing the error of the Massachusetts Supreme Judicial Court's earlier ruling in *Saikewicz, Conroy* and *Storar* acknowledge that substituted judgment is only applicable to individuals who previously were competent. *Conroy* does this by articulating a best interest standard for cases in which a decision cannot be based on the individual's previous values and preferences. The New York Supreme Court in *Storar* held that the question of what the individual would choose if competent has no sense when applied to a lifelong incompetent such as John Storar, who was profoundly retarded from birth.

According to the ethical analysis laid out in Chapter 2, each of the three developments found in the court cases discussed here marks a significant advance in legal guidance for surrogate decision making. Further progress in the law will require many more decisions, however. Rulings in one jurisdiction at most provide guidance but not precedents in other jurisdictions, and some issues have not yet been squarely joined by any higher courts. In particular, further refinements of the case law are needed to reinforce legal recognition of the fact that it is arbitrary to distinguish between respirator support and feeding (whether "natural" or "artificial") – in other words, that it is arbitrary to distinguish between technological and non-technological forms of life support. Just as importantly, additional rulings will be needed to clarify the scope and limits of the authority conferred by advance directives and to interpret rapidly developing legislation designed to give advance directives legal effect.

V. ADVANCE DIRECTIVES AND OTHER PLANNING APPROACHES: WHO USES THEM AND HOW EFFECTIVE ARE THEY?

The phrase "advance directive" usually refers to *living wills* and *durable powers of attorney,* a convention that we have followed. In Chapters 2 and 3 we set out the arguments supporting the use of advance directives and attempted to ascertain the general contours of the scope and limits of their moral authority. Here we examine critically the concrete *legal framework* in which advance directives are employed. The present chapter provides an appropriate place to do so, since advance directives will most frequently come into play in decisions for elderly patients.

A. Living wills

Two recurrent criticisms of living wills as advance directives have been that they are too general and vague to provide clear guidance on decisions to forgo life-sustaining treatment or care and that the documents themselves have no legal effect. Granted the difficulty of anticipating in detail every medical contingency, the former objection seems largely unanswerable. Natural death acts enacted in 38 states and the District of Columbia go part but not all of the way toward meeting the second objection.

For the most part, these statutes provide immunity – from criminal prosecution, from civil liability, and in some cases from professional disciplinary action – for health care providers who comply in good faith with a living will. However, like the California Natural Death Act (which in many states served as a model), these statutes do *not* impose civil or criminal penalties on a health care provider who *refuses* to comply. In some cases, the legislation states that if a physician cannot in good conscience comply, then he or she ought to facilitate transfer of the patient to the care of another physician (who will comply). But no civil or criminal liability is specified if the physician fails to do so.

In addition, some natural death acts have duplicated a much criticized error of the California statute by counting as a "qualified patient" only an individual with a "terminal condition," defined as an incurable condition in which death is "imminent" *regardless of whether life-sustaining procedures are used*. The California law also added two other conditions for a valid living will: (1) The patient must wait fourteen days after learning that his or her condition is terminal before completing the living will, and, (2) the patient must be competent to sign the living will at the time he or she does so. The obvious catch here is that very few persons will satisfy both these criteria: Few will be alive – much less competent – fourteen days after it is determined that death is "imminent" regardless of what is done. Further, to restrict valid living wills in cases in which death is imminent regardless of whether vigorous support is given or not is to rob this form of advance directive of much of its value. The purpose of a living will is not simply to enable a person to ensure that undeniably futile measures will not be taken; it also, and perhaps mainly, is designed to ensure that care will not be provided that produces only minimal benefits in proportion to the burdens it involves, or that merely prolongs unconscious life. For this reason, it is also essential that the legal validity of a living will not depend upon the individual being *terminally* ill.

B. Durable powers of attorney

Dissatifaction with living wills has led to greater interest in durable powers of attorney. Two kinds exist: general, and limited explicitly to health care.

1. General durable power of attorney: The general durable power of attorney is a document that a person, the "principal," signs in order to appoint another person or persons as "attorney in fact," with full or limited powers to act in the place of and on behalf of the principal. The general durable power of attorney can in principle be quite comprehensive, at least for financial matters. It can empower the attorney in fact to do everything that the principal could do with his or her assets: pay bills, apply for or disburse loans, sell or acquire property, and so on. Unlike the traditional power of attorney, this document is effective even if the principal is totally incapacitated and unable to make informed judgments.

The general durable power of attorney can be of two varieties. In the first type, the power to act is not effective until the principal actually becomes incompetent. In theory, the principal maintains control until he or she is no longer able to do so, and the attorney in fact cannot act before that time. A test (or set of criteria) for determining incompetence must be established and satisfied before this document will actually go into effect. The traditional and most common procedure is to have incompetence established by two physicians, including the principal's attending physician and, in some cases, an appropriate specialist. Although less formal and demanding criteria are sometimes used, they can be ambiguous and unreliable. This is particularly a problem when a dispute arises regarding an action taken by the attorney in fact. It might be objected, for instance, that the principal was not truly incompetent at the time the attorney in fact acted, and that the attorney in fact's power was therefore illegally exercised. This would render prior decisions invalid or, at minimum, questionable. Such a challenge to the attorney in fact's authority can have serious implications for third parties who rely on such documents.

The second type of general durable power of attorney becomes effective immediately and remains in effect after the principal is declared incompetent. This approach may be more appropriate for the elder who, although not yet incompetent to execute the document, is already suffering from some degree of dementia (or some other form of physical or mental illness) because its force does not depend upon a finding of incompetence.

2. Durable power of attorney for health care: A general durable power of attorney can in principle be used to appoint a proxy for health care decisions as well as for nonmedical matters such as property management. However, reliance on a general durable power of attorney in health care matters does not provide the best protection for all concerned, at least where a durable power of attorney for health care is available. Use of the general kind is liable to be challenged on two counts: General durable powers of attorney were not specifically designed for health care decisions, and there is a widespread consensus that such decisions, especially those that are a matter of life and death, require special safeguards.

More than forty states have general durable power of attorney statutes. Pennsylvania, California, and Rhode Island have statutes that create a special durable power of attorney for health care, and it is very likely that other states will soon follow suit. Because California's statute is rather carefully drawn and specific, it will serve as the focus of this discussion.[27]

The California Durable Power of Attorney for Health Care empowers a competent adult, using a rather uncomplicated printed form, to designate an agent (or "attorney in fact") to serve as his or her proxy for a broad range of health care decisions. Unlike a living will, it is not restricted to decisions concerning life-sustaining treatment or care. Five types of decisions are, however, explicitly excluded from the proxy's authority: commitment to or placement in a mental health treatment facility, electroconvulsive therapy, psychosurgery, sterilization, and abortion.

Aside from these specific exclusions, the proxy "may make health care decisions for you to the same extent you could make them for yourself . . . were you competent to do so." This last statement is at once both reassuring and unsettling. As explained earlier in this book, there is a broad consensus on the legal right of the competent person to refuse treatment, but there are still areas of disagreement. In particular, legal doctrine on the status of feeding (in various forms) as opposed to other life-sustaining measures (such as respirators) is at this point ambiguous, if not contradictory. The California Durable Power of Attorney for Health Care does not itself resolve – and should not be expected to resolve – the issue of whether a proxy may refuse feeding, or only certain methods of feeding, for an incompetent patient.

There is another unclarity in the California law concerning the forgoing of life support. Any "affirmative or deliberate act or omission to end life other than . . . to permit the natural process of dying" is explicitly forbidden. The difficulty lies in the phrase, "the natural dying process," which suggests that there is one predetermined route, with death at its end. But as many physicians have pointed out, for most patients in the final stages of a chronic terminal illness, there is almost always an opportunity to influence the time and manner of death by deliberate actions or omissions. What the law does not specify is whether, for example, refraining from administering antibiotics for pneumonia in a patient with metastatic cancer is "permitting the natural process of dying" or not. Here, as with attempts to draw moral distinctions between methods of feeding, the distinction between "natural" and "artificial" does nothing to resolve the basic moral issues. Using insulin to save a diabetic is "prolonging life by artificial means" and "interfering with the natural process of dying," but this does not make it wrong. The danger is that those physicians who tend to be overaggressive, or those who are unduly influenced by legal counsel whose sole concern is to reduce the probability of liability to zero, will respond to this ambiguity by giving it a very conservative interpretation. If this occurs, then the Durable Power of Attorney for Health Care, like the California Natural Death Act, will have achieved safety at the price of thwarting one of the main purposes of advance directives: to allow people to ensure that their lives will not be prolonged under conditions *they* find unacceptable.

The possibility that the law's unclarity concerning life-support will lead to undue prolongation of life is heightened by its lack of adequate sanctions for a health care provider's failure to comply with the proxy's decisions. A health care provider is not made subject to criminal prosecution, civil liability, or professional disciplinary action if he or she fails to "withdraw health care necessary to keep the principal alive" – even if the proxy refuses permission for such care, the patient would have refused it if competent, and a competent individual has the right to refuse it. Further, the law provides no penalty for a health care provider who, upon refusing such a request, does not facilitate transfer of patient care to another provider who will comply, stating only that refusal to comply or transfer constitutes "unprofessional conduct." Although the California statute's intention to protect the health care provider's right to conscientious refusal is laudable, this could have been achieved without undercutting the principal's right to delegate the right to refuse treatment or care.

A more balanced approach would be to impose civil liability on a provider who refuses to comply with the proxy's decision *unless* that provider takes one of two steps: transferring the patient to the care of a provider who is expected to comply (where one is available), or formally challenging the proxy's decision-making authority by seeking court intervention.

Another way to give the Durable Power of Attorney for Health Care teeth would be through the financial incentives of reimbursement mechanisms. Health care providers could be encouraged to comply with the proxy or transfer the patient by freeing the patient, the family, and the patient's insurance carrier from financial responsibility for the costs of all treatment and care that would not have been provided had the proxy's decision been honored.

The California law also lacks any provision for penalizing a proxy who disregards the instructions of the advanced directive. As with physician noncompliance, it is important to allow a proxy the opportunity to avoid doing something that he or she previously agreed to but that the proxy now finds unconscionable. However, respect for the proxy's values should not be allowed to vitiate the principal's instructions. To avoid this problem, a proxy who refuses to comply with the principal's instructions could be required by law either to relinquish authority to an alternate or to seek court appointment of a guardian (if the principal specified no alternate attorney in fact), or face civil liability.

Although a California Durable Power of Attorney for Heath Care statute includes safeguards to ensure that the execution of the document is witnessed by parties who have no conflict of interest, there is one crucial procedural issue that it leaves unresolved. It does not provide guidelines for how, and by whom, the determination of the principal's incompetence is to be made. Since the statute does not require a formal adjudication of incompetence before the attorney in fact can begin to exercise his or her powers, it leaves the impression that this determination is to be made informally – presumably with the physician and family playing a major role.[28]

The statute implicitly acknowledges the decision-relative nature of competency by including the provision that even after the attorney in fact begins to exercise decision-making authority in some areas, the principal can independently accept or refuse treatment for which he or she is capable of giving informed consent. Nevertheless, safeguards are needed to ensure the integrity of the procedure by which the principal is declared to be incompetent (or incompetent for certain decisions). Perhaps most importantly, a strong case can be made for including in the law provisions to ensure that some evidence from persons other than the individual who is to serve as proxy be required to establish the principal's incompetence. This simple procedural safeguard could help avoid the most obvious conflict of interest. Further, to minimize the possibility of collusion between the health care provider and the proxy, a determination of incompetence by an independent third party would also be appropriate.

It is to be hoped that adequate safeguards can be developed without the drastic step of requiring a judicial determination of incompetence in every or even most cases. Were this to occur, one of the main advantages of the durable power of attorney – avoidance of court intervention – would be undercut. Intrainstitutional guidelines requiring review of competence by an ethics committee, or documentation of an independent third party consultation on competence, are plausible alternatives to both the unstructured approach tacitly encouraged by the California statute and the equally unattractive option of routine recourse to the courts. The purpose of the discussion here, however, is not to focus on any one particular proposal as uniquely correct, but rather to clarify a reasonable range of policy alternatives.

There are two remaining features of the California statute that deserve comment, and that legislators in other states would do well to consider carefully before drafting similar bills. The first has already been mentioned: the exclusion of certain types of decisions from the proxy's sphere of authority. The exclusions were no doubt motivated by a recognition that there is a long and dismaying history of the abusive infliction of these procedures (for example, sterilization, commitment to a mental hospital) on incompetent or allegedly incompetent people. Neverthelsss, since various institutional and legal safeguards are now in effect that were previously lacking, it is necessary to face squarely both the costs and the benefits of such exclusionary safeguards.

One of the exclusions, electroconvulsive therapy, seems especially questionable. This treatment – which is highly successful with some individuals suffering from severe and debilitating depression who are not responsive to other forms of treatment – is not thought to be safer and less traumatic then many surgical or medical treatments that the proxy is allowed to authorize under the statute (including the use of highly toxic cancer drugs). If special safeguards are needed for certain procedures (such as electroconvulsive therapy), then a less extreme approach would be for the law explicitly to exclude them initially from the proxy's authority, but to allow the principal to sign a special authorization for any or all of them.[29]

A second, perhaps even more questionable safeguard in the California statute is that the durable power of attorney dissolves whenever the principal revokes it, either in writing or orally – *regardless of whether he or she is competent at the time of revocation*. Further, the law states that the principal's refusal of any treatment or care always overrides the proxy's decision, again even if the principal is incompetent to make that decision.

Experience with demented patients suggests that this safeguard will in some cases render the durable power of attorney useless, thwarting the principal's efforts to delegate decision-making authority to a trusted person in the event of incompetence. Some demented patients, especially those suffering from Alzheimer's disease, exhibit periods of hostility and anger in which they may stubbornly refuse virtually any form of treatment or care, no matter how beneficial, and no matter how well it serves their lifelong values. To allow this kind of behavior to undercut the proxy's ability to make coherent decisions for the patient would not only thwart the principal's purpose, it also could disrupt the continuity of medical treatment and care. Again, a less debilitating safeguard is worth considering. Attempts by the principal to revoke a durable power of attorney, or determined protests against specific treatments, could trigger a documented reevaluation of competence by an independent party.

Yet another alternative would be to preserve the safeguards of the California law, but to include an option for the principal to sign a special "Ulysses contract" stating either that certain treatments or all treatments are to be provided (or not provided) if the proxy so chooses, even if the principal at the time protests or attempts to revoke the durable power of attorney, so long as the principal is determined to be incompetent at that time. To assume, without argument, that such "self-binding" directives ought not be given statutory support is to exhibit a paternalistic bias.[30]

The purpose of these critical remarks is not to denigrate current legislation on advance directives. On the contrary, advance directives, and especially the durable power of attorney for health care, have a fundamental role to play in the development of more adequate arrangements for decision-making for elderly incompetent people. Carefully crafted legislation will not by itself suffice, however.

In addition there is a large educational task to be undertaken. In 1982, a survey conducted for the President's Commission on Medical Ethics revealed that only 8 percent of a sample of the general public had issued any type of written instructions indicating their preferences about medical treatment. Even in states with living will legislation, patients, their families, and even their physicians are unclear about the terms and procedures of living wills.[31] If anything, knowledge about proxy advance directives is probably even less widely disseminated. In spite of the educational efforts of many organizations – such as Concern for Dying, The Society for the Right to Die, the Hemlock Society, and the American Society for Law and Medicine – much more work remains to be done. It is particularly appropriate that medical societies and medical specialty groups should be in the forefront of the movement to educate the public – and their own memberships – about the opportunities for issuing advance directives. The time for most persons to start thinking about decision making in the case of their incompetence, and about their wishes concerning life-sustaining treatment in particular, is long before the need for them arises. Physicians should begin to build a record and understanding of their patient's wishes, for example by raising the issue in the course of routine care or during periodic physical examinations. Health care institutions such as hospitals and nursing homes also have a role to play in developing policies and practices to ensure that when patients have advance directives their existence becomes known and their provisions are followed.

Especially in the case of the durable power of attorney approach, most elderly people and their families will require legal counsel. The legal profession therefore has an equally important role to play both in educating the public and the medical profession and in ensuring that its own members are adequately informed about the rapidly changing law that governs advance directives. We believe that execution of advance directives should become a regular part of estate planning, and could be done when a will is drawn up or updated. Furthermore, public policy as well as codes of legal ethics should be revised, where needed, to acknowledge frankly that serious abuses can arise when an attorney represents the interests of the family rather than those of the incompetent elderly person.[32] In cases in which the interests of the incompetent individual and those of the family are in conflict, it is unethical for the same attorney to represent both. As the use of durable powers of attorney increases, new fiduciary standards must be developed, not only for the proxy and the health care provider but also for lawyers and others who participate in what may be called the surrogate system.

VI. SUMMARY

At present, most determinations of incompetence are made informally, by many different types of persons in different settings, including family members, physicians, attorneys, and nursing home personnel.

Although determinations of incompetence to make medical decisions need not routinely be accomplished through formal court proceedings, coherent institutional policies are needed within hospitals and nursing homes to ensure that incompetence is determined in an ethically and legally sound way. Such policies would:

- Articulate standards and operational criteria for determining incompetence.
- Fix responsibility on someone in the institution for establishing whether a given person is competent or incompetent to make certain decisions.
- Include effective safeguards against abuse or error.
- Provide guidance as to when court intervention is appropriate.

We have seen that recent studies of one critical type of medical decision – that concerning resuscitation – indicates that many, perhaps most health care institutions lack policies that satisfy these criteria, or have policies but fail to comply with them.

Formal determinations of incompetence appear to be more frequent with respect to nonmedical decision making, in particular concerning finance and placement in a nursing home.

There is considerable evidence of widespread confusion, error, and abuse in the "formal" legal procedures by which elderly individuals are determined to be incompetent to manage their own affairs, and by which surrogates are designated for them. These defects in guardianship and conservatorship proceedings stem from several sources, including the confusion between a diagnosis (of neurological disease or mental illness) and a determination of incompetence, a tendency to overlook the decision-relative nature of competence and to accord the surrogate plenary powers where more limited authority would be adequate, and a failure to provide effective procedural safeguards to minimize distortions due to conflict of interest. To help remedy these defects, more effective procedural safeguards must be introduced into the guardianship and conservatorship process.

In particular, adequate protection of the incompetent may require that ongoing surrogate decision making for financial management be supervised or reviewed periodically. Further, there is evidence that standards of competence applied to elders often reflect a bias against the elderly and inappropriately presuppose patterns of consumption that are reasonable for younger people but not for the elderly.

Case law concerning decision making for elderly incompetent people is rapidly evolving. Most of the more influential recent cases involve medical decisions, but the principles they enunciate have a broader application. Recent court rulings exhibit three especially important developments, all of which are improvements, although they are not yet firmly established in all jurisdictions:

- There is a growing recognition of the right of an appropriate surrogate to refuse life-prolonging treatment or care for an incompetent, even in the absence of an advance directive authorizing refusal.
- Courts are beginning to abandon the view that foregoing the use of sophisticated life-sustaining devices such as respirators is sometimes permissible but that withholding other procedures such as artificial feeding is never permissible; they are beginning to recognize that withholding feeding may sometimes be permissible as well.
- Courts are showing an increasing awareness that substituted judgment is an appropriate guidance principle only for incompetents who previously were competent, not for all incompetents.

At present, only a small minority of people execute advance directives. Legislation to give legal effect to advance directives for health care is developing rapidly. The durable power of attorney for health care provides hitherto unavailable opportunities for comprehensive planning that can maximize an individual's control over his or her future and ease the burdens of those who will care for the person when incompetent. A central issue for those drafting new legislation concerning the durable power of attorney for health care is whether additional provisions, such as the following, ought to be included:

- Clear guidance for how incompetence is to be determined and by whom.
- Effective penalties for health care providers and surrogates who refuse to follow valid advance directives, unless they seek court intervention for a determination of guardianship, or transfer care to another provider or an alternate designated surrogate who will comply.
- An opportunity for the principal to sign a special form (a "Ulysses contract") waiving the exclusion of certain procedures (such as electroconvulsive therapy) from the proxy's authority and/or the right to revoke the durable power of attorney and to refuse treatments the surrogate chooses when the principal has become incompetent (an option that would be plausible only if special safeguards are provided, such as specifying that the principal's refusal to accept treatment or the principal's attempt to revoke the durable power of attorney may only be overridden if there is first an independent, well-documented reevaluation that shows the patient to be clearly incompetent at that time).

The increasing use of advance directives in general, and of the durable power of attorney for health care in particular, necessitates the development of new ethical and legal standards for the fiduciary relationships these documents create. In particular, public policy and codes of legal ethics must recognize that attorneys may be subject to serious conflicts of interest, and that problems may arise when the same attorney represents both the incompetent individual and his or her surrogate.

A massive and diversified educational effort must be undertaken cooperatively – by medical and legal professional organizations, health care institutions, government and private organizations, legal scholars, and medical ethicists – to inform health care professionals, lawyers, judges, and the general public about the specific problems of surrogate decision making for the elderly, and about the institutional resources available for dealing with them.

7. The mentally ill

In this chapter we explore how the general accounts of competence and of the ethical decision-making framework for those judged incompetent apply to the mentally ill. We consider it a virtue of our analysis that it applies equally to the mentally ill and to the treatment of mental illness as to the more common cases of medical treatment of physical illness. Nevertheless, there are several differences in the treatment of mental illness that necessitate a separate discussion. Perhaps most important is the fact that the mental illness itself often, although by no means always, impairs the person's ability to make a competent decision about his or her need for treatment. This occurs, of course, with physical illness as well, but the difference in frequency and directness of impairment of a person's decision-making capacities is important. A second important difference is the common separation of decisions to hospitalize the patient from decisions about treatment of the patient. Some psychiatric patients are involuntarily hospitalized who at the same time are deemed competent to refuse treatment for their illness. This is one of the most controversial features of our system of care for the mentally ill. Physicians responsible for the care of these patients then understandably protest that they are being put in the punitive role of jailers, instead of their proper role as healers.

The third central difference in the care of the mentally ill is that the decision to hospitalize a person involuntarily is often made for the sake of others besides the patient when he or she is deemed dangerous to others, unlike treatment of physical illness, which is nearly always primarily for the sake of the patient. For these cases, our patient–centered model of deciding for incompetents requires extension to bring the interests of others appropriately into the decision-making process.

In what follows, we shall divide the overall discussion into decisions about hospitalization or commitment and decisions about treatment, in order to aid in clarification of the issues, even though these decisions are not always distinguished either conceptually or in practice.

I. DECISIONS ABOUT INVOLUNTARY HOSPITALIZATION OR COMMITMENT

A. The historical context of involuntary commitment

In order to understand the place at which our discussion of civil commitment enters the contemporary policy debate, it is necessary to have before us, at least in barest outline, the recent history of involuntary commitment in the United States.[1] Histories of our mental health treatment laws often describe the changes as wide pendulum swings. At one extreme there are broad or loose criteria for involuntary hospitalization emphasizing the *parens patriae* power of the state to care for those unable to care for themselves. At the other extreme lie narrow or strict criteria emphasizing the civil liberties of the mentally ill to be free from unwanted hospitalization and treatment. For brevity, we may describe this as a pendulum swing between paternalism and individual liberty.

Over most of the last three decades, the laws governing involuntary hospitalization of the mentally ill for treatment of their mental illness have been moving from the paternalistic to the individual liberty extreme, as have the practices that those laws regulate. One dramatic aspect of this shift has been the deinstitutionalization of the mentally ill. The census of patients hospitalized for mental illness declined from a high of 558,000 in 1955 to the current estimated level of less than 120,000 in 1988. In significant part this was a result of the development of powerful new psychotropic drugs that sufficiently control the symptoms of common forms of psychosis, most importantly schizophrenia, to enable most mentally ill persons who had previously required long-term hospitalization now to live and function in the community with appropriate care and support. (Appropriate care and support, however, have often not been provided, as is evident in the large proportion of the previously institutionalized mentally ill among the swelling ranks of the homeless in the United States.) While the deinstitutionalization made possible by new drugs was commonly seen as in the interests of patients, it promised as well economic savings to state governments and their departments of mental health that were the typical funding source for most long-term hospitalization of the mentally ill.

Another powerful motivating force for de-institutionalization was exposés of the squalid and miserable conditions of many hospitals and asylums in which mental patients were sometimes warehoused. Commitment was often too easy, with psychiatrists and other physicians too lax in their gatekeeping role, and too often as well little if any treatment was provided. Finally, an increasing appreciation developed that commitment often leaves patients with a lifelong stigma, a debilitating institutional dependency, and an eroded sense of self-respect. The result was a growing skepticism about the benefits of commitment together with an increased appreciation of the serious harms it did to many patients. The increasingly critical attitude toward mental hospitals, together with development of the powerful new drugs, fueled legal challenges and resultant dramatic changes in

most state laws governing the involuntary hospitalization
of the mentally ill. While the exact language of commitment laws has always varied from state to state, during the
1950s and most of the 1960s the vast majority of states had
broad criteria, judged by today's standards, for the commitment of the mentally ill. These laws typically contained
provision for the involuntary commitment of mentally ill
persons "in need of care and treatment," in addition to
those judged to be dangerous to themselves or others.
These broad substantive criteria were commonly combined with relatively loose or minimal procedural and due
process requirements for establishing that the criteria were
met. For example, in some states the certification of two
physicians, neither of whom needed to be a psychiatrist,
that a person was mentally ill and in need of care and
treatment was sufficient for lengthy involuntary commitment.

In the late 1960s and early 1970s the United States Supreme Court began to apply the strict due process, procedural safeguards of criminal law to delinquency proceedings for juveniles on the grounds that there was a
substantial deprivation of liberty at stake in both types of
cases. In the influential Wisconsin case of *Lessard v. Schmidt*
(1972),[2] constitutionally mandated due process safeguards
comparable to those in criminal proceedings were held to
be required for commitment of the mentally ill. While few
other states have gone the full route of *Lessard* in either
court cases or statutory enactments, most now have due
process requirements substantially stricter than in earlier
decades and broadly similar to criminal requirements. At
the same time, the common, broad substantive commitment criteria came under increasing attack. By the late
1960s, as one commentator notes,

> A number of factors coalesced to increase the
> attractiveness of marked limitations on the state's
> commitment powers – the legitimacy of psychiatric

diagnosis and of the concept of mental illness were under severe attack; the recognition was growing that little effective treatment was being provided in many state hospitals; and the profession itself had embraced an ideology, embodied in the community psychiatry movement, that quetioned the use of hospitalization for the treatment of psychiatric disorders.[3]

Commitment for the benefit of the patient, as in the "need for care and treatment" criteria and traditionally justified under the state's *parens patriae* power, came to be seen as unduly broad in comparison with much narrower paternalistic criteria requiring that a person be a danger of serious physical harm to him- or herself. This dangerousness criterion was often interpreted as requiring a life-threatening condition, with the suicidal person as the paradigm.

Dangerousness to others continued to be recognized as a legitimate criterion for commitment under the state's police power. In 1969 the state of California passed the Lanterman-Petris-Short Act which adopted dangerousness to self or others as the sole ground justifying commitment. The *Lessard* court in 1972, together with similar cases in other states, held that there was a constitutional requirement of a finding of dangerousness to oneself or others before mentally ill persons could be deprived of their liberty through involuntary hospitalization. Nearly all states changed their involuntary commitment laws during the 1970s to conform to the dangerousness to self or others requirement.

Whether dangerousness is legally required by the Constitution for involuntary commitment, however, remains contested. The U.S. Supreme Court has ruled only once on the issue, in *O'Connor v. Donaldson* (1977).[4] While the court in *O'Connor* clearly enunciated a right of involuntarily committed nondangerous patients to receive treatment (the "right to treatment" aspect of *O'Connor*),

its decision was ambiguous on whether nondangerous
mentally ill persons could be involuntarily committed at
all.[5] *O'Connor* has usually been read, however, as requiring dangerousness for commitment, and by the early
1980s the pendulum was probably as far in the direction of
individual liberty as it has been in this century.

In the last few years, however, there is some evidence
that the pendulum may have begun to swing again toward
paternalism. Family groups have become strong advocates
of broadening the involuntary commitment and treatment
laws in order to secure help for their seriously mentally ill,
although nondangerous, family members. In 1982, the
American Psychiatric Association adopted "Guidelines for
Legislation on the Psychiatric Hospitalization of Adults"
that added to the dangerousness criteria the alternative
criterion that the person is likely "to suffer substantial
mental or physical deterioration."[6] The APA Guidelines
interpret harm to self and substantial deterioration to include

> that, as evidenced by recent behavior, the person (1)
> is likely in the near future to inflict substantial physic-
> al harm upon himself, or (2) is substantially unable to
> provide for some of his basic needs, such as food,
> clothing, shelter, health, or safety, or (3) will if not
> treated suffer or continue to suffer severe and abnor-
> mal mental, emotional, or physical distress, and this
> distress is associated with significant impairment of
> judgment, reason, or behavior causing a substantial
> deterioration of his previous ability to function on his
> own.[7]

(Although this is sometimes called the "gravely disabled"
standard, we will refer below more specifically to 2 and 3
in the APA Guidelines as the "deterioration and distress"
standard.)

Several states have recently broadened their commitment criteria in the direction of the older "in need of care

and treatment" standard.[8] How far the pendulum is likely to continue in the future in the direction of broader, increasingly paternalistic commitment standards is, of course, uncertain. Our purpose in the preceding sketch has not been to lay the basis for speculations about the future course of commitment laws, but to place our discussion of an ethical framework for commitment decisions in at least some minimal historical context. We turn now to that framework.

B. Patient-centered commitment – danger to self versus need for care and treatment

It is important to distinguish between rationales for involuntary commitment that appeal to prevention of harm (whether broadly or narrowly construed) to the person to be committed and those that appeal to prevention of harm likely to be caused to others by the person to be committed.[9] We argued in Chapter 1 that when treatment is primarily for the benefit of the patient, the free and informed choice of the patient, including the choice of no treatment, should be accepted unless the patient has been found to be incompetent to make that decision. Criteria for involuntary commitment that appeal to the good of the person committed should always include the requirement that the person him- or herself is incompetent to make a decision about hospitalization, or "lacks the capacity to make an informed decision concerning treatment," as the APA Guidelines put it.[10] Our view that competence is task- and situation-specific implies that a person's competence to make a decision about hospitalization for treatment of mental illness cannot always be reliably inferred from his or her competence to make other non-medical decisions, such as management of financial affairs, nor even from his or her competence to make other medical treatment decisions.

The competence evaluation must address a person's capacity to decide about whether to accept hospitalization and the likely treatment(s) it will make possible. This will require a capacity to be informed about and to understand his or her prognoses both with and without hospitalization. It will also require some understanding of the nature of the expected benefits and risks of hospitalization itself and of the likely treatments to be offered in-hospital, together with their attendant probabilities. As with other medical treatment decision making, no substantial technical, biochemical understnding of treatments is commonly necessary. Instead all that is needed is an understanding of how alternative treatments, including the alternative of no treatment, are likely to affect the person's life and capacity to pursue various aims and values in life. The person must then be able to apply his or her aims and values to the available alternatives in order to decide which will be best for him or her.

The general discussion of competence in Chapter 1 divided the capacities needed for competent decision-making into three: understanding, reasoning, and applying values. Severe mental illness, in particular psychosis, can affect all three of these capacities. Delusional beliefs common in some forms of schizophrenia can lead to an inability to become adequately informed about treatment alternatives. For example, a person may persist in a fixed delusional belief that proferred medications are poison or are being used to control his or her mind. Such delusions or fixed false beliefs obviously may also impair a person's capacity to reason about whether hospitalization and treatment will on balance serve his or her well-being. Severe mental illness can also affect and seriously distort a person's underlying and enduring aims and values, his or her conception of his or her own good, that one must use in evaluating hospitalizaton and treatment for an illness. For example, severe depression can result in a person no longer caring about the aims and projects that before the onset of depression had given meaning and value to life, while mania may lead a person to pursue grandiose and unrealistic new plans and projects. Delusional belief systems can lead persons to adopt aims and behaviors that may come to dominate their lives, such as avoiding imagined persecutors, although these aims and behaviors would be senseless and worthless to them if not for their psychotic delusions.

The general point is a simple but important one: mental illness often attacks the same thought processes that are necessary for competent decisions about hospitalization. It is equally important to bear in mind, however, that even effects of mental illness like delusional beliefs can be quite focused and isolated, in some cases having no effect at all on a person's capacity for decision making about hospitalization. Consequently, in any case of questionable or borderline competence the person's specific decision making about hospitalization must be examined and evaluated, and mental illness will be a basis for a judgment of incompetence only when the mental illness seriously affects the person's reasoning about whether to accept hospitalization. More specifically, mental illness is a sufficient ground for finding a person's refusal of hospitalization incompetent *only if* it impairs decision making such that, but for that impairment either (1) the person would consent in the circumstances to hospitalization for treatment of his or her mental illness,[11] or (2) it is uncertain whether the person would consent or refuse and so a surrogate must be empowered to decide for him or her.[12]

Another important feature of our general analysis of competence was that competence is choice-specific, not merely decision-specific. Thus, a person might be competent to consent to hospitalization, but not to refuse it, and vice versa. This feature of competence determinations follows from central components of our variable-standard analysis of the level of decision-making capacity appropriately required for competence, and from our thesis that the essential function of the competence determination is to settle whether a person's voluntary choice about treatment will be respected or whether instead a surrogate must decide for him or her.

The central values at stake in that determination are respecting persons' interests in deciding for themselves when they are able (their self-determination) and protecting them from the harmful consequences of their choices when their decision making is seriously defective (their well-being). The importance of each of these values can vary considerably in different cases with mentally ill persons. The value of choosing for oneself can diminish significantly when a person's decision making is seriously distorted by mental illness. Perhaps even more important, the harm or lost benefit that will result from accepting the person's choice can very substantially, especially between choices to accept or refuse potentially beneficial treatment. The different level of competence that may be appropriate for a person's acceptance versus refusal of hospitalization, then, follows from the very different consequences for that person's well-being that can attend the two different choices of acceptance or refusal of hospitalization.

We noted about competence evaluations generally that there are two respects in which what is required may vary: first, in the degree to which the person must approximate an ideal of unimpaired, defect-free decision making; second, in the degree of certainty of the evaluator that the person meets the appropriate standard. The first judgment is often inescapably a matter of ethical controversy, and the second often leaves the evaluator with significant ineliminable uncertainty. Other things being equal, the more adverse the consequences appear for a person's well-being of accepting her refusal of hospitalization, the higher the decisionmaking standard that is reasonably imposed for her choices. Similarly, the greater the perceived risk to the individual, the more certain evaluators of competence should be that that standard is met before that person's refusal is respected.

In effect, substantive criteria embodied in law for paternalistic civil commitment specify a threshold of risk to a person's well-being if he or she refuses hospitalization – a threshold that must be met if involuntary hospitalization is to be justified. At present, this is most often done with some version of the "danger to self" criterion. The principal point of current policy controversy is whether this should be expanded to include some version of a "deterioration and distress" criterion, as recommended in the APA Guidelines.[13]

We believe that in consideration of individual cases, as opposed to broader legal policy, there is no principled ethical basis for claiming that involuntary hospitalization of the mentally ill for their own good should be limited by a narrowly interpreted "danger to self" criterion, understood as meaning the imminent likelihood of life-threatening or other serious physical harm. A balancing of the effects on a person's well-being of accepting his or her refusal of hospitalization requires an assessment of all such effects, not simply the threat of violent or suicidal behavior. Those effects may include other non-life-threatening harms to the person's health or other important interests. In addition, it is important to take into account the loss of whatever benefits in restoration of function hospitalization and treatment would likely bring. The examples of homeless mentally ill persons who are able to meet their basic needs sufficiently so as not to satisfy dangerousness requirements, but who are overwhelmed and imprisoned by their illness and delusional states, show that not all serious harm to self is physical harm.

A narrow "danger to self" criterion may reflect the conclusion that involuntary hospitalization, at least for a significant period of time, is always a serious infringement of a person's important liberty interest and so requires a substantial threshold of harm prevention to be justified.

While this may be granted, there is little reason to believe
that only a threat of serious bodily harm, much less only a
suicidal threat to life itself, is a substantial enough threat to
a person's well-being to justify even a short period of
involuntary hospitalization and treatment.

The two most important categories of mentally ill persons missed by a "danger to self" criterion are nondangerous   chronic   schizophrenics   and   nondangerous
manic-depressives. Consider the familiar case of a young
chronic schizophrenic whose symptoms are managed reasonably well on medication, but who then ceases to comply with treatment. To satisfy a narrow dangerousness
standard, such a person may have to deteriorate substantially—while the mental health professionals treating
the person and the person's concerned family members can
only look on powerless to intervene—until he or she
reaches a point where the illness becomes life-threatening
or threatens other serious bodily harm. Likewise, chronic
manic-depressives often do not reach a point where they
are a "danger to self" during severe manic episodes,
although their behavior before they reach this extreme
may leave them and their families in a financial and emotional shambles from destroyed careers and marriages,
squandered savings, and the like.

It seems likely that many persons, perhaps most, would
want treatment for themselves, including involuntary
hospitalization when that is necessary to treat their mental
illness, in the event that they were to become noncompliant schizophrenic or manic-depressive persons of
this sort. The point is simply that nearly anyone with the
usual regard for him- or herself would fhave a concern for
these other serious effects on his or her well-being, not
simply the threat of serious physical harm. A person
would be concerned about *all* the significant adverse
effects or risks of involuntary hospitalization and treatment, which will vary from case to case and in many
instances may be substantial, as well as about *all* the likely

and significant harms prevented and benefits secured by hospitalization and treatment. Few would deny that there are many nondangerous mentally ill persons, such as young chronic schizophrenics or manic-depressives, who on balance could be substantially benefitted by a period of involuntary hospitalization. Few also would deny that there are any such persons whose decision to refuse hospitalization is so seriously disordered by their illness that acting to protect or promote their well-being is more important than respecting their expressed refusal of hospitalization. If criteria for civil commitment aimed paternalistically at only the benefit of the patient are justifiably restricted to narrow "danger to self" criteria, this cannot be because there are no nondangerous individuals who could be sufficiently benefitted by commitment.

Support for narrow paternalistic criteria limited to the serious danger to self requirement comes largely from two sources. The first source is an historical appreciation of some of the conditions that led to the earlier tightening of commitment requirements—the miserable conditions in some hospitals, the inadequate or negligible treatment often provided in them, and the lasting stigma and dependency often left by commitment—together with a concern lest they be allowed to recur. This concern fuels the second worry that a general legal policy of committing the nondangerous would not be justifiable because of likely misuse or abuse of the policy.

But whether only narrow danger-to-self criteria are justified even as a matter of general legal policy is highly problematic. The argument for these narrow criteria would have to be that broader criteria, such as the APA's "deterioration and distress" version, although they would permit involuntary hospitalization in some individual cases in which it is justified, would inevitably also lead to its use in individual cases in which it is ethically unjustified, *and* that these latter cases would likely be sufficiently frequent and serious so as to make broader commitment criteria on balance ethically unjustified.[14] It is an important feature of the policy debate on this specific issue that it turns importantly on at least four different kinds of contested points. First, there is disagreement about where and how sharp the boundary is between the mentally ill, who might be subject to involuntary treatment, and others with unusual, eccentric, or even weird beliefs and characters, but without mental illness. Second, there are disputes, with deeply interwoven empirical and evaluative components, about the nature and value of the treatment that would be administered under broadened commitment laws. Third, there are the speculative empirical issues about the *number* of persons with mental illness of specific types and degrees of seriousness who cannot now be committed under "danger to self" criteria but who would be benefitted by commitment under broader criteria, as opposed to the *number* and types of persons who would not be sufficiently benefitted by commitment under broader criteria, but who nevertheless inevitably would be unjustifiably committed and harmed under them. Fourth, there are conflicting ethical judgments of the relative *seriousness* of failing to hospitalize some mentally ill persons who would be significantly benefitted by hospitalization, as compared with involuntarily hospitalizing some persons who are not sufficiently benefitted by that hospitalization.

Even setting aside the first two disputes about the nature of mental illness and its treatment, the policy disagreement about broadening commitment criteria will likely remain intractable because of the very limited data available for settling these empirical issues, and because of the sharp disagreements in our society about the relative ethical seriousness of wrongfully depriving some persons of their liberty as opposed to failing to hospitalize and treat some mentally ill persons in need of care.[15] It is doubtful that this ethical disagreement can be resolved fully, even if greater clarity of argument and empirical evidence are brought to bear on it, although these would surely help somewhat. On the empirical issues, well-designed studies could substantially improve on the present paucity of relevant data. It is also important to bear in mind that any data concerning the kinds and numbers of persons who would or would not be committed under "danger to self" criteria and under broader "deterioration and distress" criteria are always relative both to the specific procedural and due process safeguards employed with those criteria and to the economic and other incentives to which participants in the commitment process are subject. We do not address in this book the many details of legal and institutional design of procedures appropriate for decisions about involuntary hospitalization of the mentally ill. Our focus instead is primarily on the prior conceptual and ethical issues that ought to guide the design of procedures. However, if the common current restriction to the dangerousness standard is abandoned in favor of broader "deterioration and distress" or "need for care and treatment" criteria for civil commitment, then well-designed and relatively strict procedural and due process requirements will become increasingly important. Such procedural requirements would be necessary in order to provide reasonable assurance that the wider net cast by the broader criteria does not catch too many persons for whom involuntary hospitalization is not warranted.

C. Society-centered commitment— dangerousness to others

Most states include among their criteria for involuntary commitment some version of the condition that the person by reason of mental illness represents a serious danger to others. While it is generally assumed that hospitaliztion will entail treatment of the person hospitalized although this is not always so, as we shall see in Section II and that the treatment will be of benefit to the patient, it is specifically the protection of *others* that here warrants the person's involuntary confinement and treatment in a hospital.

The patient-centered account of deciding for others developed earlier in this volume is not adequate for these other-regarding decisions. Its analysis of competence as a variable standard makes the proper level of decision-making capacity required for a particular choice depend on a balancing of two values—protecting the patient from the harmful consequences of his or her choice about treatment when the patient's decision making is seriously defective while also respecting his or interest in making important decisions about his or her own life when able to do so. Moreover, the principal ethical values that we have argued should guide surrogates when deciding for persons deemed to be incompetent to decide for themselves are these same values of patient self-determination and patient well-being. Just as the informed consent doctrine in general excludes the interests of others from the physician-patient relationship and from health care treatment decision making when the patient is competent (except to the extent the patient him- or herself gives weight to others' interests), so our account of the determination of patient incompetence and of principles for surrogate decision making for incompetent patients excludes the interests of others as well. (Considerations of distributive justice, which sometimes require exceptions to this general approach, were discussed in detail in Chapter 4.)

Our general ethical framework for deciding for others when they are incapacitated from deciding for themselves attempts to replicate, so far as possible, the decision the paitent would have made in the circumstances were he or she competent, and thus the guiding values are *patient* self-determination and *patient* well-being. It cannot likewise be assumed for all mentally ill patients who are dangerous to others, however, that were their decision making not affected by their mentall illness they would choose to have themselves involuntarily committed because of the danger they pose to others. Some persons who are mentally ill and a danger to others might well choose, were they competent and not mentally ill, to give less or no weight to the danger they pose to others when weighed against their own loss of liberty if involuntarily hospitalized and treated. While it might be reasonable to assume that disinterested third parties would give equal weight to the interests of mentally ill persons and to the interests of any other person to whom they pose a danger, it is not reasonable to assume that any mentally ill person him- or herself would, if competent, give equal weight to his or her own and another's interests, much less give overriding weight to the other's interests. Some persons might do so, but it is surely not reasonable to assume that all would do so, given the obvious fact that most persons who *are* competent and not mentally ill choose most of the time to give greater weight to their own interests than to the interests of most others.

The involuntary commitment of mentally ill persons on grounds of dangerousness to others requires, therefore, not an ethical framework for deciding *for* others, but an ethical framework for deciding *about* others. There should be no pretense that such decisions are always paternalistic decisions under the state's *parens patriae* power to care for persons unable to care for themselves and guided only by the interests of the mentally ill person. They are decisions taken under the state's *police* power for the purpose of protecting the others to whom the mentally ill person poses a serious danger.

One important implication of this view is that a finding of incompetence, that is, of the mentally ill person's incapacity to make an informed decision about hospitalization, should *not* be required for all involuntary commitment of mentally ill persons who pose a serious danger to others.[16] The operative requirement in these cases is their dangerousness to others by reason of their mental illness, independent of their capacity to make a decision about their need for hospitalization and treatment.[17] But this immediately raises two related questions: What is the relevance of the persons' mental illness? Why are persons who are dangerous to others treated differently depending on whether or not they are also mentally ill?

These questions are more pressing still once we notice how great the difference is between how mentally ill and non-mentally ill dangerous persons are dealt with.[18] The critical difference is that dangers posed to others by non-mentally ill persons are dealt with largely through the criminal law which prohibits various actions, such as assault and homicide, that cause harms to others. Instead of employing preventive detention of dangerous persons before they act to harm others, however, intervention under the criminal law is either prevention only of the criminal act itself or punishment of the wrongdoer after the prohibited action has taken place. Civil commitment of the mentally ill who are judged to be dangerous to others, on the other hand, is *always* preventive detention, since even when a history of violence or other harmful acts towards others is required, it is required only as evidence in support of the determination that the person now poses a danger of acting to cause harm to others in the future.

The underlying assumption of the criminal law is that persons are generally capable of understanding and conforming their behavior to the rules of criminal law that prohibit actions causing specific harms to others. The criminal law then can be understood as what H. L. A. Hart has called a choosing system, announcing to those governed by it either to refrain from proscribed acts like homicide or suffer punishment.[19] Understood in this way, only those who have in fact chosen to violate the criminal prohibitions, not those who might do so at some unspecified time in the future, *deserve* punishment. The criminal law announces that certain acts are not to be done, but then leaves persons free to choose whether to conform, and holds them accountable for their decisions. Of course, police will prevent, for the protection of the victim, a criminal act in process, but that is vastly different from detention to prevent some possible criminal act at some unspecified time in the future. The excuses that relieve a person of accountability for criminal punishment—roughly, coercion, inability to conform to the law, and non-culpable ignorance of the nature of one's action—are to insure that the lawbreaker's action was intentional and voluntary, and so in turn that he is *fairly* held accountable for his behavior. Use of the criminal law instead of measures of preemptive prevention to control behavior harmful to others reflects the substantial value our society places on individual self-determination, liberty, and responsibility.

If the dangerous mentally ill are justifiably treated differently, it must be because they are not capable of responsibly controlling their behavior that is dangerous to others as required by criminal prohibitions. As a result, they are not subject to the "do it or else" criminal law, but instead to a cost/benefit calculus of protection and prevention. To put the point overdramatically, we lock them up as we would a dangerous animal because their behavior cannot be controlled by means of laws appropriate for rational agents. This is why many involuntary commitment statutes quite properly require that a person be dangerous to others *by reason of* mental illness. More specifically, the requirement should be understood to be that persons' mental illness causes them to be both dangerous to others and not in control of nor thus responsible for their dangerous behavior as required under the criminal law.

Finally, it is crucial to note the well-known difficulties in predicting dangerous behavior whether to the mentally ill persons themselves or to others. The fallibility of such predictions raises serious challenges to commitment under the dangerousness standard. There are several aspects of the difficulty. First, the category of behavior judged to be a sufficient danger to warrant involuntary hospitalization must be restricted and specified. In general, homicide, rape, and other acts of violence causing serious harm or injury to persons are the appropriate sorts of acts to be prevented. Merely bizarre or offensive behavior should not be included under a dangerousness standard.[20]

Second, when the category of dangerous behavior is appropriately restricted in this way, dangerous acts are of quite infrequent occurrence. As a result, even an extremely accurate test of clinical predictive procedure for indentifying people as dangerous will produce significantly more false predictions that a person is dangerous (false positives) than correct predictions that a person is dangerous (true positives). For example, if only one out of every 1,000 persons will commit a dangerous act of the required sort and we have a predictive procedure that is accurate 99 percent of the time in identifying persons as dangerous or nondangerous, then for each person it correctly identifies as dangerous, at least ten others will be incorrectly identified as dangerous. To protect through the involuntary commitment of a single truly dangerous person either that person or the others that he or she might harm, it would be necessary to commit involuntarily ten other persons who are in fact not dangerous. Moreover, no predictive test or clinical method for establishing dangerousness has been demonstrated even to approach the level of accuracy assumed in the example. Of course, if the mentally ill are much more dangerous than the general public, then the incidence of violent behavior among them is much higher than the example assumes. Available evidence suggests, however, that the mentally ill overall are not more dangerous than the general public.[21]

It may be possible to identify narrower categories of mental illness, for example certain forms of paranoia, or categories of persons exhibiting specific kinds of behavior associated with a substantially higher frequency of violence and for which sufficiently accurate predictive methods might be developed. However, it seems that so far no such methods have been demonstrated to have a reasonable false positive/true positive rate. What evidence there is suggests that psychiatrists' clinical predictions substantially overpredict dangerousness, so that several persons will be predicted to be dangerous to others who will turn out not to be dangerous for each correct prediction of dangerousness, although there is controversy about just what the rate of over-prediction is.[22]

The actual calculation of the expected benefits and burdens produced by the use of any particular predictive method for involuntary commitment of mentally ill persons believed to be dangerous to others would have to be more complex than our discussion has indicated. It would have to take into account the expected treatment of persons' mental illness necessary to make them nondangerous, together with its expected benefits and burdens. At least as important is the expected length of time of persons' involuntary commitment. When dangerousness to others is used as the basis for short-term emergency commitment (for example, a few days or at most weeks) the predictable cost or harm of false positives, that is commitment of persons believed to be dangerous who in fact are not, is substantially less, and so more reasonably borne, than when it is used for long-term commitment. We will not explore these and related details further here. Instead, we want to emphasize that decisions to hospitalize involuntarily persons dangerous to others by reason of mental illness move beyond our ethical framework of deciding *for* incompetents *for their* benefit to decisions *about* incompetents *for others'* benefit.

II. DECISIONS TO REFUSE
TREATMENT BY INVOLUNTARILY
COMMITTED PATIENTS

A. The historical context of treatment refusal by involuntarily committed patients

How does our analysis of competence and our ethical framework for treatment decision making for incompetent persons apply to the mentally ill? Here again, a very brief sketch of recent developments in medical practice and the law will be helpful in placing our analysis in historical context.[23] Unitl the mid- to late 1970's it was common practice for involuntarily hospitalized mental patients to be subjected as a matter of course to involuntary treatment as well. Particular forms of treatment, such as ECT (electro-convulsive therapy), lobotomies, and other forms of psychosurgery, have at various times drawn special attention from the public, the courts, and/or the medical profession and been made subject to special restrictions.[24] Since hospitalization is presumably *for* treatment, however, the practice, where necessary, of focibly treating involuntarily hospitalized patients had a certain natural plausibility, and involuntary hospitalization was considered to carry with it authorization also for involuntary treatment. In some states, moveover, one necessary condition for involuntary hospitalization for treatment of mental illness was an inability to decide for oneself about one's need for treatment. A 1974 summary article on developments in civil commitment law observed:

> Inherent in an adjudication that an individual should be committed . . . is the decision that he can be forced to accept treatments . . . ; it would be in incongruous if an individual . . . could frustrate the very justification for the state's action by refusing such treatment.[25]

Within the last decade two prominent cases which reached
the United States Supreme Court for review, *Rogers v.
Okin* (1979)[26] and *Rennie v. Klein* (1983),[27] have rejected
this assumption and initiated the articulation of a right of
involuntarily committed mental patients to refuse treatment.

Both the *Rogers* and *Rennie* decisions addressed the use
of psychotropic drugs, which have become the standard
form of treatment of most serious forms of mental illness,
whether for voluntarily or involuntarily hospitalized
patients. The antipsychotic effect of psychotropic drugs
was first discovered in the early 1950s, and the drugs came
rapidly into regular use in mental hospitals for both treatment and control of seriously ill patients. As noted earlier,
the development of the psychotropics, with their capacity
to control psychotic patients' delusions, hallucinations,
and general agitation, made it possible for vast numbers
of institutionalized mental patients to exist safely outside
the hospital, and was probably the single most important
factor in the dramatic deinstitutionalization movement
from the mid-1950s into the 1980s.

By the time the *Rogers* and *Rennie* cases were begun in
the mid-1970s there had thus been two decades of experience with psychotropic medications. It had become clear
that these drugs were not the panacea some had once
hoped, as reservations developed about both their benefits
and their risks. On the benefit side, many patients on these
medications relapsed and the drugs often proved more
effective at controlling behavior than at curing the underlying mental illness and restoring patients to normal
function. On the risk side, these drugs were gradually
recognized frequently to have a wide range of physical,
psychological, cognitive, and behavioral side effects that
contributed to many patients' unwillingness to continue
their use. Besides their antipsychotic effect in reducing
many of the symptoms of schizophrenia, the neuroleptics

also have a strong sedative effect. Among the common side effects that are found to be particularly distressing by patients are the extrapyramidal side effects such as akenesia, which involves general slowing of movement and feelings of drowsiness and lifelessness, and akisthesia, which involves extreme and irresistable restlessness manifested in pacing and shaking of the extremities. Tardive dyskinesia, characterized by involuntary and often grotesque movements of the face, mouth, tongue, and limbs, is generally considered the most serious side effect because of its high frequency in long-term users of the neuroleptics, its usual irreversibility even after discontinuance of the medication, and the often disabling and humiliating social impact on its sufferers.[28] While there is considerable variability in the presence, severity, and toleration of the side effects of the psychotropic drugs, many patients find their effects intolerable and resist their continued administration. Nevertheless, there are still today no alternative forms of treatment with significant effectiveness in the treatment of much schizophrenia and other severe mental illness, and the psychotropic drugs continue to be the mainstay of treatment of the symptoms of severe psychosis.

These side effects had a significant impact on the *Rogers* and *Rennie* decisions. In both cases, the federal district courts and, on appeal, the first and third federal circuit courts, respectively, held that patients have a constitutional right to refuse medication. Insofar as this finding resulted from appeal to a principled distinction between a person satisfying conditions for hsopitalization, focusing usually on dangerousness, and satisfying conditions for competence, it was not a new right that was being asserted. The underlying right was to self-determination, as exemplified in the context of medical treatment by the doctrine of informed consent. What was new was its application to patients involuntarily hospitalized for mental illness. The right was held to be limited. It

could be overridden when the patient is dangerous to him-
or herself or to others, is incompetent to make a decision
about treatment, or in an emergency. The courts diverged
on whether review procedures for overriding the right can
be located in the hospital or must utilize the courts.

Both cases were appealed to the United States Supreme
Court at the time it was deciding a case concerning a
resident of an institution for the mentally retarded, *Youngberg v. Romeo.*[29] The Supreme Court declined to rule on
whether patients have a constitutional right to refusal
medications, and in *Romeo* in essence held that patients
have a right only to the review of treatment decisions to
which they object, the purpose of the review being to
ascertain that treating physicians have exercised "professional judgment" in those decisions. As a result of
Romeo and subsequent federal court decisions, one commentator has concluded,

> The right has become a right to object and to have
> one's treatment decision reviewed. It is no longer in
> some federal courts a right to refuse, if by "refusal" is
> meant the power to prevent the state from com-
> pulsorily medicating a patient except within rea-
> sonably well-defined exceptions for dangerousness,
> incapacity, and deterioration.[30]

At the same time, in some state courts, including Massachusetts in its redecision of *Rogers,*[31] the right of patients to
refuse treatment, except in emergencies threatening
dangerousness, has been affirmed, unless *the courts* have
found the patient incompetent to make the treatment
decision. Thus, the legal right of involuntarily committed
mental patients to refuse treatment in the United States
today can only be summarized as uncertain and contested,
varying according to locale, and still in a period of definition. Indeed, even the direction, not just the ultimate desti-
nation, of the evolution of the right, remains unclear.
Moreover, there is little reliable data at this point about

actual practice in dealing with patients' refusals of psychotropic medication.[32]

B. An ethical framework for treatment refusal by involuntarily committed mental patients

1. Persons dangerous to others. Our choice-specific analysis of competence provides clear and firm support for the courts' distinction between commitment and competence.[33] The distinction is clearest when only dangerousness by reason of mental illness is required as the substantive criterion for commitment. As one influential commentator, himself a psychiatrist, has noted of many patients committed for dangerousness,

> such patients, many of whom manifest character type problems, are not incompetent to consent or to refuse treatment.[34]

He adds, regarding dangerous persons hospitalized under an emergency commitment while violent,

> it is not clear that preventive treatment may continue once the emergency is controlled. This leaves in limbo the treatment of mentally ill persons who have been assaultive, who are judicially committed, but who are not assaultive in the hospital. Unfortunately, this type of person rather than the person who can profit from treatment, is the paradigm of commitment under the dangerousness to others' approach, honestly applied.[35]

It was noted earlier that persons mentally ill and dangerous to others might be competent to decide about hospitalization, but reject it because they view the burdens treatment imposes on them not to be adequately compensated for by any protection it provides other persons likely to be the objects of their violent behavior. Moreover, we argued that incompetence to decide about hospitalization should not be a requirement for persons committed because dangerous to others by reason of mental illness. The same distinction holds in principle between their commitment and their competence to consent to or to refuse particular treatments once hospitalized. In actual practice, as the second quotation above indicates, it frequently occurs that persons, initially committed for dangerousness at a time when they were violent and may have been incompetent to decide about hospitalization, after some period of hospitalization become competent to decide about their treatment.

The treatment refusal cases in the law that have generated the strongest protests within the psychiatric profession concern this kind of patient who is committed because dangerous to others but also deemed competent to decide about treatment. If the patient's competent refusal of treatment is accepted, then the hospital seems to become only a jail, and the physicians who staff it the patient's jailers instead of doctors. This is an inappropriate role for the medical profession, it is argued, one that society cannot justifiably impose on it. Does this imply that such persons should not be involuntarily hospitalized? We rejected that conclusion in arguing above that society can be justified in committing persons judged to be imminently dangerous to others by reason of mental illness, despite their competent refusal of hospitalization, at least if such commitments are combined with adequate procedural safeguards. Should such persons then be treated against their will, despite their competent refusal of treatment? We believe the proper answer is, "Almost never."

What is required for such patients is what Loren Roth has called a "segregation model" of involuntary commitment.[36] Patients who are dangerous to others by reason of mental illness would be segregated against their will from others in order to protect those others to whom they are dangerous. They should be offered treatment, but if they are competent to refuse treatment, they should not be forcibly treated against their will. The discussion with the person of possible treatments should, as always, cover the risks, benefits, and side effects of treatments, together with their probabilities. But in this case it should also include the information that if all treatment is refused the person will remain involuntarily confined so long as he or she continues to meet the commitment criteria of being dangerous to others by reason of mental illness. Such segregation should take place in a separate facility, or at least a separate part of a hospital facility, so as to make clear to all concerned that the person, having exercised a competent refusal of treatment, is confined for the protection of others and not for treatment.

While confinement would be for segregation and not for treatment, it would also not be punitive. The penal system requires a finding of responsibility for the behavior for which the person is to be punished, while segregation for dangerousness to others by reason of mental illness should be reserved for potential behavior for which the person would not properly be held to be criminally responsible.

Would a person deemed dangerous to others but competent to decide about treatment be able to give *voluntary* consent to treatment, as required for effective consent, if the only alternative to consenting could be indefinite confinement? Such a choice would commonly be a "forced choice" in the sense of a choice of what the person considers a lesser evil, with both alternatives viewed as very undesirable.[37] Moreover, it would be a choice forced on the person by other persons and social institutions, not by "nature," and so would not in that respect be an unavoidable choice. But if the consent would be involuntary and therefore not valid, would that imply that the patient cannot receive treatment despite his or her competent choice to undergo it? Or would it imply instead that a surrogate must decide for the person because his or her choice is ineliminably involuntary? And how would such a surrogate decide following the substituted judgment principle, if not exactly as the person him- or herself actually has competently decided in the circumstances?

It is difficult to see the rationale for a surrogate decision-maker if the person him- or herself is capable of a competent choice. The central issue for the voluntariness and in turn validity of the consent is whether others are justified in structuring the person's choice so that it is a choice between these lesser evils. Is this case closer to the gunman who unjustifiably "offers" the choice, "your money or your life," or to the state director of health who justifiably "offers" a person either treatment for a highly contagious disease or quarantine for the protection of others? In arguing above that in some circumstances it is justifiable to commit involuntarily persons dangerous to others by reason of mental illness but competent to refuse hospitalization, we essentially argued for construing this decision along the lines of the quarantine model. The preventive confinement model is justified for persons dangerous to others by reason of mental illness when their mental illness makes them not responsible for the dangerous behavior and so unsuitable for the alternative of control under the criminal law. The choice of a person involuntarily committed because dangerous to others by reason of mental illness of whether to submit to treatment or remain confined, consequently, is a forced but justified choice, and so is not incompatible with effective consent.

Our answer above to whether a person should ever be treated against his or her will who is dangerous to others, but competent to decide about and to refuse treatment, was "Almost never," but not simply "Never." This is because of third-party interests in this physician and patient treatment decision, which again require an extension of our patient-centered model of deciding for others. We have already recognized that considerations of distributive justice can place limits on the claims to social resources for the provision of health care that competent patients, or incompetent patients' surrogates, can justifiably make. Similarly, there are limits to the burdens that persons can justifiably impose on others by their competent choices about treatment, including choices to refuse treatment. For example, a possible alternative to quarantine of the person with the highly contagious disease who refuses treatment is to leave him or her at liberty and require others to take whatever steps are necessary to avoid any contacts with the person who might infect them. One moral reason others generally are not required to pursue this alternative is that doing so would in most cases impose unreasonably large burdens on them, in comparison with treating or quarantining the person with the contagious disease. Likewise, the costs to society of long-term confinement of a person dangerous to others by reason of mental illness who makes a competent choice to refuse treatment might be sufficiently great, while the burdens and risks imposed on the patient from treatment sufficiently small, that a social choice to impose treatment instead of long-term confinement would be justified.

Some might object that a competent person's right to refuse treatment cannot be justifiably overridden merely by showing that a utilitarian, cost/benefit analysis favors not respecting the right. As Ronald Dworkin, among many others, has argued, rights "trump" considerations of social utility.[38] However, this objection misunderstands our position. We are not arguing that any gain in social utility, no matter how small, from infringing a person's right to refuse treatment would justify infringing the right, but only that the costs of long-term, indefinite confinement could become sufficiently great to warrant the alternative of at least some kinds of involuntary treatment. The moral right to refuse treatment, like other moral rights, is not absolute and does not justify the imposition of unlimited costs and burdens on innocent third parties. At the present time, however, involuntary treatment on these grounds seems largely a theoretical possibility since the competent but dangerous refuser is sufficiently uncommon, and the usual treatments of severe mental illness are sufficiently intrusive and burdensome to the patient to make segregation by confinement the morally preferable alternative.

While we have supported the principled place for a competent choice to refuse treatment by patients involuntarily hospitalized because dangerous to others by reason of mental illness, it bears emphasizing that a large majority of involuntarily committed patients are not likely to turn out to be competent to decide about treatment because the same psychotic illness, with its attendant delusions and hallucinations, that causes them to be dangerous to others also affects their capacity to make a competent decision about treatment. How should these patients' surrogates, whether family members or court-appointed guardians, decide together with the patient's treating physician about treatment? Specifically, do the general patient-centered guidance principles for the selection of treatment offered in Chapter 2 apply without any qualification here?

The reason for thinking they may not is that the earlier decision to commit the patient involuntarily was made for the benefit, that is the protection, of *others,* not for the patient's benefit. Why then cannot a patient while involuntarily hospitalized because dangerous to others also be *treated* for the benefit of others? And once he or she has been hospitalized because dangerous to others, can "treatment" then include any effective steps to make him or her non-dangerous?

The important point to bear in mind is that commitment is not simply for dangerousness to others, but for dangerousness to others *by reason of mental illness,* that is, for dangerousness *caused* by mental illness. Thus, treatment should address and seek to cure or ameliorate the patient's mental illness, still directed by our patient-centered guidance principles. The physician's role should remain that of a treater of illness—not simply an incapacitator of the dangerous. Surrogates making treatment decisions for such patients must take into account that the patient's interest in release from confinement and in returning to a functional life at liberty in the community can now only be sered by treatment that will make him or her no longer dangerous when returned unsupervised to the community.

Adjusted for this difference, however, the ordered set of principles elaborated in Chapter 2—advance directive, substituted judgment, and best interests—remain the proper guidance principles for surrogates making treatment decisions for mentally ill persons, whether involuntarily hospitalized because dangerous to others or on other grounds. The substituted judgment principle, with the mentally ill as with other adults, has priority over the best interests principle, although long-term, chronic mental illness may often make it difficult or impossible to determine what treatment the patient would have consented to if competent, and so require resort to the best interests principle. This treatment decision-making model remains patient-centered, with the intersts of others entering only indirectly in this way into treatment decisions for patients dangerous to others, just as they may enter indirectly into decisions about the treatment of other mental or physical illness.

This leaves open whether there may be some forms of "treatment" of such patient's mental illness, for example that reduce or eliminate the mental illness and its resultant dangerousness only by substantial mental and/or vocational incapacitation, that by their very nature should be forbidden even if necessary to enable the patient to be released from the hospital. This issue is important and concerns treatment of persons dangerous either to others or to themselves, and it is addressed in Section III.D of this chapter.

2.   *Persons dangerous to themselves or in need of care and treatment.*   Are persons mentally ill and involuntarily

hospitalized on paternalistic grounds, either because of danger to themselves on strict paternalistic criteria or because they are in need of care and treatment on broader paternalistic criteria, also morally entitled to make a competent choice to refuse treatment? If so, it cannot be for the same reason as for persons who are dangerous to others by reason of mental illness, but competent and insufficiently concerned for the well-being of others they endanger. In our general analysis of competence and incompetence in Chapter 1, we argued that the crucial outcome of the competence evaluation is to determine whether a person's decision-making capacities, as exercised on a particular occasion, are sufficient to support respecting his or her choice about treatment or whether instead a surrogate must decide for the person to protect his or her well-being. If the person has already been involuntarily committed on self-regarding, paternalistic grounds, hasn't a decision already been made that his or her own choices about treatment will be set aside and another designated to decide for him or her?

If the paternalistic commitment criteria were restricted solely to the issue of dangerousness to oneself by reason of mental illness, however, the question of the person's competence to decide about treatment need never have arisen or been addressed. Dangerousness to oneself because of mental illness will itself be dispositive regarding involuntary commitment.

We argued, in Section I.B. that involuntary commitment on self-regarding, paternalistic grounds should require a determination of incompetence to the effect that the person lacks sufficient capacity to make an informed decision about hospitalization for him- or herself. If this is required, then how could a person be competent now to refuse treatment? The answer lies in recalling the choice-specific nature of the competence determination. A person's decision-making competence can vary from decision to decision because the decision-making demands of different decisions can vary substantially, because the patient's decision-making capacities can improve or deteriorate substantially over time due to the effects on those capacities of illness, its treatment, and other factors, and finally because the level of decision-making capacity appropriately required will vary depending, most importantly, on the consequences for the patient's well-being of accepting a particular choice. Thus, although he or she will have been found incompetent intitially to decide about his or her need for hospitalization can treatment, either the nature of the decision or the nature of the patient's decision-making capacities may have changed sufficiently to enable him or her now to make a competent decision about treatment. If the patient now competently refuses a particular form of treatment, that treatment should not be forced on the patient, but other treatments pursued instead.

Just because the right of hospitalized patients to refuse treatment for mental illness is so strenuously and widely opposed by psychiatrists, it bears emphasis that this is no different from the constraint physicians practice under in the rest of medicine, where a patient may competently refuse what the attending physician believes is the optimal form of treatment, and so other alternative treatments must be pursued instead. If there are no other alternative treatments that the patient will accept, or is not incompetent to refuse, and that promise significantly to benefit the patient or reduce the patient's danger to him- or herself, then the rationale for involuntary hospitalization itself is called into question and must be reassessed. This too is not different from the situation in nonpsychiatric medical practice where a patient may sometimes competently refuse all proferred treatments, with the result that no treatment can be carried out and the patient signs out of the hospital "against medical advice."

While we have supported the right in principle of involuntarily hospitalized mental patients to make a competent decision to refuse treatment, the independence in practice of the decision to hospitalize involuntarily from the decision about treatment should not be exaggerated. An initial decision to seek involuntary hospitalization will virtually always be a decision, however explicit, to seek hospitalization in order to provide some kind(s) of planned treatment for the patient once hospitalized. If the patient is involuntarily committed on paternalistic grounds, we have argued that this should require a determination that the person is not competent to make a decision about hospitalization *for that treatment*. Thus, the person's competence to decide about the planned treatment should be addressed *at the time of initial commitment*. To this extent, competence at that time to decide about hospitalization and competence to decide about planned treatment should in practice commonly not be distinct determinations.

However, a change in the planned treatment, in the circumstances relevant to the treatment decision, or in the patient's decision-making capacities, can give rise to the possibility of a competent refusal of treatment by a patient justifiably involuntarily committed on paternalistic grounds. Moreover, to the extent that incompetence continues in practice not to be a necessary condition for involuntary commitment on paternalistic grounds, but only dangerousness to self by reason of mental illness or need for care and treatment is required, then even in practice the patient's competence may be addressed only at the point that a decision about treatment must be made.

Our discussion of treatment refusal until now has assumed that the patients in question are involuntarily hospitalized, and certainly the cases most troubling to psychiatrists are those in which courts have upheld both the patient's involuntary hospitalization and their refusal of treatment. While it might seem that treatment refusal is not an issue for voluntary patients because they can always leave the hospital if faced with unwanted treatment, there are three reasons to be concerned about refusals of, and even sometimes consents to, treatment by patients *voluntarily* admitted to hospitals. The first is that there is often a significant degree of coercion or manipulation in what is formally a voluntary admission by the patient. Voluntary patients have sometimes been threatened by family members or treating professionals with involuntary commitment or other unwanted consequences if they do not agree to voluntary hospitalization. Similar threats are sometimes made with voluntary patients who indicate a wish or intention to leave the hospital. Deception and other forms of manipulation have also been used to achieve what is formally a voluntary, but in substance an involuntary admission. Thus, patients who are formally admitted to the hospital as voluntary patients may fail to meet any true standard of voluntariness. The secon reason for concern is that in many states minors may be "voluntarily" admitted to hospitals for treatment of mental illness against their will, but with the consent of their parents or guardians. Thirdly, some hospitals for the mentally ill, especially some state-run public hospitals, continue to be what Erving Goffman called "total institutions"[39] in which patients are highly dependent on and at the mercy of their caretakers and in which abuses continue involving administration of care not in the patient's interests. Therefore, there are strong reasons for some relatively formal determinations of the incompetence of patients in such facilities, whether voluntary or involuntary, before treatment is administered against their will. While formal court review is perhaps the most obvious institutional practice for review of patients' competence to refuse or consent to treatment, various states have used other means such as mental health advocates charged with protecting the rights and interests of patients being treated for mental illness.

III. SOME RESIDUAL ISSUES IN DECISIONS FOR THE MENTALLY ILL

A. The least restrictive alternative condition

Many states' mental health treatment laws, court decisions, and policy proposals include the requirement that either involuntary hospitalization itself, or the particular treatment to be pursued involuntarily, be the least restrictive alternative available for the patient. The general least restrictive alternative doctrine has been applied in many areas of the law and holds "that governmental action must not intrude upon constitutionally protected interests to a greater degree than necessary to achieve a legitimate governmental purpose."[40] Whether it applies as a matter of law in the area of commitment and/or treatment of the mentally ill has been a specific point of legal controversy, on which we take no position here.[41] Our concern here is with what role, if any, it should play in our ethical framework for decisions about commitment and treatment of the mentally ill. We believe that there is a defensible interpretation of the least restrictive alternative requirement, but that on that interpretation, strictly speaking, it is superfluous within our general ethical framework for deciding for others, although perhaps often a useful explicit reminder in practice. However, this requirement is sometimes employed in a confused or indefensible manner.

The general legal doctrine of the least restrictive alternative has commonly been used to strike down state actions that impinge on constitutionally protected rights, such as first amendment rights, when the *same* state purpose can be achieved by means that impinge less on the protected right. Extrapolating to commitment of the mentally ill, the doctrine would seem to require that involuntary hospitalization not be employed when the purposes of treating the patient in paternalistic commitments, or of protecting others in police power commitments, could be *equally* well served without the restriction of liberty that involuntary hospitalization involves. Likewise, with treatments such as seclusion and the use of restraints, they would not be permissible if *equally* efficacious treatment is possible without them or with less restrictive means. In order to apply the doctrine to treatments like psychotropic medications, it has been extended by some proponents to require the use of *equally* efficacious treatments that are *less intrusive,* not just *less restrictive,* on the person and mind of the patient.

We have highlighted the key condition in each of these three applications of the first interpretation of the doctrine—that efficacious but less restrictive or intrusive alternative treatments must be pursued if they are *equally* efficacious. So interpreted, the doctrine seems to be plausible and acceptable. Since an involuntary hospitalization or treatment that is "restrictive" or "intrusive" is in that respect burdensome to the patient, a simple assessment of the benefits and burdens of alternative treatments (using the patient's values when he or she was competent and so far as they are known) will *always* support the less restrictive or intrusive alternative. (When the restrictiveness itself provides a benefit for the patient, as is sometimes the case with hospitalization or seclusion, then an alternative without that restriction will, other things equal, be less efficacious.) The least restrictive alternative doctrine on this interpretation is strictly an unnecessary and redundant addition to our general ethical framework requiring an assessment of the benefits and burdens of alternative treatments for the patient—it yields no different treatment selections, and so its only role is likely to be to remind those considering involuntary commitment or alternative treatments to weigh their restrictiveness or intrusiveness in the decision.

The only controversial aspect to the least restrictive alternative doctrine, on this interpretation, is its exclusion from consideration of any inconvenience, cost, or other burdens to persons other than the patient. While there may be a few extreme cases in which such an exclusion is unreasonable, in the vast majority of cases this seems an acceptable implication of our patient-centered ethical framework and of the least restrictive alternative doctrine which it incorporates.

This interpretation that no *equally* efficacious but less restrictive or intrusive alternative be available is probably what is intended in the APA Guidelines statement of the condition:

> Consistent with the least restrictive alternative princi-
> ple means that . . . each patient committed solely on
> the ground that he is likely to cause harm to himself
> or to suffer substantial mental or physical deteriora-
> tion shall be placed in the *most appropriate and thera-
> peutic* available setting, that is, a setting in which
> treatment provides the patient with a realistic oppor-
> tunity to improve and which is no more restrictive of
> his physical or social liberties than is believed con-
> ducive to the *most effective* treatment for the patient
> . . ." [emphasis added].[42]

Interpreted literally, although probably not as the APA intended, this would bar adoption of a treatment alterna-tive believed to be only slightly less effective than the treatment believed to be most effective, even if the less effective treatment was *vastly less* restrictive or intrusive. This is hardly a plausible interpretation of the least restric-tive alternative requirement.

A stronger interpretation of the least restrictive alterna-tive requirement is that less restrictive (or intrusive) alternatives must be taken even at some significant cost in the expected effectiveness or benefits of treatment. Only on this interpretation does the requirement result in any choices different from those of our general framework for the assessment of benefits and burdens to the patient. But if the least restrictive alternative requirement is understood to require a less restrictive (or intrusive) alternative even in some cases in which an overall assessment of the benefits and burdens (including the burdens of restrictiveness or intrusiveness) to the patient of alternatives favors the more restrictive alternative, then we believe that it is not defensible. If the alternative of involuntary hospitalization, or of alternative treatment A over treatment B, is judged to be, all things considered, more beneficial for the patient, then why should a least restrictive alternative requirement bar commitment or require treatment B simply because it is less restrictive (or intrusive)? We conclude that the least restrictive alternative requirement is either superfluous in our ethical decision-making framework or indefensible, and that its only useful role seems to be as an indirect, although admittedly sometimes important and much-needed, reminder that the mere convenience of others, such as family or treatment staff, does not justify employing significantly more restrictive (or intrusive) treatment alternatives.

B. Advance directives by the mentally ill

The use of advance directives in health care planning is increasingly common, but remains restricted largely to life-sustaining treatment for the critically ill or dying. Such directives, either in the form of a living will or an appointment of a durable power of attorney for health care, are made when a person is competent to issue such directives, and take effect only when the person becomes incompetent to make his or her own health care decisions (although, as we saw in Chapter 6, there are commonly additional requirements before the directives take effect, such as that the person be "terminally ill"). There is an important, but as yet largely untapped, opportunity for the use of advance planning and advance directives in the care of some mentally ill persons.

Most state law, as we noted in Section I of this chapter, currently restricts commitment to the dangerousness standard, requiring the person to be a danger either to self or others by reason of mental illness. Patients suffering from two common kinds of chronic mental illness—certain forms of schizophrenia and major affective disorders such as manic depression—are much of the time not dangerous and so not committable when the dangerousness standard is honestly and accurately applied. Both kinds of patient can usually be stabilized and their illnesses brought into some degree of remission by medication, but these patients often become noncompliant with treatment after some period of time and stop taking their medications. With schizophrenic patients, this is then commonly followed by predictable periods of deterioration as the patients become increasingly psychotic until sufficiently delusional or unable to care for themselves that they are then a danger to themselves or others and can be committed involuntarily for treatment. With manic-depressive patients, as they become increasingly manic their behavior often wreaks serious havoc in their own lives and the lives of others, even to the point of destroying their careers or families. In each case the period of deterioration that begins when the patients stop using medications can be a matter of weeks and often months in which others, including both the patients' treating psychiatrists and families, must stand by helplessly as the patients become increasingly ill before treatment can be involuntarily reinstituted; indeed, they must do so even if the patients had earlier implored them to disregard their treatment refusals in just these circumstances.

Because of their common cyclic pattern, together with patients' common periodic noncompliance with treatment, both of these forms of mental illness lend themselves to the use of long-range planning and advance directives. Patients commonly go through significant periods of nondangerousness when they are complying with treatment, their illnesses are in remission, and they are competent to make decisions about their treatment. As a result of the cyclic pattern of their illness, these patients commonly have personally experienced the onset of non-compliance with treatment, their consequent deterioration, and the way in which their illness then affects their ability to recognize their need for, and capacity to make decisions about, hospitalization or treatment. It would thus be possible for these patients to utilize their periods of competence, while their illness is stabilized by treatment and in remission, to plan for and give directives about their treatment should they cease to comply with treatment, suffer relapse, and become incompetent to decide about their care. It is crucial to see that criteria for their hospitalization and treatment in these circumstances need not be restricted to the dangerousness standard, but could be the serious recurrence of their illness, together with their incompetence to make decisions about its treatment.

We suggested earlier that a principal objection to broadening criteria for involuntary commitment from the dangerousness standard to "deterioration and distress" criteria is the increased risk of well-intentioned misuse, or ill-intentioned abuse, of commitment. The use of broader commitment criteria restricted to *voluntary* commitment contracts between a patient and a treating physician or facility should substantially reduce that risk. Most importantly, such agreements would insure that the involuntary commitment and treatment were in accordance with the patient's own wishes when the patient was competent. The general objection made by some critics to all *parens patriae,* paternalistic commitment is that it risks imposing on persons someone else's view, which they do not share even when competent, of whether hospitalization and treatment are best for them. This would be an instance of the more general form of morally objectionable paternalism—failure to respect persons' own conception of their good and substituting instead another's conception of what is best for them.

However, this objection does *not* apply to these voluntary commitment contracts. The person's own values, aims, and conception of his or her good, while he or she is competent and with the illness in remission, would always be guiding and controlling. Moreover, the evidence that the patient would have wanted hospitalization and treatment in these circumstances would be of the strongest sort possible—the patient's own decision, while competent and with the illness in remission, in favor of that hospitalization and treatment—as compared with the more uncertain and unreliable inferences required by the substituted judgment principle about what he or she would likely have wanted in the present circumstances when competent. As a safeguard, at least one past episode of treatment noncompliance and deterioration to the point of hospitalization could be required before a voluntary commitment contract could be made. If this requirement were met, patients making these contracts would always do so on the basis of some personal experience of the treatment noncompliance and deterioration the contract seeks to prevent.

Howell et al.[43] have proposed a number of restrictions and procedural safeguards in order to provide increased assurance against abuse of these contracts. They would limit the contracts to persons with mental illnesses that "involve psychosis, are recurrent, and are amenable to treatment. Major affective disorders (such as bipolar and manic-depressive affective disorders, recurrent mania, and psychotic depression) and certain forms of schizophrenia are examples of psychiatric disorders that might qualify."[44] Contracts would be made only while the person is competent to do so and in remission from the illness, and must be entered into voluntarily without coercion from others, including family members and treating health care professionals. Further, Howell et al. propose that a third party, such as the individual's lawyer or a court-appointed lawyer, be involved to insure that the contract is fully voluntary and in the person's best interests. The contract could only be made with a physician who knows the patient and his or her clinical situation well, and could be subject to review by medical-legal boards. Contracts would specify clearly the conditions for invoking them and the treatment plans that could be employed, would be for a specified period of time such as one year, and would be revocable or revisable unless the person is in relapse. The patient would retain the right to a hearing before involuntary treatment was begun under the contract. Moreover, and importantly, involuntary treatment under the contract would be limited to no longer than a relatively short period such as three weeks. This is usually long enough to achieve remission in most cases in which such contracts would be invoked.

Our purpose here is not to provide all of the details that would be required in the legislative drafting of such a proposal; instead, we have referred to some of the details of Howell et al.'s version to illustrate the kinds of safeguards and restrictions that could be employed. Even with such safeguards, however, proposals for legally enforceable voluntary commitment contracts have come under criticism. Rebecca Dresser has argued that they would probably have higher costs (understood broadly as bad effects, not just financial costs) than the problem for which they are proposed.[45] The general form of her criticism is that much judgment and interpretation would be required of those seeking to invoke these contracts, which would lead to mistakes and abuse. Psychiatrists would have to determine when the patient's disorder is in remission and when he or she has relapsed, when irrational or unwise behavior such as indiscriminate spending is due to relapse, when the person is likely to deteriorate and to suffer significant harm in the future without treatment, and so forth. Moreover, some of the safeguards, such as the third party involvement by an attorney and the hearing before enforcement, would look only to whether the terms of the contract now applied, not to whether it was in the person's interest. Dresser also argues that this paternalistic, state-enforced interference with a person's liberty would be invoked against persons who have not been found to be incompetent.

There are two ways or responding to this last objection. The first response appeals to our decision-specific account of incompetence in Chapter 1 and imposes a requirement that at the hearing before enforcement of the contract the patient be determined then to be incompetent to make a decision about the proposed treatment, and incompetent to revoke or revise the contract. The fact that the patient's advance directive applies to the circumstances in question is evidence that he or she considered protection of his or her well-being more important than respecting a current exercise of self-determination in refusing treatment. Thus the patient's *own* balancing of the values at stake in the competence determination supports a finding of incompetence, the setting aside of his or her current choice, and the transfer of decision-making authority to the advance directive.

The second response accepts the idea of enforcing such contracts on persons who have not been found to be incompetent, or even would not be found incompetent, at least as competence is now often defined. On this alternative, the condition of relapse of the illness, but not of incompetence to decide about treatment, would be required to invoke the contract. But enforcing the contract in the event of relapse and without the person's incompetence would be justified by the person's earlier choice, while the illness was in remission, that this be done. The second response to Dresser's objection would require making the implementation of these advance directives an exception to the important and deeply entrenched general legal principle that the informed and voluntary treatment refusal of a competent patient must be respected. It would also make these advance directives of the mentally ill unlike other advance directives for health care treatment that can only be implemented when their issuer has later been determined to be incompetent. Consequently, we favor the first response, especially because we believe that our own analysis of competence supports a finding of incompetence when the patient's refusal of treatment is reasonably believed to be a product of the relapse of his or her illness.

Nevertheless, Dresser's general concern about abuse is well-taken: Feasible procedural safeguards, here as elsewhere, would not eliminate all abuses and mistakes. But it is important to remember as well that there appear to be thousands of seriously mentally ill persons who now cannot receive adequate and appropriate treatment which, when their judgment is not affected by their illness, they have clearly stated they want for themselves. The issue is what the likely *balance* would be of mistakes and abuse as against provision of desired and beneficial treatment. In the absence of actual experience with advance directives in this area of health care, neither opponents nor proponents of them can offer solid evidence for their position, and the issue remains highly speculative.

In fact, durable powers of attorney for health care designed principally for life-sustaining treatment decisions might seem already to give legal validity to this form of advance directive for the care of the mentally ill. However, as was noted earlier, these durable powers commonly contain a provision that treatment will not be either provided or withheld over the objection of the patient, despite the patient's incompetence. While perhaps understandable for advance directives about life-sustaining treatment, for example as a response to persons' worries about changing their minds, this provision makes them legally impotent for involuntary treatment of just the kinds of mentally ill patients in question here. Moreover, since procedural safe-guards appropriate for advance directives concerning treatment of mental illness are probably significantly different than for life-sustaining treatment, a separate kind of legal instrument is desirable.

Forms of advance planning and advance directives such as Howell et al. have proposed are potentially important and valuable aids in treatment decision making for the mentally ill. They are legal devices to carry out what people more commonly do in informal, everyday contexts in which they anticipate impaired judgment. For example, a man who knows from experience that he tends to drink too much alcohol at parties may give his car keys to a friend with instructions not to return them later in the evening even if he then asks for them; or a wife dieting may put particularly tempting and fattening foods in the hands of her husband with instructions not to serve her more than a specified amount even if she later asks for more. Precisely because mental illness so often affects persons' capacities for judgment regarding their need for treatment, but also leaves those same persons intermittently competent to decide about their treatment (as a result either of treatment or of the cyclic pattern of the illness), we consider advance directives to be the natural device for extending mentally ill persons' self-determination to cover their treatment when they are seriously ill but not dangerous. By relying on the person's own prior, competent choice, these voluntary commitment contracts could provide the strongest ethical basis for involuntary hospitalization and/or treatment of any criteria now commonly in use. The appropriate response to the legitimate concerns of Dresser and others about possible abuse and mistakes is the careful monitoring of the actual effects of such voluntary commitment contracts when employed on a trial basis, rather than barring their use on the basis of highly speculative worries.

C. Involuntary outpatient commitment

A number of states in recent years have adopted a new form of involuntary treatment of the mentally ill—the involuntary commitment, by court order, of mentally ill persons to *outpatient* treatment, usually treatment with antipsychotic medications.[46] Outpatient commitment has usually come about through reliance on statutory legislation explicitly authorizing it, although it may be possible in some jurisdictions to construe "least restrictive alternative" requirements of general involuntary commitment and treatment laws as authorizing it. However it is legally authorized, if a patient opposes hospitalization and can be treated effectively as an outpatient in the community, then outpatient treatment should promise the patient comparable benefits to involuntary hospitalization, as well as treatment with lesser burdens. Here again, our concern is not with the details of legislative drafting and institutional procedures of an outpatient commitment program, but with how our general ethical framework for deciding for others helps illuminate the central ethical issues concerning outpatient treatment. Perhaps the two most controversial aspects of outpatient commitment, besides the question of whether it is desirable in any form, are whether it should require a judgment of the patient's incompetence to decide about treatment and what the other substantive commitment criteria for it should be.

The use of court-ordered outpatient treatment commonly is restricted to persons deemed capable, with treatment, of remaining safely in the community without danger to themselves or others, but who have demonstrated an unwillingness to comply adequately with their treatment porgram on a voluntary basis. Because there appear to be significant numbers of such patients, outpatient commitment is a potentially important policy alternative that could assure treatment to patients who otherwise either would not comply with treatment voluntarily or would have to receive it involuntarily in a vastly more restrictive inpatient setting.

A finding of incompetence to decide about treatment is commonly held to be a necessary condition for a court order to outpatient treatment. When commitment is for the benefit of the patient under *parens patriae* powers, our analysis in Section II.B.2 supports the requirement that the person be found incompetent to make a decision about the proposed treatment, and our general analysis of the nature of competence determinations applies intact here. If outpatient commitment is on grounds of dangerousness to others, on the other hand, for the reasons developed in Section I.C., our analysis would *not* require a finding that the patient is incompetent to decide about treatment. Instead, all that would be necessary is that the patient be dangerous to others and that this dangerousness be due to mental illness. Just as with inpatient commitment, to require a finding of incompetence to decide about outpatient treatment would allow an unacceptable outcome: a patient who is dangerous to others by reason of mental illness competently refusing treatment and not being committable or treatable.

This may be little more than a theoretical possibility, however, since it seems extremely unlikely in practice that the courts would find a person otherwise deemed a serious danger to others by reason of mental illness to be at the same time competent to refuse both inpatient and outpatient treatment. Nevertheless, imposing an incompetence requirement on police power commitments of patients dangerous to others by reason of mental illness is a mistake, whether the commitment is in- or outpatient, and doing so only promotes conceptual confusion in an area of policy already rife with it.

Should the criteria for court-ordered outpatient commitment be restricted to the dangerousness standard, or should broader criteria such as the APA's proposed "deterioration and distress" condition be adopted? The justification within our patient-centered ethical framework for any medical treatment should always depend on the patient's, or the incompetent patient's surrogate's, assessment of the benefits and burdens for the patient of the proposed treatment and its alternatives. Since the loss of liberty that involuntary hospitalization involves is generally a substantial burden of inpatient commitment, when comparably efficacious treatment can be provided on an involuntary outpatient basis the overall burdens of treatment are substantially reduced.

This implies that commitment to outpatient treatment can be justified at a lower threshold of expected benefit to be provided or harm to be prevented to the patient than should be required for involuntary inpatient treatment. Consequently, criteria for commitment that are broader than the dangerousness standard are justified for court-ordered outpatient treatment. For example, criteria along the lines of the relatively broad "deterioration and distress" criteria recommended in the APA Guidelines, even if rejected as overly broad for *inpatient* commitment, in our view can provide an expected benefit to patients that warrants the coercion of involuntary *outpatient* treatment. Understood as applying to involuntary outpatient treatment, criteria following these guidelines have the potential of assuring treatment to an important group of patients that often does not meet a dangerousness standard—chronic schizophrenics who frequently become noncompliant with treatment, but must go through a substantial period of deterioration before they satisfy the dangerousness standard.

Sometimes it is argued that if inpatient involuntary commitment criteria are restricted to the dangerousness standard, then outpatient criteria should be as well, so that the threat of involuntary inpatient commitment will always be available as a sanction for noncompliance with court-ordered outpatient treatment. This argument is, however, unpersuasive, since it is not clear either that this is the only possible sanction for noncompliance or that without a sanction of this kind there would be inadequate compliance with the outpatient order. It is proper that some patients who are noncompliant with court-ordered outpatient treatment under a broad deterioration and distress standard would not qualify under a stricter dangerousness standard for inpatient commitment, and so might go without treatment. That is a straightforward implication of the policy judgment implicit in the vast majority of current state mental health laws that only the benefit of treatment for persons who constitute a serious danger to themselves is sufficient to warrant imposing on paternalistic grounds the severe restriction of involuntary hospitalization.

D. Special limits on surrogate consent for "inhumane" treatments

Finally, we want to consider whether there are some kinds of treatment of the mentally ill, usually the dangerous mentally ill, that should not be employed even with the decision of the surrogate deciding for the patient (or perhaps even with the consent of a competent patient). In particular, are there some ways of treating mentally ill patients so as to make them nondangerous that are nonetheless ethically unacceptable?

Two examples will help make this issue more concrete. From the 1930s into the 1950s a crude form of psychosurgery called prefrontal lobotomy was common treatment for some kinds of mental illness.[47] While these procedures usually made the patient less, or no longer, dangerous, they often did so only at the cost of massive impairment of the patient's general cognitive and volitional capacities; they seemed less a specific treatment of the patient's mental illness than global social control through incapacitation, and their use seems sometimes to have been more for the benefit of the staff of mental hospitals than for the patients.

While this crude form of psychosurgery is no longer in use, some professionals still advocate use of more sophisticated forms of psychosurgery for some mentally ill persons.[48] A second example of ethically controversial treatment is still currently in use for severely mentally ill persons who are unresponsive to more conventional treatments: Aversive therapies that include pinchings, restraints, water sprayed in the face, subjections to "white noise," and the like, are employed with patients, usually young persons, suffering from severe autism, some otherwise untreatable forms of schizophrenia, and mental retardation, often in an attempt to control the patient's seriously self-destructive behavior. The parents of these patients often support the use of these seemingly cruel measures, perceiving them to be a last hope for their children after all other treatments have been tried and have failed.

Within the framework of deciding *for* others, and so for their benefit, are such treatments ever ethically acceptable, or are they instead intolerably inhumane? In the best-known, latter-day psychosurgery legal case, *Kaimowitz v. Department of Mental Health* (1973),[49] the court rejected the legal adequacy of the consent of a mental patient, involuntarily confined as a criminal sexual psychopath, to experimental psychosurgery. It held that none of the three components of an adequate consent were satisfied: The highly experimental nature of the surgery militatated against even the possibility of an informed choice; the patient's mental illness, together with the effects of institutionalization, called into question his competence to make the choice; and the inherently coercive nature of his involuntary institutional confinement undermined the voluntariness of his choice. The court held as well that even with the patient's consent, the psychosurgery's profound and irreversible effects on the patient's mental capacities would violate his First Amendment right, as the court put it, to generate ideas, as well as his constitutionally protected right to privacy. While much of the court's reasoning in *Kaimowitz* was problematic, its concerns were typical of the *legal* concerns that are raised to special forms of treatment like psychosurgery.[50] However, they fail to capture other aspects of typical, although often largely unarticulated, *ethical* concerns. It would be a lengthy task that would take us too far afield to try to elaborate fully the nature of these concerns, but we can at least gesture in their general direction.

The first ethical concern is brought out by the case of psychosurgery, and especially early crude, prefrontal lobotomies. While these procedures often may have been effective in controlling the patient's dangerousness, they did so only by diffuse, profound, and irreversible effects on the patient's general mental and volitional capacities. They commonly controlled the patient's violent behavior only through massive and generally incapacitating changes in central capacities distinctive of our humanity and personhood—our capacities for rational thought and purposeful action. To so reduce or destroy these capacities was not treatment for the patient's benefit or in the patient's interest as a human being or person, just because of its destructive effect on these distinctly and centrally important human capacities.

The second ethical concern is brought out by the example of the use of aversives, and has at least three somewhat distinct components. One component is that many of the techniques used in these therapies seem, at least on the surface, to come perilously close to techniques used in one of the most ethically abhorrent practices devised by human beings—torture. It is a widely held ethical conviction that deliberate torture of other human beings is wrong, virtually no matter what and how laudable the goal of its use might be. This same surface association with torture, we believe, contributes to the vehement denunciation made by some of electroconvulsive therapy (ECT), despite its well-documented benefits in the treatment of delusional and severe endogenous depression.[51] That ECT is often a selected and justified treatment of severe depression, using either the substituted judgment or best interest principles, illustrates the hazards of accepting superficial and misleading understandings of the nature and effects of some treatments for the mentally ill. Here as elsewhere, sound treatment decision making by surrogates must overcome misleading symbolism and be based on a well-informed understanding of the nature and consequences of the treatments under consideration.

A second component of this ethical concern is that these aversive techniques seem sometimes to be, or to have been, used not as a mode of treatment for the patient's benefit, but as a punitive means of behavior control for the benefit of others besides the patient. Finally, a third component of this ethical concern is that the deliberate behavioral conditioning processes used in aversive therapies on patients commonly unable even to understand their purpose, much less to give consent for their use, is much closer to the way we train and control wild or dangerous animals that to the way we nurture and help humans to develop. It responds to and acts on the subject's animal nature, not his or her rational capacities.

Each of these ethical concerns about special forms of treatment of the mentally ill, and about others consenting to, or participating in, the use of such treatments, raises serious and legitimate questions about these therapies that deserve more elaboration and development than we can give them here. They do not, however, require special constraints on our general ethical framework for deciding for others. Instead, they provide an important and sometimes much needed reminder to look more deeply and broadly at the harms particular treatments for the mentally ill may cause. At the same time, it would be a mistake to let these legitimate ethical concerns blind us to the benefits treatments such as aversives or ECT sometimes provide to desperately ill people for whom more conventional and accepted therapies have failed. The assessment of the expected benefits and burdens of a specific treatment to a specific patient remains the centerpost of deciding about treatment for mentally ill others.

Looking forward

Our aim in the final paragraphs of this detailed examination of the ethics of decision making for and about incompetents is not to repeat the material already presented in the overview sketched in the introduction or in the more detailed and focused summaries found in the various chapters. Instead, we wish to emphasize a few selected implications of our study for the future of research and public policy in this complex area.

- There is a vital need for a more systematic implementation of the decision-specific concept of competence. Some progress in this regard has already been made in the law concerning older minors and in the use of limited conservatorships for the elderly, but there is much more to be done. Especially in less formal, medical contexts, efforts must be made to ensure that the actual practice of decision making reflects the fact that competence is decision-relative and often fluctuating. A first step toward this goal is for those in charge of the training of health care professionals to ensure that nurses, interns, and residents are properly educated as to the nature and importance of competence determinations, and are able to understand and apply sound principles of surrogate decision-making.
- It is not enough to educate individual health care professionals; more responsible *institutional* arrangements in health care facilities must be developed (1) for determining competence, (2) for locating and following

valid advance directives, (3) for identifying suitable surrogates, and (4) for ensuring that suitable surrogates are properly informed about the decisions they are entitled to make and are free to make those decisions without interference, duress, or manipulation.

- Health care and legal professionals can play a crucial role by helping to promote the wider and more responsible use of various techniques of planning for crisis: from DNR, do not hospitalize, do not feed by tube orders, and do not administer antibiotics orders, to limited conservatorships and living trusts, living wills, and durable powers of attorney. The use of such devices will require greater attention to effective liaison and communication among caregivers, and more concerted efforts to achieve continuity of care than presently exist in most contexts. Nothing less than a new conception of the responsibilities of the health care provider will be needed.

- More careful drafting of advance directive legislation (especially for durable power of attorney for health care) is needed, and much can be learned from criticisms of the few existing statutes. Most jurisdictions currently lack durable power of attorney for health care statutes, but this is almost certain to change. The wider use of durable power of attorney for health care statutes presents an opportunity to remedy the well-known defects of most existing living will or natural death act statutes, since the former can include provisions for instructions as well as for the designation of a proxy, and could in principle be explicitly formulated to supersede the latter.

- As our frequent reference to the paucity of data indicates, a great deal of empirical research is needed to determine how competence judgments are actually made, especially in contexts less formal than that of legal competence hearings. Accurate information in this regard is required before reasonable, concrete efforts to implement the decision-relative concept of competence can be successfully formulated.

- If a sound ethical framework for decision making for incompetents is to be successfully implemented, careful attention will have to be paid to the difficult but essential task of embedding the appropriate ethical principles in the relevant institutions in such a way that key agents will have effective *incentives* to abide by them. The U.S. health care system (like those of several developed countries, at least in the West) is currently undergoing rapid changes in the very structure of health care delivery, the fundamental organization of medical practice, and the basic forms of reimbursement. Whether or not physicians and others reasonably can be expected to comply with sound ethical principles will depend in large part on the character of the incentive structure within which they work. On the one hand, a sober appreciation of limits on the range of feasible arrangements may require us to reduce somewhat our expectations as to what degree of compliance with sound ethical principles is the acceptable minimum. On the other hand, our choice among feasible arrangements should be guided at least in part by an accurate estimate of the extent to which the various alternatives include incentives that facilitate compliance with sound ethical principles. Much creative analysis, informed by a sure grasp of the scope of institutional innovation in the health care sector, is needed to ascertain the "ethical impact" of rapidly emerging new types of health care systems, including their impact on incompetent patients.

- If significant progress in the care and treatment of the incompetent is to be made, it will not suffice for hospitals and other facilities such as nursing homes and mental hospitals to formulate and announce sound policies. Experience with DNR policies, as well as the continuing failure of many health care professionals even to recognize the rights of *competent* patients (both of which are documented above), make it all too clear that much more must be done to ensure that sound policies are actually being followed. Too often, the work of hospital ethics committees and other bodies that formulate ethical policies ends with the production of inscriptions on paper rather than with genuine institutional change. The development of policies concerning the treatment of incompetent individuals must be accompanied by concrete plans for assigning appropriate institutional roles and attendant responsibilities, integrated into the working administrative structure of the facility, along with effective procedures for monitoring compliance.

Appendix 1. Living trust and nomination of conservatorship[1]

There are two other important, legally recognized instruments, by which a person, when competent, may exert control over decisions that are made after he or she becomes incompetent: a *living trust* and *nomination of conservator*. Although neither of these devices provides comprehensive control over future decisions, each is useful for limited purposes for some individuals.

I. LIVING (INTERVIVOS) TRUST

A Trust is a disarmingly simply concept. Once viewed as a preserve of the wealthy, millions of middle-income and older Americans in general are now taking advantage of its benefits.

A valid Trust is created by a written agreement in which a person, the "settlor," places some assets in the Trust for the benefit of him or herself or any other person. This latter person is called the "beneficiary." Someone must also be appointed as "trustee" to manage and control the assets.

Perhaps most typical is the Intervivos or Living Trust. Such a Trust is expressly revocable, which means that the settlor can modify or revoke the terms of the agreement so

[1]Reprinted from Buchanan, A., & Brock, D., with Gilfix, M. (1986). *Deciding for others: The ethics of decisionmaking for elderly individuals who are incompetent or of questionable competence* (Background study). Washington, DC: U.S. Congress, Office of Technology Assessment.

370

long as that person retains legal capacity. Thus the settlor retains control even after the Trust is created, so long as he or she is competent.

The settlor (or settlors – often husband or wife) may create a Trust for one or more reasons. The first, and probably most common, is to avoid probate. The probate process, by which a decedent's assets are passed along to heirs, is expensive and typically very time-consuming. By placing assets in a Living Trust, the settlor has created an alternative mechanism for passing along his or her estate. The Intervivos Trust also avoids conservatorship. In a typical Trust, the creators are the initial trustees. This means that they have complete, unrestricted control of their assets just as if they had not set up a Trust. In their Trust agreement, they also name "alternative trustees," who will take over management of the Trust in the event that the initial trustees – who may be the beneficiaries – become incapacitated. No conservatorship of the estate is needed because someone has complete legal control of the assets without recourse to the courts.

Another factor in setting up a Trust is that, unlike the probate process, it maintains the privacy of those involved. In the probate process, the will becomes something of a public document – barring special court orders, anyone can look at a probate file, which includes the decedent's will and listing of assets. Unwanted media attention sometimes results and, much more significantly, unscrupulous "con artists" have access to the names of the beneficiaries. Unlike the probate file, however, the Intervivos Trust is a private document. Uninvolved persons have no access to the Trust agreement, and therefore have no way of learning anything about the size or disposition of a deceased person's estate.

The Intervivos Trust also allows the settlor to monitor the performance of the trustee. By initially naming a person or entity (such as a bank trust department), the still competent settlor can evaluate the trustee's performance to decide if that particular trustee does an adequate job, and, if not, name another trustee instead. The Trust also can serve as a vehicle for minimizing inheritance taxes.

Finally, a Trust can be used to plan for such things as Medicaid eligibility. Although this subject is beyond the scope of this book, there are numerous planning steps that can be taken to preserve a substantial portion of an older person's estate, particularly in the event of nursing home placement. The noninstitutionalized spouse thus need not become destitute before Medicaid will pay for nursing home and other medical care costs. The Intervivos Trust can provide an effective device for an elder – particularly one diagnosed as having Alzheimer's or Parkinson's disease, who may face institutional placement – to ensure that his or her care will not bankrupt the family.

II. NOMINATION OF CONSERVATORSHIP

The conservatorship usually is a court-ordered taking of independence and control from the elderly person – another person (or entity) is given control over the assets and/or person of the elder. Unlike an Intervivos Trust, the conservatorship is public in nature. Accountings (delineations of assets, income, and expenditures) must be filed, and are open to anyone's review. Although this may be viewed as an invasion of privacy, its purpose is to shield the elder from undue risk – without control of his or her own assets, the older person cannot be preyed on by con artists or unscrupulous businesspeople.

Provisions for a conservatorship also may be made by an older person while still competent. The California Durable Power of Attorney for Health Care Statute, described in detail below, includes a place for nominating a conservator. A conservator may also be nominated in a very simple independent document or in a general durable power of attorney document (one not specifically limited to health care). Although a judge is not legally bound to honor such a nomination, it is unlikely that it would be disregarded without a weighty reason for doing so.

Notwithstanding its often intrusive nature, conservatorship plays an important role in protecting the elderly incompetent person. Although conservatorship by a person nominated in advance by the conservatee is not a substitute for the more extensive control possible with an Intervivos Trust or a Durable Power of Attorney, it provides somewhat greater scope for self-determination than when a conservator is appointed independently.

Appendix 2. Durable power of attorney for health care

(California Civil Code Sections 2410–2443) *GUIDE-
LINES FOR SIGNERS*

I. WHAT IS A DURABLE POWER OF ATTOR-NEY FOR HEALTH CARE?

A "Durable Power of Attorney for Health Care" is a document that you can use to appoint another person, such as a family member or friend, who can make health care decisions for you if you become unable to make the decisions on your own. The person may make all decisions about your health care, subject only to limitations you specify on that person's authority and several restrictions imposed by law.

II. WHY COMPLETE A DURABLE POWER OF ATTORNEY FOR HEALTH CARE?

A Durable Power of Attorney for Health Care will be helpful even if you have executed a "Living Will" or a "Directive to Physicians" since it applies to all health care decisions and allows you to appoint a person who can carry out your wishes if you become incapable of making your own decisions. The other primary reasons for completing a Durable Power of Attorney for Health Care are to avoid court proceedings, possible delays in receiving needed medical

374

care, and emotional and financial stress on family or friends. These benefits are available because a Durable Power of Attorney for Health Care can be executed by simply completing this form, without going to court. It may be advisable to execute a Durable Power of Attorney for Health Care before surgery or other medical care. Persons with chronic conditions that may "flare up" and leave them unable to make decisions might also consider executing a Durable Power of Attorney. Persons with no close relatives living nearby may want to identify a close friend to make medical decisions for them in the event they should become unable to make such decisions for themselves. As a practical matter, many people may want to keep a Durable Power of Attorney for Health Care in effect at all times, just as they maintain insurance to protect their interests in the event of unforseen occurrences.

III. WHO CAN COMPLETE A DURABLE POWER OF ATTORNEY FOR HEALTH CARE?

Any person who is a California resident, is at least 18 years old, is of sound mind, and is acting of his or her own free will may execute a Durable Power of Attorney for Health Care.

IV. CAN A PERSON APPOINTED IN A DURABLE POWER OF ATTORNEY FOR HEALTH CARE MANAGE MY FINANCIAL AFFAIRS?

A person appointed in a Durable Power of Attorney for Health Care is allowed only to make health care decisions, arrangements for medical services, and related decisions. If you want to appoint a person to handle your other financial or legal affairs, you should consult with an attorney about completing a

Durable Power of Attorney for such matters or using alternative methods for taking care of these matters.

V. HOW DO I COMPLETE A DURABLE POWER OF ATTORNEY FOR HEALTH CARE?

Simply fill out this form, which will name your health care agent and set forth the limits imposed by you and by law on his or her authority. Read the form carefully before filling it out.

VI. MUST THE APPOINTED PERSON BE AN ATTORNEY?

Although the Durable Power of Attorney for Health Care has the term "attorney" in the title, and the person appointed to make decisions is called an "attorney-in-fact," he or she does not need to be an attorney. There are only a few limits on who may be appointed. These are set forth in the form below.

WARNING TO PERSON EXECUTING THIS DOCUMENT

THIS IS AN IMPORTANT LEGAL DOCUMENT. IT CREATES A DURABLE POWER OF ATTORNEY FOR HEALTH CARE. BEFORE EXECUTING THIS DOCUMENT, YOU SHOULD KNOW THESE IMPORTANT FACTS:

1. THIS DOCUMENT GIVES THE PERSON YOU DESIGNATE AS YOUR ATTORNEY-IN-FACT-THE POWER TO MAKE HEALTH CARE DECISIONS FOR YOU. THIS POWER IS SUBJECT TO ANY LIMITATIONS OR STATEMENT OF YOUR DESIRES THAT YOU INCLUDE IN THIS DOCUMENT. THE POWER TO MAKE HEALTH CARE DECISIONS FOR YOU MAY

INCLUDE CONSENT, REFUSAL OF CONSENT, OR WITHDRAWAL OF CONSENT TO ANY CARE, TREATMENT, SERVICE, OR PROCEDURE TO MAINTAIN, DIAGNOSE, OR TREAT A PHYSICAL OR MENTAL CONDITION. YOU MAY STATE IN THIS DOCUMENT ANY TYPES OF TREATMENT OR PLACEMENTS THAT YOU DO NOT DESIRE.

2. THE PERSON YOU DESIGNATE IN THIS DOCUMENT HAS A DUTY TO ACT CONSISTENT WITH YOUR DESIRES AS STATED IN THIS DOCUMENT OR OTHERWISE MADE KNOWN OR, IF YOUR DESIRES ARE UNKNOWN, TO ACT IN YOUR BEST INTERESTS.

3. EXCEPT AS YOU OTHERWISE SPECIFY IN THIS DOCUMENT, THE POWER OF THE PERSON YOU DESIGNATE TO MAKE HEALTH CARE DECISIONS FOR YOU MAY INCLUDE THE POWER TO CONSENT TO YOUR DOCTOR NOT GIVING TREATMENT OR STOPPING TREATMENT WHICH WOULD KEEP YOU ALIVE.

4. UNLESS YOU SPECIFY A SHORTER PERIOD IN THIS DOCUMENT, THIS POWER WILL EXIST FOR SEVEN YEARS FROM THE DATE YOU EXECUTE THIS DOCUMENT AND, IF YOU ARE UNABLE TO MAKE HEALTH CARE DECISIONS FOR YOURSELF AT THE TIME WHEN THIS SEVEN-YEAR PERIOD ENDS, THIS POWER WILL CONTINUE TO EXIST UNTIL THE TIME WHEN YOU BECOME ABLE TO MAKE HEALTH CARE DECISIONS FOR YOURSELF.

5. NOTWITHSTANDING THIS DOCUMENT, YOU HAVE THE RIGHT TO MAKE MEDICAL, AND OTHER HEALTH CARE DECISIONS FOR YOURSELF SO LONG AS YOU CAN GIVE INFORMED CONSENT WITH RESPECT TO THE PARTICULAR DECISION. IN ADDITION, NO TREATMENT MAY BE GIVEN TO YOU OVER YOUR OBJECTION, AND HEALTH CARE NECESSARY TO KEEP YOU ALIVE MAY NOT BE STOPPED IF YOU OBJECT.

6. YOU HAVE THE RIGHT TO REVOKE THE APPOINTMENT OF THE PERSON DESIGNATED IN THIS DOCUMENT TO MAKE HEALTH CARE DECISIONS FOR YOU BY NOTIFYING THAT PERSON OF THE REVOCATION ORALLY OR IN WRITING.

7. YOU HAVE THE RIGHT TO REVOKE THE AUTHORITY GRANTED TO THE PERSON DESIGNATED IN THIS DOCUMENT TO MAKE HEALTH CARE DECISIONS FOR YOU BY NOTIFYING THE TREATING PHYSICIAN, HOSPITAL, OR OTHER HEALTH CARE PROVIDER ORALLY OR IN WRITING.

8. THE PERSON DESIGNATED IN THIS DOCUMENT TO MAKE HEALTH CARE DECISIONS FOR YOU HAS THE RIGHT TO EXAMINE YOUR MEDICAL RECORDS AND TO CONSENT TO THEIR DISCLOSURE UNLESS YOU LIMIT THIS RIGHT IN THE DOCUMENT.

9. IF THERE IS ANYTHING IN THIS DOCUMENT THAT YOU DO NOT UNDERSTAND, YOU SHOULD ASK A LAWYER TO EXPLAIN IT TO YOU.

★★★

1. CREATION OF DURABLE POWER OF ATTORNEY FOR HEALTH CARE.

By this document I intend to create a durable power of attorney by appointing the person designated below to make health care decisions for me as allowed by the California Civil Code. This power of attorney shall not be affected by my subsequent incapacity.

2. DESIGNATION OF HEALTH CARE AGENT.

(Your attorney-in-fact, i.e., your agent, must be an adult and a California resident. Insert the name, address, and telephone number of the person you wish to designate as your agent to make health care decisions for you. None of the following may be designated as your agent: (1) your treating health care provider, (2) an employee of your treating health care provider, (3) an operator of a community health care facility, or (4) an employee of an operator of a community health care facility. For example, your agent may not be your physician, your nurse, an employee of your nursing home, or an operator of a board and care home.)

I, _____ do hereby designate and appoint:

Name: _____

Address: _____

_____

Telephone Number: (____) _____ as my agent to make health care decisions for me as authorized in this document.

3. GENERAL STATEMENT OF AUTHORITY GRANTED.

If I become incapable of giving informed consent with respect to health care decisions, I hereby grant to my

agent full power and authority to make health care
decisions for me including: consent, refusal of consent, or withdrawal of consent to any care, treatment,
service, or procedure to maintain, diagnose, or treat a
physical or mental condition, and to receive and to
consent to the release of medical information, subject
to the limitations and special provisions, set forth in
Paragraph 6 below.

4.   CONTRIBUTION OF ANATOMICAL GIFT

(You may choose to make a gift of all or part of your
body to a hospital, physician, or medical school, for
scientific, educational, therapeutic, or transplant purposes. Such a gift is allowed by California's Uniform
Anatomical Gift Act. If you do not make such a
gift, you may authorize your agent to do so, or a
member of your family may make a gift unless you
give them notice that you do not want a gift made.
In the space below you may make a gift yourself
or state that you do not want to make a gift. If
you do not complete this section, your agent will
have the authority to make a gift of all or part
of your body under the Uniform Anatomical Gift
Act.)

If either statement reflects your desires, sign the box
next to the statement. You do not have to sign either
statement. If you do not sign either statement, your
agent and your family will have the authority to make
a gift of all or part of your body under the Uniform
Anatomical Gift Act.

(_____) Pursuant to the Uniform Anatomical
Gift Act, I hereby give, effective upon
my death:

□ Any needed organ or parts; or

□ The parts or organs listed:

_____

_____

_____

(_____) I do not want to make a gift under the Uniform Anatomical Gift Act, nor do I want my agent or family to do so.

5. SPECIAL PROVISIONS AND LIMITATIONS.

(By law, your agent is not permitted to consent to any of the following: commitment to or placement in a mental health treatment facility, convulsive treatment, psychosurgery, sterilization, or abortion. In every other respect, your agent may make health care decisions for you to the same extent that you could make them for yourself if you were capable of doing so. If there are any special restriction you wish to place on your agent's authority, you should list them in the space below. If you do not write in any limitations, your agent will have the broad powers to make health care decisions on your behalf which are set forth in Paragraph 3, except to the extent that there are limits provided by law.)

In exercising the authority under this durable power of attorney for health care, the authority of my attorney-in-fact is subject to the following special provisions and limitations:

_____

_____

_____

_____

_____

6. DESIGNATION OF ALTERNATE AGENT.

(You are not required to designate any alternative
agents but you may do so. Any alternative agent must
meet the requirements set forth in Paragraph 2 above.
Any alternative agent you designate will be able to
make the same health care decisions as the agent designated in Paragraph 2 above in the event that he or
she is unable or unwilling to act as your agent. Also, if
the agent designated in Paragraph 2 is your spouse,
his or her designation as your agent is automatically
revoked by law if your marriage is dissolved.)

If the person designated in Paragraph 2 as my agent is
unable to make health care decisions for me or is
disqualified by law from so doing, then I designate
the following persons to serve as my agent to make
health care decisions for me as authorized in this
document, such persons to serve in the order listed
below:

A. First Alternative Agent
   Name: _____
   Address: _____

   _____
   Telephone Number: (____) _____
B. Second Alternative Agent
   Name: _____
   Address: _____

   _____
   Telephone Number: (____) _____

7. DURATION

I understand that this power of attorney will exist for
seven years from the date I execute this document
unless I establish a shorter time. If I am unable to

make health care decisions for myself when this power of attorney expires, the authority I have granted my agent will continue to exist until the time when I become able to make health care decisions for myself.

(Optional) I wish to have this power of attorney end before seven years on the following date:_____

8.   PRIOR DESIGNATION REVOKED.

I revoke any prior durable power of attorney for health care.

(YOU MUST DATE AND SIGN THIS POWER OF ATTORNEY)

I sign my name to this Durable Power of Attorney for Health Care on _____ at _____,
                               (Date)   (City)
_____.
          (State)

_____
          (Signature)

_____
THIS POWER OF ATTORNEY WILL NOT BE VALID FOR MAKING HEALTH CARE DECISIONS UNLESS IT IS EITHER (1) ACKNOWLEDGED BEFORE A NOTARY PUBLIC IN CALIFORNIA OR (2) SIGNED BY AT LEAST TWO QUALIFIED WITNESSES WHO PERSONALLY KNOW YOU AND ARE PRESENT WHEN YOU SIGN OR ACKNOWLEDGE YOUR SIGNATURE.

CERTIFICATE OF ACKNOWLEDGEMENT
, OF NOTARY PUBLIC

(You may use acknowledgment before a notary public instead of the statement of witness.)

STATE OF CALIFORNIA)
) ss.
COUNTY OF_____)

,
On this _____ day of_____, in the year _____

before me, a Notary Public in and for the State of California, personally appeared _____
personally known to me (or proved to me on the basis of satisfactory evidence) to be the person whose name is subscribed to this instrument, and acknowledged that he or she executed it. I declare under penalty of perjury that the person whose name is subscribed to this instrument appears to be of sound mind and under no duress, fraud, or undue influence.

NOTARY SEAL   _____
                           (Signature of
                           Notary Public)

STATEMENT OF WITNESSES

(If you elect to use witnesses instead of having this document notarized, you should carefully read and follow this witnessing procedure; otherwise this document will not be valid.)

(You must use two qualified adult witnesses who personally know you. None of the following may be used as a witness: (1) a person you designate as your agent, (2) a health care provider, (3) an employee of a health care provider, (4) the operator of a community care facility, (5) an employer of an operator of a community care facility. For example, your witness may not be a physician, a nurse, a hospital employee, a nursing home employee, or an operator of a board and care home. At least one of the witnesses must make the additional declaration set out following the place where the witnesses sign.)

I declare under penalty of perjury under the laws of California that the principal is personally known to me, that the principal signed or acknowledged this durable power of attorney in my presence, that the principal appears to be of sound mind and under no duress, fraud, or undue influence, that I am not the person appointed as attorney-in-fact (agent) by this document, and that I am not a health care provider, an employee of a health care provider, the operator of a community care facility, nor an employee of an operator of a community care facility.

Signature:_____ Residence Address: _____
Print Name:_____ _____
Date:_____ _____
Signature:_____ Residence Address: _____
Print Name:_____ _____
Date:_____ _____

(AT LEAST ONE OF THE ABOVE WITNESSES MUST ALSO SIGN THE FOLLOWING DECLARATION.)

I declare under penalty of perjury under the laws of California that I am not related to the principal by blood, marriage, or adoption, and to the best of my knowledge I am not entitled to any part of the estate of the principal upon the death of the principal under a will now existing or by operation of law.

Signature: _____
Optional Second Signature: _____

SPECIAL REQUIREMENTS

(Special additional requirements must be satisfied for this document to be valid if (1) you are a patient in a skilled nursing facility or (2) you are conservatee under the Lanterman-Petris-Short Act and you are appointing the conservator as your agent to make health care decisions for you. If you are not sure whether you are in a skilled nursing facility, which is a special type of nursing home, ask the facility staff.)

1. If you are a patient in a skilled nursing facility (as defined in Health and Safety Code Section 1250(c) at least one witness must be a patient advocate or ombudsman. The patient advocate or ombudsman must sign the witness statement and must also sign the following declaration.

I declare under penalty of perjury under the laws of California that I am a patient advocate or ombudsman as designate by the State Department of Aging and am serving as a witness as required by subdivision (a) (2)A of Civil Code 2432.

Signature:_____ Address:_____
Print Name:_____ _____
Date:_____ _____

COPIES: You should retain the executed original document and give a copy of the executed original to your agent and any alternative agents. You may also wish to give a copy to your doctor or to members of your family. Photocopies of this document can be relied upon as though they were originals.

Pursuant to California Civil Code §2421, I expressly eliminate the authority of any of my or my wife's children or grandchildren to petition the court under this article for one or more of the purposes enumerated in Sections 2412 or 2412.5 of the California Civil Code.

Notes

INTRODUCTION

1. Congress of the United States, Office of Technology Assessment. (1987). *Losing a Million Minds: Confronting the Tragedy of Alzheimer's Disease and Other Dementias* (pp. 3–4). Washington, DC: U. S. Government Printing Office.
2. President's Commission for the Study of Ethical Problems in Medicine and Biomedical and Behavioral Research. (1983). *Deciding to Forego Life-Sustaining Treatment* (pp. 17–18). Washington, D.C: U. S. Government Printing Office.
3. Bedell, S., & Delbanco, T. (1984). Choices about Cardiopulmonary Resuscitation in the Hospital. *New England Journal of Medicine, 310,* 1089–93. Lidz, C. W., Meisel, A., Zerubavel, E. (1984). et al. *Informed Consent: A Study of Decision Making in Psychiatry* (pp. 1–3). New York: Guilford Press. Evans, A. & Broady, B. A. (1985). The Do Not Resuscitate Order in Teaching Hospitals. *Journal of the American Medical Association, 253,* 2236–45.
4. Faden, R. & Beauchamp, T. L. (1986). *A History and Theory of Informed Consent.* New York: Oxford University Press.
5. Childress, J. F. (1982). *Who Should Decide?* New York: Oxford University Press. Feinberg, J. (1986) *Harm to Self.* New York: Oxford University Press. Kleinig, J. (1984). *Paternalism.* Totowa, N J. Rowman & Allanheld. VanDeVeer, D. (1986). *Paternalistic Intervention.* Princeton, NJ: Princeton University Press.
6. Mill, J. S. (1974). *On Liberty* (1859). New York: Penquin Books.
7. President's Commission for the Study of Ethical Problems in Medicine and Biomedical and Behavioral Research. (1981) *Defining Death.* Washington, DC: U. S. Government Printing Office.
8. Buchanan, A. (Summer 1979). Medical Paternalism or Legal Imperialism: Not the Only Alternatives for Handling *Saikewicz*-type Cases. *American Journal of Law and Medicine, 5,* 97–117.

387

9. Buchanan, A. (forthcoming). The Ethics of Allocation of Health
    Care Resources. In R. Veatch (ed.), *Medical Ethics*. Boston, MA:
    Jones and Bartlett. Brock, D. (1986). The Value of Prolonging
    Human Life. *Philosophical Studies, 50,* 401–28.
10. For a thoughtful discussion of Rawls's notion of wide reflective
    equilibrium see: Daniels, N. (1979). Wide Reflective Equilibrium
    and Theory Acceptance in Ethics. *Journal of Philosophy, 76,* 256–
    82.
11. Buchanan, A. Personal communication.

CHAPTER 1

1. The basic position, and even on occasion some of the language, of
    our account of competence in this chapter bears a close relation at
    some points to the treatment of decision-making capacity in the
    reports of the President's Commission for the Study of Ethical
    Problems in Medicine and Biomedical and Behavioral Research.
    (1982). *Making Health Care Decisions: The Ethical and Legal Im-
    plications of Informed Consent in the Patient-Practitioner Relationship*
    Vol. 1: report) Washington, DC: U. S. Government Printing
    Office, and *Deciding to Forego Life-Sustaining Treatment.* (1983).
    Washington, DC: U.S. Government Printing Office. However,
    our account is developed in considerably greater detail and carries
    the analysis of the President's Commission substantially further in
    a number of important respects. Both of us contributed to the
    second work and one of us (Brock) was also a member of the staff
    team that drafted the first, together with an earlier unpublished
    Commission discussion paper on competence, with special
    responsibilities for some of the philosophical issues discussed
    there, including the account of competence. That report was truly
    a team effort and Brock's views on competence are deeply in-
    debted to the other members of that team, Alexander M. Capron,
    Joanne Lynn, Marion Osterweis, and Alan J. Weisbard, although
    none of them can, of course, be held responsible for our account
    developed here.
2. A global conception of decision-making competence is defended
    by Abernathy, V. (1984). Comparison, Control, and Decisions
    About Competency. *American Journal of Psychiatry, 141,* 53–60,
    largely on the basis that it is less subject to the abuse of un-
    warranted removal of decisions from patients. We believe that the
    evidence about abuse of decision-specific standards does not war-
    rant the inflexibility of a global standard. Among recent influential
    decision-relative accounts are the President's Commissions' re-

ports, *Making Health Care Decisions, op. cit.,* and *Deciding to Forego Life-Sustaining Treatment, op. cit.;* Jonsen, A., Siegler, M., & Winslade, W. (1982). *Clinical Ethics.* New York: MacMillan Publishing Co.; and the report of the Hastings Center. (1987). *Guidelines on the Termination of Treatment and the Care of the Dying.* Briarcliff Manor, NY: Author. A good review of the use in the law of selective competency with children can be found in Holder, A. (1985). *Legal Issues in Pediatrics and Adolescent Medicine.* New Haven: Yale University Press.

3. This presumption is displayed in the legal doctrine of informed consent for medical care. An excellent historical survey of that doctrine can be found in Faden, R. & Beauchamp, T. L. (1986). *A History and Theory of Informed Consent.* New York: Oxford University Press, especially chapters 2, 4, pp. 23–49, 114–150.

4. The long line of legal cases in the first half of this century enunciating the requirement of consent for medical care, and later in the second half of this century of *informed* consent, have consistently appealed in one form or other to a right of self-determination. In probably the most often-cited consent case, Schloendorf v. Society of New York Hospital, 211 N.Y. 125, 105 N.E. 91, 95 (1914), Justice Cardozo stated

   "Every human being of adult years and sound mind has a right to determine what shall be done to his own body; and a surgeon who performs an operation without his patient's consent commits an assault, for which he is liable in damages."

   Nearly half a century later in the important case of Natanson v. Kline, 186 Kan. 393, 350 P.2d. 1093 (1960), The Kansas Supreme Court made an equally ringing appeal to self-determination.

   "Anglo-American law starts with the premise of thorough-going self-determination. It follows that each man is considered to be master of his own body, and he may, if he be of sound mind, expressly prohibit the performance of life-saving surgery, or other medical treatment. A doctor may well believe than an operation or form of treatment is desirable or necessary, but the law does not permit him to substitute his own judgment for that of the patient by any form of artifice or deception."

5. President's Commission, *Making Health Care Decisions* (pp. 58–9), *op. cit.*

6. For a subtle discussion of a number of difficulties in assessing competence in clinical contexts, cf., Appelbaum, P. S. & Roth, L. (1981). Clinical Issues in the Assessment of Competency. *American*

Journal of Psychiatry, 138, 1462–67, and Roth, Appelbaum, & Sallee, et al (1982). The Dilemma of Denial in the Assessment of Competency to Consent to Treatment, *American Journal of Psychiatry, 139,* 910–13.

7. Brock, D. W. (1987). Informed Consent. in T. Regan & D. VanDeVeer (eds.), *Health Care Ethics* Philadelphia: Temple University Press. Among the most important and useful extended treatments of informed consent are: Faden and Beauchamp; President's Commission, *Making Health Care Decisions;* Appelbaum, P. S., Lidz, C. W., & Meisel, A. (1987). *Informed Consent: Legal Theory and Clinical Practice.* New York: Oxford University Press. The most important empirical study of informed consent is Lidz, C. W., Meisel, A., Zerubavel, E. et al. (1984). *Informed Consent: A Study of Decision-making in Psychiatry.* New York: The Guilford Press; cf. also Meisel, A. & Roth, L. H. (1981). What We Do and Do Not Know About Informed Cconsent. *Journal of the American Medical Association, 246,* 2473–77; and Roth, L. H., Lidz, C. W., Meisel, A., et al (1982). Competency to Decide About Treatment or Research: An Overview of Some Empirical Data. *International Journal of Law and Psychiatry, 5,* 29–50. The exceptions to the legal requirement of informed consent are discussed in Meisel, A. (1979). The Exceptions to the Informed Consent Doctrine: Striking A Balance Between Competing Values in Medical Decision-making. *Wisconsin Law Review* (1979), 413–88.

8. Probably the most penetrating discussion of many of the obstacles to attaining this ideal in practice is Katz, J. (1984). *The Silent World of Doctor and Patient.* New York: The Free Press.

9. Faden and Beauchamp (pp. 287–8), *op. cit.,* make this point in characterizing competence as a "gatekeeping concept," "competence judgments function to distinguish persons from whom consent *should* be solicited from those from whom consent need not or should not be solicited." For reasons that will become clear as our analysis proceeds, we would substitute "accepted" for "solicited" since in hard cases it commonly cannot be clear whether a person is competent for the decision in question until he or she has gone through the process of making, or attempting to make, that decision.

10. For a perceptive discussion of the distinction between comparative and threshold conceptions of competence, see Wikler, D. (1983). Paternalism and the Mildly Retarded. In R. Sartorius (Ed.), *Paternalism* (pp. 83–94). St. Paul, MN: University of Minnesota Press.

11. Probably the most subtle and detailed recent discussion of alterna-

tive theories of the good for persons is Griffin, J. (1986). *Well Being*. Oxford: Oxford University Press.

12. For an explanation and defense of the hedonist, specifically, happiness, theory of the good for persons, cf. Brandt, R. (1979). *A Theory of the Good and the Right* (pp. 246–65). Oxford: Oxford University Press, Chap. 13.

13. This view is discussed in Griffin (pp. 7–20), *op. cit.*

14. Cf. Goodin, R. (1986). Laundering Preferences. In J. Elster & A. Hylland (Eds.), *Foundations of Social Choice Theory* (pp. 95–101). Cambridge: Cambridge University Press.

15. Parfit, D. (1984). *Reasons and Persons*. Oxford: Oxford University Press. Cf. espec. Appendix I (pp. 493–502).

16. Brock,. D. W. (1983). Paternalism and Promoting the Good. In R. Sartorius, *op. cit.*

17. See, for example, Griffin, chap. 1 (pp. 7–20), *op. cit.*

18. Cf. Buchanan, A. (1983). Medical Paternalism. In R. Sartorious, *op. cit.*

19. Cf. n. 4 above. For an extended argument that informed consent law inadequately protects inc' .dual autonomy, and a proposal of a distinct and independently protected legal interest in patient autonomy, see Schultz, M. M. (Dec. 1985). From Informed Consent to Patient Choice: A New Protected Interest. *Yale Law Review, 95*(2), 219–99. A good discussion of autonomy in the clinical context, with attention to the obstacles to it there, is Katz, chaps. 5–6 (pp. 104–64).

20. But among more important discussions, see Dworkin, G. (1988). *The Theory and Practice of Autonomy*. Cambridge: Cambridge University Press; Benn, S. (1976). Freedom, Autonomy, and the Concept of a Person. *Proceedings of the Aristotelian Society, 12*, 109–130; Frankfurt, H. (1971). Freedom of the Will and the Concept of a Person. *Journal of Philosophy, 68*, 5–20; Haworth, L. (1986). *Autonomy*. New Haven, CT: Yale University Press; Rawls, J. (1980). Kantian Constructivism in Moral Theory. *Journal of Philosophy, 77*, 515–72; Young, R. (1980). Autonomy and Socialization. *Mind, 89*, 565–76; and Young, R. (1980). Autonomy and the Inner Self. *American Philosophical Quarterly, 17*, 35–43.

21. This notion of balancing two kinds of errors is used by Drane, J. who develops a conception of competence similar in a number of respects to our own: Drane, J. (1985). The Many Faces of Competency. *Hastings Center Report, 15*(2) 17–21.

22. Feinberg, J. (1986). *Harm to Self*. Oxford: Oxford University Press. Other accounts that reject balancing autonomy against

other values include Shuman, S. 1979. Informed Consent and the "Victims" of Colonialism. In W. L. Robison (Ed.), *Medical Responsibility* (pp. 75–100). Clifton, NJ: Humana Press and Goldstein, J. (1975). For Harold Lasswell: Some reflections on Human Dignity, Entrapment, Informed Consent, and the Plea Bargain. *Yale Law Journal 84,* 683–703.

23. But see also VanDeVeer, D. *Paternalistic Intervention, op. cit.,* and Kleinig, J. *Paternalism, op. cit.*

24. Feinberg, (p. 115), *op. cit.*

25. *Ibid.,* (p. 117).

26. *Ibid.,* (p. 57).

27. *Ibid.,* (p. 161).

28. *Ibid.,* (p. 117).

29. *Ibid.,* (p. 119).

30. See especially Roth, L. H., Meisel, A., & Lidz, C. W. (1977). Tests of Competency to Consent to Treatment. *American Journal of Psychiatry, 134,* 279–84; what they call "tests" are what we call "standards". An excellent discussion of competence generally, and of Roth, et al.'s tests for competence in particular, is Freedman, B. (1981). Competence, Marginal and Otherwise. *International Journal of Law and Psychiatry, 4,* 53–72.

31. Cf. Freedman, *op. cit.*

32. For example, John Rawls makes such claims for an objective and interpersonal account of "primary goods" to be used in evaluating persons' well-being within a theory of justice; cf. Rawls, J. (1971). *A Theory of Justice.* Cambridge, MA: Harvard University Press. Cf. also Scanlon, T. (1975). Preference and Urgency. *Journal of Philosophy, 72,* 655–69.

33. This second kind of decision-making defect illustrates the inadequacy of the tests that Roth, Meisel & Lidz call "the ability to understand" and "actual understanding" tests (cf. Roth, et al. (pp. 281–82), *op. cit.* The clinically depressed patient may evidence no failure to understand the harmful consequences of his choice, but instead evidence indifference to those consequences as a result of his depression.

34. Appelbaum, P. S., & Roth, L. H. (1982). Treatment Refusal in Medical Hospital. In President's Commission for the Study of Ethical Problems in Medicine and Biomedical and Behavioral Research, *Making Health Care Decisions: The Ethical and Legal Implications of Informed Consent in the Patient-Practitioner Relationship: Vol. 2. Appendices.* Washington, DC: U. S. Government Printing Office.

35. The necessity for such balancing at the deepest theoretical level

even in moral theories that may seem to eschew it by appeal to a
general right to self-determination is argued in Brock, D. W.
(1983). Paternalism and Promoting the Good. In R. Sartorious,
op. cit.

36. Culver, C. M. & Gert, B. (unpublished). The Inadequacy of
Incompetence.
37. *Ibid.,* (p. 6).
38. *Ibid.,* (p. 12).
39. *Ibid.,* (p. 12).
40. *Ibid.,* (p. 13).
41. Nelson, A., Fogel, B. S., & Faust, D. (1986). Bedside Cognitive
Screening Instruments: A Critical Assessment. *Journal of Nervous
and Mental Disease, 174*(2), 73–83.
42. Folstein, M. F., Folstein, S. E., & McHugh, P. R. (1975). Mini-
Mental State. *Journal of Psychiatric Research, 12,* 189–98.
43. Jacobs, J. W., Bernhard, M. R., Delgado, A., & Strain, J. J.
(1977). Screening for Organic Mental Syndromes in the Medically
Ill. *Annuals of Internal Medicine, 86,* 40–46.
44. Mattis, S. (1976). Mental Status Examination for Organic Mental
Syndromes in the Elderly Patient. In L. Bellak & Karasu, T. E.
(Eds.), *Geriatric Psychiatry.* New York: Grune and Stratton.
45. Kahn, R. L., Goldfarb, A. I., Pollack, M., & Peck, A. (1960).
Brief Objective Measures for the Determination of Mental Status
in the Aged. *American Journal of Psychiatry, 117,* 326–8.
46. Gardner, R., Oliver-Munoz, S., Fisher, L., & Empting, L. (1981).
Mattis Dementia Rating Scale: Internal Reliability Study Using a
Diffusely Impaired Population. *Journal of Clinical Neuropsychology,
3,* 271–5.
47. Their reliability and validity are reviewed in Nelson, Fogel, &
Faust, *op. cit.*
48. Except as noted below, these limitations are all discussed in Nelson, Fogel & Faust, *op. cit.*
49. This failure to address affective components of decision making is
discussed at length by White, B. C. (1989). *Competence to Consent.*
Unpublished doctoral dissertation, Rice University.
50. For a general discussion of informed consent in the research setting see Appelbaum, Lidz, & Meisel, chaps. 11, 12 (pp. 211–60),
op. cit. Since our concern with research in this study is limited, we
make no attempt systematically to cite the very large literature in
this area. Important additional sources are the various reports of
the National Commission for the Protection of Human Subjects
of Biomedical and Behavioral Research, as well as the journal
IRB, published by the Hastings Center.

51. Horstman, P, (1978). Protection Services for the Elderly: The Limits of Parens Patriae. *Missouri Law Review, 40,* 215–78.
52. Cf. Wikler, (1983). in R. Sartorius (Ed.), *op. cit.*

CHAPTER 2

1. Buchanan, A. (1985). Competition, Charity and the Right to Health Care. In Attig, R. et al. (Eds.), *The Restraint of Liberty* (pp. 129–43). Bowling Green, OH: The Applied Philosophy Program, Bowling Green State University.
2. See, for example: President's Commission. (1983). *Deciding to Forego Life-Sustaining Treatment* (pp. 89–90). Washington, DC: U. S. Government Printing Office.
3. *In re* Brooks Estate, 32 Ill. 2d 361 205 N.E.2d 435 (1965). *In re* Osborne, 294 A.2d 372 (D.C. Appl. 1972). *In re* Yetter, 62 d & C.2d 619 (C.P. Northampton County, PA, 1973).
4. Angell, M. (1984). Respecting Self-determination of Competent Patients. *New England Journal of Medicine, 310,* 1115–6. Evans, A. & Brody, B. A. (1985). The Do Not Resuscitate Order in Teaching Hospitals. *Journal of the American Medical Association, 253,* 2236–45.
5. In some cases, a death hastened by dehydration and malnutrition may in fact even be less painful than the discomfort and terror of asphyxiation that sometimes follow removal of a respirator. In either case, however, appropriate sedation can prevent unnecessary pain once the decision to withhold support has been made. President's Commission (pp. 277–94), *op. cit.*

The fact that feeding is one of the first and most familiar forms of caring experienced by human beings endows it with considerable symbolic significance, at least for some people. This symbolic significance, when combined with the tendency of those who characterize termination of nutritional support as "starving" the patient, has served to obscure the fact that there is no ethical distinction per se between removing a respirator and removing a feeding tube or even ceasing ordinary feeding. The term "starvation" functions only as prejudicial rhetoric, because of its associations with cases outside of the medical setting in which deliberately withholding food from an individual involves malicious or callous neglect. But the immorality of these other, quite different cases is irrelevant to the moral status of withholding nutritional support when this is freely chosen by a competent and informed patient who does so only to bring a quicker end to what he or she believes to be futile suffering.

The competent patient, then, has the moral right to refuse nutritional support, whether by ordinary feeding or by artificial means. Since such support might more aptly be called care rather than treatment, it may be more useful to say that a the competent individual has the right to refuse medical treatment and care. A number of important recent court rulings have clearly affirmed a legal right to refuse artificial feeding as well as respirator support. See Barber v. Superior Court, 147 Cal. App. 3d. 1006, 195 Cal. Rptr. 484 (Ct. App. 1983). Brophy v. New England Sinai Hospital, Inc., 398 Mass. 417, 497 N.E.2d. 626 (1986). *In re* Conroy, 98, N.J. 321, 486 A.2d. 1209 (1985). *In re* Jobes, No. A-108/109 (N.J. June 24, 1987). *In re* Peters, No. A-78 (N.J. June 24, 1987). Rasmussen v. Fleming, no. CV-86-0450 PR (Ariz. July 23, 1987). The reasoning the courts have used to justify this conclusion also tends to support the broader conclusion that there is a legal right to refuse "natural" feeding as well, although the courts themselves have not yet explicitly drawn this implication.

Although the factors that justify withholding "artificial" feeding in principle justify withholding "natural" (spoon) feeding under the same circumstances, it can be argued that social policy and the law should treat the two differently. The vast majority of patients who can be fed without artificial means are either able to make their own decisions about whether to accept food or are not so ill that a surrogate could properly conclude that continued feeding would be of no benefit to them. Withholding "natural" feeding thus has a greater potential for error and abuse than the withholding of "artificial" feeding. Consequently, it may be prudent to require stricter protections against decisions to forgo "natural" feeding for incompetent patients, to minimize the risk of unsound decisions. See Lynn, J. & Childress, J. (1983). Must patients always be given food and water? *Hastings Center Report, 13,* 21–23. Brock, D. & Lynn, J. (1986). The Competent Patient Who Decides Not to Take Nutrition and Hydration. In J. Lynn (Ed.), *By No Extraordinary Means: The Choice to Forego Life-Sustaining Food and Water* (pp. 202–15). Bloomington, IN: Indiana University Press.

6. Daniels, N. (1985). *Just Health Care* (pp. 36–85). Cambridge, England: Cambridge University Press. Englehardt, H. T. (1986). The foundations of bioethics (pp. 336–65). New York: Oxford University Press. President's Commission for the Study of Ethical Problems in Medicine and Biomedical and Behavioral Research. (1983). *Securing Access to Health Care, Vol. 1: Report* and *Vol. 2: Appendices.* Washington, D.C.: U. S. Government Printing Office.

7. *Ibid.,* Vol. 1 (p. 32).
8. There are, of course, special ethical and legal positive rights, including rights to specific medical treatments, that arise in the contractual or quasi-contractual relationships between a particular physician and patient. A recent highly publicized case illustrates the importance of distinguishing between special and general rights in this context. Elizabeth Bouvia was a young woman paralyzed with cerebral palsy. See Bouvia v. Superior Court of the State of California for the County of Los Angeles, No. BO19134 (Cal. Ct. App., 2d. Dist., April 16, 1986). She voluntarily admitted herself to a psychiatric hospital inpatient ward, and then refused nourishment with the announced intention of ending a life of disability that she professed was intolerable. But not only did she refuse life-sustaining nutrition, which she clearly had the right to do, she also demanded that the hospital continue to provide her with a place to stay and with palliative and hygienic care during the period of her anticipated death by malnutrition.

    In the absence of a general right to health care, her basis for this demand would have to be a special right generated by the contractual relationship between her and her physician. There are two ways in which such a special right might be generated by entering into the physician-patient relationship: (1) by virtue of explicit agreement by both parties or (2) implicitly in virtue of reasonable expectations based on a clear standard of care that provides the background for the contract. The first source of the alleged special right is not plausible, since no evidence of any explicit agreement to provide palliation while withholding nutritional support between Bouvia and her health care providers was produced.

    A somewhat stronger case might be made that Bouvia had a reasonable expectation of receiving the mix of care she chose because it was recognized as part of the accepted standard of professional care, for it does seem to be part of the standard of good professional practice to provide palliative care to patients who have refused life-sustaining care and so are dying.

    However, the practice in question needs to be more carefully described to see if it does in fact support Bouvia's claim. It is widely recognized that palliative care is to be provided to patients who have refused life-sustaining care (or treatment). But in the cases in which this is considered least controversial the patient is terminally ill or terminally ill and in intractable pain. Bouvia, however, satisfied neither of these conditions.

    Nevertheless, the Bouvia case does raise troubling doubts about the scope of patients' rights of self-determination. Although she was neither terminally ill nor in intractable pain, Elizabeth Bouvia had decided, apparently after considerable reflection on her condition, that her disability made her life not worth living. We cannot simply dismiss this decision as irrational nor take it as evidence of incompetence. Her decision may well have been a genuine exercise of self-determination, a sincere and well-informed expression of her desire to be self-determining.

If we concentrate only on the value of individual self-determination here, however, we place the physician in the position of being a passive vendor required to provide whatever mix of services the competent patient chooses. At least where the accepted professional standard of care does not require that he or she accede to the patient's wishes, and in the absence of explicit contractual agreement, a proper regard for the physician's integrity and self-determination permits him or her to refuse some requests on grounds of conscience.

It must be emphasized that it does not follow that the patient had no right to refuse nutritional support and that forcible feeding was permissible. Instead, the physician could acknowledge the right to refuse treatment by transferring the patient to another physician, or to family or friends who would be willing to withhold nutritional support while providing palliative and hygienic care. As the Bouvia case clarifies, the proper justification for a physician's refusal to withhold nutritional support is not that the right of self-determination does not include the right to refuse food, but rather that the right of self-determination is not a right to force health providers to provide whatever mix of care and withholding of care a patient demands, regardless of the moral scruples of the providers and prevailing professional standards of care.

9. However, at least one Western European country, The Netherlands, has now legalized voluntary active euthanasia under certain conditions, not through explicit legislation authorizing it, but through an agreement among courts and the medical profession that it is permissible.

10. Anderson, C. G. et al. (1984). Have Nurses and Physicians Signed Living Wills? (Letter). *New England Journal of Medicine, 311,* 678.

11. Sartorius, R. E. (Ed.). (1983). *Paternalism.* Minneapolis, MN: University of Minnesota Press.

12. President's Commission (pp. 136–37), *op. cit.*

13. *In re* Quinlan, 70 N.J. 10, 355 A.2d. 647, *cert. denied sub non.* Garger v. New Jersey, 429 U. S. 922 (1976).

14. Superintendent of Belchertown State School v. Saikewicz, 373 Mass. 728, 370 N.E.2d. 417. 1977.

15. *In re* Spring, 380 Mass, 629, 405 N.E.2d. 115 (1980).

16. Annas, G. & Glantz, L. Brief *amicus curiae (Spring)* on behalf of the American Society of Law and Medicine, Inc. (1980), 5.

17. Buchanan, A. (1983). The Limits of Proxy Decision-Making. In Sartorius, R. (p. 158), *op. cit.*

18. President's Commission (pp. 132–3), *op. cit.*

19. *In re* Conroy, 98 N.J. 3211, 486 A.2d. 1209 (1985).

20. Buchanan, A. (Summer 1979). Medical Paternalism or Legal Imperialism: Not the Only Alternatives for Handling *Saikewicz*-type Cases. *American Journal of Law and Medicine, 5,* 97–117.

21. Saikewicz, 430–2, *op. cit.*

22. (Thursday, May 23, 1985). *Boston Globe.*

23. Brock, D. (February 1988). Distributive Justice and the Severely Demented Elderly. *The Journal of Medicine and Philosophy, 13,* 79–80. Buchanan, A. (1987). The Treatment of Incompetents. In Regan, T. & VanDeVeer, D. (Eds.), *Health Care Ethics* (pp. 230–32). Philadelphia, PA: Temple University Press. Feinberg, J. (1984). *Harm to Others* (Chap. 1, pp. 31–64). Oxford, England: Oxford University.

24. President's Commission (pp. 178–9), *op. cit.*

25. Steinbock, B. (1983). The Removal of Mr. Herbert's Feeding Tube. *Hastings Center Report, 13,* 12–5.

26. Strunk v. Strunk, 445 S.W. 2d. 145 (Ky. Ct. App. 1969). Hart v. Brown, 289 A.2d. 386 (Conn. 1972). Little v. Little, 576 S.W. 2d. 493 (Tex. Civ. App. 1979). Robertson, J. (1976). Organ Donations by Incompetents and the Substituted Judgment Doctrine. *Columbia Law Review, 76,* 48–68.

27. President's Commission (pp. 135–6), *op. cit.*

28. Buchanan, A., *op. cit.*

29. Buchanan, A. In Sartorius (pp. 161–3), *op. cit.*

30. Baron, C. (1978). Assuring "Detached But Passionate Investigation and Decision": The Role of Guardians Ad Litem in Saikewicz-type Cases. *American Journal of Law and Medicine, 4*(2), 111–30.

31. Buchanan, A. (1984). Limitations on the Family's Right to Decide for the Incompetent Patient. In R. Crawford & E. Doudera (Eds.), *Institutional Ethics Committees and Health Care Decision Making* (p. 211). Ann Arbor, Michigan: Health Administration Press

32. We believe that decisions to terminate life-support for permanently unconscious patients should not routinely be subjected

to special scrutiny, once this prognosis has been confirmed by an independent, qualified physician (preferably a neurologist), at least if a reasonable waiting period has passed (for example, two or three weeks, though this may vary depending upon the presumed cause of the patient's loss of consciousness, his or her age, or other factors relevant to the possibility of recovery).

CHAPTER 3

1. Perry, J. (1975). The Problem of Personal Identity. In J. Perry (Ed.), *Personal Identity* (p. 10). Berkeley, CA: University of California Press.
2. For an influential recent discussion of the psychological continuity view, see Parfit, D. (1986). *Reason and Persons* (especially 204–9). New York: Oxford University Press. See also Grice, H. P. (1986). Personal Identity. In J. Perry (pp. 73–95), *op. cit.*
3. Dresser, R. (1986). Life, Death, and Incompetent Patients: Conceptual Infirmative and Hidden Values in the Law. *Arizona Law Review, 28,* 379–81.
4. Premise ii in the slavery argument is *not* offered as a claim about which individuals *the law* presently considers to be persons. Instead, the argument is intended to express a severe limitation on the *moral* authority of advance directives, a limitation which the law, if it is to be morally sensitive, *ought* to recognize.
5. For examples, see Feinberg, J. (1982). The Problem of Personhood (pp. 108–16) and Warren, M. A. (1982). On the Moral and Legal Status of Abortion (pp. 25–60). Both in T. L. Beauchamp & L. Walters (Eds.), *Contemporary Issues in Bioethics* (2nd ed.). Belmont, CA: Wadsworth Publishing Co.
6. Congress of the United States, Office of Technology Assessment. (1987). *Losing a Million Minds: Confronting the tragedy of Alzheimer's Disease and Other Dementias* (pp. 68–83). Washington, DC: U.S. Government Printing Office. This chapter also includes a bibliography on Alzheimer's disease.
7. Parfit, D. (1973). Later Selves and Moral Principles. In Montefiore, A. (Ed.), *Philosophy and Personal Relations* (pp. 137–69). Montreal, Canada: McGill-Queen's University Press.
8. *Ibid.* (pp. 137–42).
9. It is perhaps worth re-emphasizing that Durable Powers of Attorney are currently revokable at will by the principal whether he or she is competent or not.

CHAPTER 4

1. Daniels, N. (1986). Why Saying No to Patients in the United States Is So Hard – Cost Containment, Justice and Provider Autonomy. *New England Journal of Medicine, 314,* 1380–83.
2. The most prominent example is in Callahan, D. (1987). *Setting Limits. Medical Goals in an Aging Society.* New York: Simon and Schuster. Perhaps the most systematic approach to the problem of setting limits on care at the end of life that has seemed to some to be especially promising is the *prudent allocator model.* According to this view, in order to determine whether it is permissible to withhold beneficial health care services from those in the last stages of terminal chronic illness we are to think of a person as making a rational, self-interested choice among different insurance policies providing different mixes of preventive and curative services as well as medical and nonmedical support services, to be supplied over an entire lifetime. Because different persons would choose different insurance policies tailored to their own particular health care needs if they could make probabilistic calculations about those needs, the prudent allocator approach can yield a single answer to the question of how care may be limited only if the chooser is barred from utilizing information about his or her own particular characteristics so far as these influence health status and information about the person's particular preferences for health versus other goods, as well as his or her attitude toward risk. Thus it is necessary to impose a veil of ignorance – a set of informational constraints – upon the choice. One writer has suggested that it is necessary to think of a person as choosing among policies prior to his or her own conception, since from conception on our health prospects diverge. (See Gibbard, A. (1983). Prospective Pareto Principle and Equity of Access to Health Care. In President's Commission for the Study of Ethical Problems in Medicine and Biomedical and Behavioral Research, *Securing Access to Health Care: vol. II. Appendices* (pp. 153–78). Washington, DC: Government Printing Office. Given such a restriction, the choice of an insurance policy would be based only on general statistical information about average morbidity and mortality rates, and so on, for the chooser's society.

   As Norman Daniels has noted, one advantage of the prudent allocator approach is that it enables us to transform our thinking about allocational decisions in a way that makes them less morally problematic (see Daniels, N. (1987) *Am I My Parents' Keeper?* (New York/Oxford: Oxford University Press. For example, we tend to think of the question of whether to increase Medicare benefits or to use the same resources to improve perinatal care as a problem of *inter*personal allocation – as a zero sum game in which serving the interests of one group (the young) can only come at the expense of another group (the elderly) and vice versa. The prudent allocator approach promises to enable us to identify and justify an appropriate allocation from the perspective of a *single* individual's nonmoral, that is, prudential choice.

There are, however, a number of serious limitations on this approach; only two will be sketched here. First, recall that the approach to how a prudent allocator would ration a fixed amount of resources for health care over a lifetime is supposed to *justify* policies of withholding some forms of beneficial care from persons at the end of life. Presumably the *justificatory* force of the model depends on this assumption: having more resources available at earlier stages is worth enough, from the standpoint of the prudent allocator, to compensate him or her for not having certain resources available at the end of life. But the whole exercise appears to collapse as a justification for rationing if the person from whom the care is withheld does not in fact receive the benefit of that saving. Yet if such a policy were implemented today, some of the elderly people from whom care would be withheld *would* certainly have enjoyed access, in earlier stages of their lives, to the expensive sort of care that a prudential allocator would forego at the end of life in order to obtain it at an earlier stage. In other words, the attempt to use the prudent allocator model to justify rationing by recasting a zero sum interpersonal competition for resources as a problem of rational budgeting for a single individual cannot succeed if the costs of prudential budgeting fall on some while the benefits accrue to others.

Second, the fact that *past* allocational policies can have a significant effect on the quality of life at certain stages of life implies another important limitation on the prudent allocator model as a justification for age-related rationing policies. The problem is this. How a prudent allocator would budget resources across different stages of life depends on how he or she would value life within those stages; yet how he or she would value life at a given stage will depend upon the quality of life at that stage, and this in turn will depend in part on what resources are available at that stage. If one budgets $N for the final stage of life, then the total available for all earlier stages is $T - $N. But whether one is willing to forego access to $N in the final stage of life in order to have an additional $N available at some earlier stage will depend upon how much one values an extension of life in the final, stage. And this will depend upon one's estimate of the quality of life in the final stage. Now if our society has failed to actualize technological possibilities for improving the quality of life in the final stage of the normal life span, or if many elderly people in our society have lacked access to quality of life-enhancing care, then we may under-estimate the comparative quality of life in the final stage of life when we perform the prudent allocator thought experiment. For after all, how we regard the comparative quality of life in old age is determined by our cultural experience of what old age is like, and what old age is like in our culture depends in part upon what resources are typically available to the elderly. Thus, if lack of access to health care or the failure to utilize effectively technologically feasible care leads to a lower quality of life for significant numbers of the elderly, then our conception of what old age is like will be adversely influenced. But if, *for these reasons,* we assign a lower quality of life to old age than we otherwise would, then we will conclude that the extension of an elderly life is not worth the loss of certain resources at earlier, more highly valued, stages. If the resources thus withheld would have so improved the quality of life in old age that we would not have had such a low opinion of the quality of life at that stage, then the prudent allocator approach will have produced a circular result and will simply exacerbate current irrational allocation patterns and cannot justify the rationing policy in question. These two problems, as well as others which cannot be explored here, should make it clear that even if we could ascertain that a prudent allocator would budget health care resources so as to limit care at the end of life, this alone would *not* provide an adequate justification for age-related rationing in our society at the present time. (For a review essay on Callahan's and Daniels's books, see Brock, D. (Summer 1989). Justice, Health Care, and the Elderly. *Philosophy and Public Affairs.* Forthcoming.)

3. The most ambitious attempt to develop such a theory for health care is Daniels, N. (1985). *Just Health Care.* Cambridge: Cambridge University Press.
4. Daniels, *op. cit.*
5. Callahan, D. (1985). What Do Children Owe Their Elderly Parents? *Hastings Center Report, 15,* 32–7.
6. Public Broadcasting System. (May 21, 1985). *Frontline.* "What About Mom and Dad?"

CHAPTER 5

1. A good source of data and discussions on research involving children is National Commission for the Protection of Human Subjects of Biomedical and Behavioral Research (1977). *Research*

Involving Children: Appendix. Washington, DC: U.S. Government Printing Office.

2. For the account in this section of the developmental evidence about children's capacities, we rely heavily on the excellent review by Grisso, T. & Vierling, L. (1978). Minors' Consent to Treatment: A Developmental Perspective. *Professional Psychology, 9,* 412–27, and also on Melton, G. B. (1983). Psychological Issues in Increasing Children's Competence (pp. 21–40), on Lewis, C. E. (1983). Decision Making Related to Health: When Could/Should Children Act Responsibly? (pp. 75–91), on Groden, M. A. & Alpert, J. J. (1983). Informed Consent and Pediatric Care (pp. 93–110), and on Weithorn, L. A. (1983). Involving Children in Decisions Affecting Their Own Welfare: Guidelines for Professionals (pp. 235–260). All in Melton, G. B., Koocher, G. P. & Saks, M. J. (Eds.), *Children's Competence to Consent.* New York: Plenum Press. Also see Weithorn, L. A. & Campbell, S. B. (1982). The Competency of Children and Adolescents to Make Informed Treatment Decisions. *Child Development, 53,* 1589–98, and Leiken, S. (1987) Minor's Assent or Dissent in Medical Treatment. In President's Commission for the Study of Ethical Problems in Medicine and Biomedical and Behavioral Research, *Making Health Care Decisions: Vol. 3. Medical Treatment* (pp. 175–91). Washington, DC: Government Printing Office.

3. Grisso and Vierling, 417, *op. cit.*
4. *Ibid.,* 418.
5. Lewis, in Melton, Koocher, & Saks (p. 84).
6. See Piaget, J. (1965). *The Moral Judgment of the Child.* New York: Free Press, *The Child's Conception of the World* (1972). Totowa, NJ: Littlefield, Adams, and Piaget, J. & Inhelder, B. (1969). *The Psychology of the Child.* New York: Basic Books.
7. Grisso & Vierling, 419, *op. cit.*
8. *Ibid.,* 419.
9. Leiken, in President's Commission (p. 180), *op. cit.*
10. Grisso & Vierling, 419, *op. cit.* This is also consistent with the findings of Weithorn & Campbell, *op. cit.,* that nine-year-olds were able to reach reasonable conclusions, but were not able to attend to all relevant factors in complex cases and instead focused on a few prominent factors.
11. Grodin & Alpert, in Melton, Koocher, & Saks (p. 96), *op. cit.*
12. Cf. Leiken, in President's Commission, *op. cit.* and Weithorn and Campbell, in Melton, Koocher, & Saks, *op. cit.*
13. Melton, quoting Keith-Spiegel, P. (1976). Children's Rights as Participants in Research. In G. P. Koocher (Ed.), *Children's Rights and the Mental Health Professions* (p. 24). New York: Wiley.

14. See, among many of his writings on this subject, Erikson, E. (1963). *Childhood and Society* (2d Ed.). New York: W. W. Norton.

15. Strictly, the assumption is that the person either now or at some time past had the capacities necessary for self-determination. It is possible to respect a person's past choices for his or her present treatment even if the person currently lacks the capacities for self-determination.

16. Representative philosophical discussions of this issue can be found in Aiken, W. & LaFollette, H. (Eds.). (1980). *Whose Child? Children's Rights, Parental Authority, and State Power*. Totowa, NJ: Littlefield, Adams and Blustein, J. (1982). *Parents and Children: The Ethics of the Family*. New York: Oxford University Press.

17. Both Grisso & Vierling, *op. cit.*, and Weithorn, *op. cit.*, for example, assert the relevance of this interest.

18. See Schoeman, F. (1985). Parental Discretion and Children's Rights: Background and Implications for Medical Decision-Making. *Journal of Medicine and Philosophy, 10*, 45–62.

19. Among other explicit defenses of a variable standard of competence for adults is Drane, J. (April 1985). The Many Faces of Competency. *Hastings Center Report, 15*(2), 17–21. Gaylin, W. (1982). Competence: No longer All or None. In *Who Speaks for the Child*. W. Gaylin & R. Macklin (Eds.). New York: Plenum Press defends a variable standard for children.

20. Capron, A. M. (1982). The Competence of Children as Self-deciders in Biomedical Interventions. In Gaylin & Macklin, *op. cit.* Book contains an excellent review of the law regarding children's competence, as well as a very useful appendix detailing the standards in the different states.

21. See Meisel, A. (1979). The "Exceptions" to the Informed Consent Doctrine: Striking a Balance Between Competing Values in Medical Decision-making. *Wisconsin Law Review*, 413–88.

22. Capron, A. M, in Gaylin & Macklin (p. 94), *op. cit.*

23. *Ibid.*, Appendix.

24. Cf. Holder, A. (1985). *Legal Issues in Pediatric and Adolescent Medicine* (2nd ed.) (pp. 133–35). New Haven: Yale University Press.

25. Capron argues that as a matter of law this presumption is undergoing change and erosion.

26. Grisso & Vierling, 424, *op. cit.*

27. Feinberg, J. (1980). The Child's Right to an Open Future. In Aiken & LaFollette (pp. 124–153), *op. cit.*

28. Buchanan, A. (1983). The Limits of Proxy Decision-making. In R. E. Sartorius (Ed.), *Paternalism* (pp. 153–70). Minneapolis: University of Minnesota Press.

29. Stinson, R. & P. (1981). On the Death of a Baby. *Journal of Medical Ethics,* 7(5), 5–18. Reprinted with commentary from *Atlantic Monthly,* July 1979.

30. Goldstein, J. (June 1985). Lecture presented at a conference on bioethics sponsored by the Arizona Humanities Council, Phoenix, Arizona.

31. Feinberg, J. (1982). The Problem of Personhood. In T. L. Beauchamp & L. Walters (Eds.), *Contemporary Issues in Bioethics* (2nd ed.) (p. 113). Belmont, CA: Wadsworth.

32. For an extended treatment and criticism of the potentiality principle, see Tooley, M. (1983). *Abortion and Infanticide* (Chap. 6). Oxford: Oxford University Press.

33. See, as an example of the radical view rejecting personhood for infants, Englehardt, H. T. (1986). *The Foundations of Bioethics* (pp. 115–21). New York: Oxford University Press.

CHAPTER 6

1. National Institute on Aging. (1977). *Our Future Selves: A Research Toward Understanding Aging.* Washington, DC: National Institutes of Health.

2. Jarvik, L. (1980). Diagnosis of Dementia in the Elderly: A 1980 Perspective. *Annual Review of Gerontology and Geriatrics, 1,* 44–60.

3. Roth, M. (1983). Senile Dementia and Related Disorders. In J. Wertheimer and M. Marasi. (Eds.). *Senile Dementia: Outlook for the Future* (p. 32). New York: Alan R. Liss, Inc.

4. State of New York, Deputy Attorney General for Medicaid Fraud Control. (March 20, 1984). News release. Albany, NY: Author.

5. Cranford, Dr. R. E. (1986). Personal communication to Allen Buchanan. Department of Neurology, Hennepin County General Hospital, Minneapolis, MN.

6. Evans, A. & Brody, B. A. (1985). The Do Not Resuscitate Order in Teaching Hospitals. *Journal of the American Medical Association, 253,* 2236–45.

7. Bedell, S. & Delbanco, T. (1984). Choices about Cardiopulmonary Resuscitation in the Hospital. *New England Journal of Medicine, 310,* 1089–93.

8. Kapp, M. & Lo, B. (1986). Legal Perceptions and Medical Decision Making. *Milbank Quarterly, 64*(Suppl. 2), 175.

9. Buchanan, A. (1985). Personal communication.

10. Buchanan, A. (1980). Personal communication.

11. President's Commission for the Study of Ethical Problems in Medicine and Biomedical and Behavioral Research. (1983). *Decid-*

ing to Forego Life-Sustaining Treatment (pp. 234–5). Washington, DC: U.S. Government Printing Office.

12. Wadleigh, E. et al. (Eds.). (1979). *Aging and the Law, Curriculum Materials, Part XII: Protective Services.* Palo Alto, CA: Senior Adults Legal Assistance.
13. *Ibid.,* (p. 40).
14. *Ibid.,* (pp. 37–42).
15. California Probate Code, Section 18016.
16. For example, California Probate Code, Section 1801a.
17. Gilfix, M. (1986). Personal Communication to Allen Buchanan. Gilfix Associates, Palo Alto, CA.
18. Bartling v. Superior Court, 163 Cal. App.3d. 186, 209 Cal. Rptr. 220 (Ct. App. 1984).
19. Appelbaum, P. S., Lidz, C. W., & Meisel, A. (1987). *Informed Consent: Legal Theory and Clinical Practice.* (pp. *1–3).* New York: Oxford University Press.
20. Evans and Brody, *op. cit.,* 2245.
21. *In re* Quinlan, 70 N.J. 10, 355 A.2d. 647, *cert. denied sub nom.* (1976).
22. *In re* Eichner (*In re* Storor), 52 N.Y.2d. 363, 420 N.E.2d. 64, 438 N.Y.S.2d. 266, *cert. denied,* 454 U.S. 858 (1981).
23. Severns v. Wilmington Medical Center, Inc., 421 A. 2d. 1334 (Del. 1980). *In re* Severns, 425 A.2d. 156 (Del. Ch. 1980).
24. *In re* Conroy, 98 N.J. 3211, 486 A.2d 1209 (1985).
25. *In re* Conroy, *op. cit.*
26. *In re* Storar, 52 N.Y.2d. 363, 420 N.E.2d. 64, 438 N.Y.S.2d. 266, *cert. denied,* 454 U.S. 858 (1981).
27. See Appendix 2: California Durable Power of Attorney For Health Care Act.
28. Lo, B. & Steinbrook, R. (1984). Decision Making for Incompetent Patients by Designated Proxy. *New England Journal of Medicine, 310,* 1598–1601.
29. Electroconvulsive therapy is discussed further in Chapter 7.
30. Howell, T. et al. (1982). Is There a Case for Voluntary Commitment? In T. L. Beauchamp & L. Walters (Eds.), *Contemporary Issues in Bioethics* (pp. 163–8). Belmont, CA: Wadsworth. For an opposing view, see Dresser, R. (1984). Bound to Treatment: The Ulysses Contract. *Hastings Center Report, 14,* 13–6. Ulysses contracts are also discussed in Chapter 7.
31. President's Commission. *Making Health Care Decisions, Vol. Two: Appendices* (p. 242), *op. cit.*
32. This important point is due to Michael Gilfix; Gilfix, M., *op. cit.*

CHAPTER 7

1. Among the helpful sources on which we have relied in this section
   are Appelbaum, P. (1984). Civil Commitment. In J. O. Cavenar,
   Jr. (Ed.), *Psychiatry (Vol. 3,* Chap. 32, pp. 1–18). Philadelphia: J.
   B. Lippincott; Dershowitz, A. (1974). The origins of Preventive
   Confinement in Anglo-American Law, Part II: The American
   Experience. *University of Cincinnati Law Review, 43,* 781–846;
   Appelbaum, P. & Kemp, K. N. (1982). The Evolution of Commitment Law in the Nineteenth Century: A Reinterpretation. *Law
   and Human Behavior, 6,* 343–54.
2. Lessard v. Schmidt, 349F. Supp 1078 (E.D.Wis. 1972).
3. Appelbaum. (1984). In J. O. Cavenar (p. 5), *op. cit.*
4. O'Connor v. Donaldson, 422 U.S. 563 (1975).
5. Appelbaum. (1984). In J. O. Cavenar (pp. 5–6), *op. cit.* Cf. also
   Appelbaum, P. (1984). Is the Need for Treatment Constitutionally Acceptable as a Basis for Civil Commitment? *Law,
   Medicine and Health Care, 12,* 144–9.
6. American Psychiatric Association. (May 1983). Guidelines for
   Legislation on the Psychiatric Hospitalization of Adults. *American
   Journal of Psychiatry, 140:5,* 672–9. Cf. also Special section on
   APA's Model Commitment Law. (1985). *Hospital and Community
   Psychiatry 36* 966–89.
7. American Psychiatric Association, 673, *op. cit.*
8. Cf. Durham, M. L. (1985). Implications of Need-for-Treatment
   Laws: A Study of Washington State's Involuntary Treatment Act.
   Hospital and Community Psychiatry, 36, 975–7 and Pierce, G. L.,
   Durham, M. L., & Fisher, W. H. (1985). The Impact of
   Broadened Civil Commitment Standards on Admissions of State
   Mental Hospitals. *American Journal of Psychiatry, 142,* 104–7.
9. A classic paper in the literature on civil commitment is Livermore,
   J. M., Malmquist C. P., & Meehl, P. E. (1968). On the Jus-
   tifications for Civil Commitment. *University of Pennsylvania Law
   Review, 117,* 75–96. One of the most extensive criticisms of involuntary commitment is Morse, S. J. (1982). A Preference for
   Liberty: The Case Against Involuntary Commitment of the Mentally Disordered. *California Law Review, 70,* 54–106.
10. American Psychiatric Association, 694, *op. cit.*
11. For a discussion of problems in employing this substituted judg-
    ment standard with the mentally ill, see Gutheil, T. G. & Appel-
    baum, P. S. (April 1985). The Substituted Judgment Approach: Its
    Difficulties and Paradoxes in Mental Health Settings. *Law Medi-
    cine and Health Care, 13,* 61–4.

12. For a similar position about the specific effects of mental illness relevant to incompetence, see Annas, G. J., & Densberger, J. E. (1984). Competence to Refuse Medical Treatment: Autonomy vs. Paternalism. *Toledo Law Review, 15,* 580. Their position differs from our own, however, in several respects; most importantly, they support a standard of competence that requires only that the patient be able to understand and appreciate the nature and consequences of his or her decision. We believe that this standard incorrectly ignores other serious effects of mental illness on persons' decision making about their treatment; for example, the deeply depressed person who understands how his decision harms his interests, but because of his depression "no longer cares."

13. Another variant of the APA proposal for broadening commitment criteria is presented in Treffert, D. A. (1985). The Obviously Ill Patient in Need of Treatment: A Fourth Standard for Civil Commitment. *Hospital and Community Psychiatry, 36,* 259–64. Reliance on the dangerousness standard is criticized in Chodoff, P. (1976). The Case for Involuntary Hospitalization of the Mentally Ill. *American Journal of Psychiatry, 133,* 496–501, and Treffert, D. A. (1973). Dying With Their Rights On. *American Journal of Psychiatry, 130,* 1041.

14. An account of some of the historical abuses that have fueled this concern is Ennis, B. (1972). *Prisoners of Psychiatry.* New York: Harcourt, Brace, Jovanovich.

15. Cf. Durham, M. L. and LaFond, J. (1985). The Empirical Consequences and Policy Implications of Broadening Statutory Criteria for Civil Commitment. *Yale Law and Policy Review, 3,* 395–446.

16. It is remarkable how few commentators have recognized this point. Some do not make incompetence to decide about the need for hospitalization and treatment a requirement for self-regarding *or* other-regarding commitment. While commentators increasingly support the requirement of a finding of incompetence to decide about hospitalization and treatment for self-regarding commitment, due no doubt in significant part to recent court cases requiring it (cf. the second section of this chapter), they rarely argue as well that incompetence to decide about treatment should *not* be required for other-regarding commitment. One exception who clearly perceives the difference is Roth, L. (1979). A Commitment Law for Patients, Doctors, and Lawyers. *American Journal of Psychiatry, 136,* 1121–7.

17. This account conforms to the power possessed by most state directors of health to confine a person, by quarantine where neces-

sary, who poses a serious health threat to others or to the public health. The exercise of this power turns on the danger the person poses to others, and not on whether the person is competent to make a decision about his or her need for treatment or confinement.

18. These differences are explored in more detail in Brock, D. W. (1980). Involuntary Civil Commitment: The Moral Issues. In B. A. Brody & H. T. Endelhardt, Jr. (Eds.). *Mental Illness: Law and Public Policy* (pp. 147–173). Dordrecht, Holland/Boston: D. Reidel Publishing Co.

19. Cf. Hart, H. L. A. (1961). *The Concept of Law*. Oxford: Oxford University Press and Hart, H. L. A. (1968). *Punishment and Responsibility*. Oxford: Oxford University Press, *passim*.

20. Articulating a distinction between harm and mere offense is a difficult matter. For a thoughtful attempt to do so and to argue for not only harm, but also "profound offense" as a ground for liberty-limitation, see Feinberg, J. (1985). *Offense to Others*. Oxford: Oxford University Press.

21. Cf. Rapport, J. R., & Lassen G. (1964). Dangerousness—Arrest Rate Comparisons of Discharged Patients and the General Population. *American Journal of Psychiatry, 121,* 776.

22. Cf. Cocozza, J. J. & Steadman, H. (1974). Some Refinements in the Measurement and Prediction of Dangerousness. *American Journal of Psychiatry, 131,* 1012–4; Monahan, J. (1981). *Clinical Prediction of Violent Behavior*. Rockville, MD: National Institutes of Mental Health; snf Kozol, H., Boucher, R., & Garofolo, R. (1973). The Diagnosis and Treatment of Dangerousness. *Crime and Delinquency, 18,* 371–92. Appelbaum (1984) in J. O. Cavenar (pp. 7–8), *op. cit.,* concludes that there are significant methodological difficulties in most studies of prediction of dangerousness and that little is known about emergency room prediction, perhaps the most important context in which such predictions are actually made.

23. A very large literature has developed on this issue in a relatively short period of time. Among more useful sources are: Cavanaugh, J. L., & Rogers, R. L. (Eds.). (1986). *Behavioral Sciences and the Law,* 4(3), the entire issue of which is devoted to the right to refuse treatment; Doudera, A. E. & Swazey, J. P. (Eds.). (1982). *Refusing Treatment in Mental Health Institutions—Values in Conflict*. Ann Arbor, MI: AUPHA Press; Rapoport, D., & Parry, J. (1986). *The Right to Refuse Antipsychotic Medication*. Washington, D.C.: American Bar Association; Rhoden, N. K. (1980). The Right to Refuse Psychotropic Drugs. *Harvard Civil Rights-Civil Liberties Law Re-*

view, 15, 363–413; Mills, M. J., Yesavage, & Gutheil, T. G. (1983). Continuing Case Law Development in the Right to Refuse Treatment. *American Journal of Psychiatry, 140,* 715–9; and Appelbaum, P. (1988). The Right to Refuse Treatment With Antipsychotic Medications: Retrospect and Prospect. *American Journal of Psychiatry, 145,* 413–9.

24. For example, a referendum in the City of Berkeley, California was passed several years ago prohibiting any use, whether with voluntary or involuntary patients, of ECT within the city. The widespread use of lobotomies received public attention and concern as a result of media publicity and fictional treatments such as Ken Kesey's *One Flew Over the Cuckoo's Nest.* A prominent example of the courts' concerns with special kinds of treatment is Kaimowitz v. Department of Mental Health, No. 73-19434-AW (Cir. Ct. of Wayne County, Mich., July 10, 1973), concerned with the use of psychosurgery for involuntarily committed mental patients, and discussed briefly in Section III.D. of this chapter.

25. (1974). Developments in the Law—Civil Commitment of the Mentally Ill. *Harvard Law Review, 87,* 1190–406, and quoted in Gutheil, T. G. (1986). The Right to Refuse Treatment: Paradox, Pendulum and the Quality of Care. *Behavioral Sciences and the Law, 4,* 268.

26. First decided as Rogers v. Okin, 478 F. Supp. 1342 (D. Mass 1979). Decided on appeal to the First Circuit Court of Appeals as Rogers v. Okin, 634 F.2d 650 (1st Cir. 1980). Decided on appeal to the United States Supreme Court as Mills v. Rogers, 457 U.S. 291 (1982).

27. Rennie v. Klein 462 F. Supp. 1131 (D.N.J. 1978) and 476 F. Supp. 1294 (D.N.J. 1979). Appealed to the Third Circuit Court of Appeals in Rennie v. Klein, 653 F.2d 836 (3d Cir. 1981) *(en banc)* and then to the United States Supreme Court, which remanded the case back to the Third Circuit in Rennie v. Klein, 458 U.S. 1110 (1982). The Third Circuit redecided in Rennie v. Klein, 720 F.2d 266 (3d Cir. 1983) *(en banc).*

28. There is considerable controversy concerning the frequency and irreversibility of the effects of tardive dyskinesia. See, for example, Kane, J. M., Woerner, M., Lieberman, J., & Kinon, B. (1984). Tardive Dyskinesia. In D. P. Jeste & R. P. Wyatt (Eds.). *Neuro-Psychiatric Movement Disorders.* Washington, DC: American Psychiatric Press.

29. Youngberg v. Romeo, 457 U.S. 307, 102 S. Ct. 2452, 73 L. Ed.2d 28 (1982).

30. Brooks, A. D. (1986). Law and Antipsychotic Medications. *Behavioral Sciences and the Law, 4,* 259.

31. Rogers v. Commissioner, 390 Mass 489, 458 N.E.2d 308 (1983).

32. But see Brooks's discussion of data concerning current practices in Oregon, New Jersey, and Ohio, 259–61, *op. cit.*

33. One state, Utah, has avoided this distinction between commitment and competence in practice by making incompetence to decide about treatment a requirement for involuntary commitment. Cf. Lebegue, B. & Clark, L. D. (1981). Incompetence to Refuse Treatment: A Necessary Condition for Civil Commitment. *American Journal of Psychiatry, 138,* 1075–7.

34. Roth, L. H., 324, *op. cit.*

35. *Ibid.,* 325.

36. Roth, L. H. (1977). Involuntary Civil Commitment: The Right to Treatment and the Right to Refuse Treatment. In R. J. Bonnie (Ed.), *Psychiatrists and the Legal Process: Diagnosis and Debate* (pp. 50–76). New York: Insight Communications.

37. A detailed and very subtle analysis of forced choices and of consent given in that context is contained in Feinberg, J. (1986). *Harm to Self* (chaps. 23–4). Oxford: Oxford University Press.

38. See Dworkin, R. (1977). *Taking Rights Seriously* (esp. Chap. 7). Cambridge, MA: Harvard University Press.

39. Goffman, E. (1961). *Asylums.* New York: Doubleday.

40. Dudzik, C. J., Jr. (1982–3). The Scope of the Involuntarily Committed Mental Patient's Right to Refuse Treatment with Psychotropic Drugs: An Analysis of the Least Restrictive Alternative Doctrine. *Villanova Law Review,* 28, 129. This paper contains an extended analysis and defense of the application of the least restrictive alternative doctrine to the legal right to refuse treatment for mental illness. Cf. also Klein, J. I. (1982). The Least Restrictive Alternative: More about less. In L. Grinspoon (Ed.). *Psychiatry 1982: The American Psychiatric Association annual review* Washington, DC: American Psychiatric Association Press.

41. See, for example, the *Rennie v. Klein* decision of the Federal Third Circuit Court of Appeals, in which the Court held that the doctrine did apply to questions of treatment refusal, while four members of the *Rennie* court who concurred in the majority decision strongly rejected the application of the least restrictive alternative doctrine in the case.

42. APA Guidelines, 672–3, *op. cit.*

43. Howell, T., Diamond, R. J., & Wikler, D. (1982). Is There a Case for Voluntary Commitment? In T. Beauchamp & L. Walters

(Eds.). *Contemporary Issues in Bioethics* (pp. 163–168). Belmont, CA: Wadsworth, is the most detailed proposal for the use of such advance directives.

44. *Ibid.* (p. 165).

45. Dresser, R. (June 1984). Bound to treatment: The Ulysses Contract. *The Hastings Center Report, 14*(3), 13–6. A more detailed analysis is presented in Dresser, R. (winter 1982). Ulysses and the psychiatrists: A Legal and Policy Analysis of the Voluntary Commitment Contract. *Harvard Civil Rights-Civil Liberties Review, 16*(3), 777–854.

46. Miller, R. D. (1985). Commitment to Outpatient Treatment: A national survey. *Hospital and Community Psychiatry, 36,* 265–67; Keilitz, I., & Hall, T. (1985). State Statutes Governing Involuntary Outpatient Civil Commitment. *Mental Disability Law Reporter, 9,* 378–97. Miller, R. D. and Fiddleman, P. B. (1984). Outpatient Commitment: Treatment in the Least Restrictive Environment? *Hospital and Community Psychiatry, 35,* 147–51, discuss the experience in North Carolina and the obstacles to wider use of outpatient commitment.

47. Valenstein, E. S. (1986). *Great and Desperate Cures, The Rise and Decline of Psychosurgery and Other Radical Treatments for Mental Illness.* New York: Basic Books.

48. Mark, V. H., & Ervin, F. R. (1970). *Violence and the Brain.* New York: Harper and Row, argue that a significant amount of violence is due to brain pathology that could be eliminated by psychosurgery. Cf. also Valenstein, E. S. (Ed.). (1980). *The Psychosurgery Debate.* San Francisco: W. H. Freeman.

49. No. 73-19434-AW (Mich. Cir. Ct., Wayne County, July 10, 1973).

50. For a discussion of *Kaimowitz* and other legal cases concerning psychosurgery, see Kopesky, J. P. (1978–9). Psychosurgery and the Involuntarily Confined. *Villanova Law Review, 24,* 949–91.

51. Cf. (1985, October 18). Consensus Conference: Electroconvulsive Therapy. *Journal of the American Medical Association, 254*(15), 2103–8.

Index